Death, Grief, and Mourning

Death, Grief, and Mourning

Individual and Social Realities

John S. Stephenson

THE FREE PRESS
A Division of Macmillan, Inc.
NEW YORK

Collier Macmillan Publishers
LONDON

The Free Press
A Division of Macmillan, Inc.
866 Third Avenue, New York, N.Y. 10022

Collier Macmillan Canada, Inc.

Printed in the United States of America

printing number
1   2   3   4   5   6   7   8   9   10

Library of Congress Cataloging in Publication Data

Stephenson, John S. (John Samuel)
    Death, grief, and mourning.

    Bibliography: p.
    Includes index.
    1. Death—United States—Psychological aspects.
2. Death—Social aspects—United States. 3. Bereavement—
Psychological aspects. I. Title.
BF789.D4S735   1985   306'.9   85-1571
ISBN 978-1-4165-7356-2   ISBN 1-4165-7356-9

For Johnny

Still with his eyes on the world Christopher Robin put out a hand and felt for Pooh's paw.

"Pooh," said Christopher Robin earnestly, "if I—if I'm not quite—" he stopped and tried again—Pooh, *whatever* happens, you *will* understand, won't you?"

"Understand what?"

"Oh, nothing." He laughed and jumped to his feet. "Come on!"

"Where?" said Pooh.

"Anywhere," said Christopher Robin.

—*A. A. Milne*

Contents

Preface

THE INTERDISCIPLINARY NATURE of this book grew as much out of the demands of the subject matter as the author's biases. A topic as broad as death is best understood in the light of studies in many disciplines. History provides an understanding of the roots of many of our contemporary behaviors and attitudes. Sociology is valuable when examining our contemporary institutions and behavior, and psychology aids in understanding individual responses to death. One of my primary objectives has been to unite these perspectives in a framework within which the many dimensions of death and dying may be viewed, and the relations between them explored.

Central to the book's theoretical perspective is the concept of the image—that inner schema through which we understand and act in the world. The image of death that people held in earlier times affected the ways in which they felt and acted, as we see when we examine the history of American attitudes and behaviors surrounding death. Our contemporary social response to death is an institutional one; death is relegated to the hospital, hospice, and nursing home. These institutions reflect the larger collective image as they function to respond to death. Socially valued people are treated differently from the less socially desirable. Individual behavior does not take place in a vacuum; it takes place within a social context which both affects the person's actions and is in turn affected by those actions.

Grief—the individual's response to loss—is a function of the individual's as well as the larger society's understanding of the loss. Neither a strictly sociological nor psychological explanation will allow us to fully understand grief; it is necessary to take into account both the person and the social environment in order to understand why the grief-stricken behave and feel as they do. We will also examine the effects of grieving upon various categories of people such as the widowed and the family unit.

The ceremonies of death are discussed for several reasons. They not only serve as a collective response; they also manifest the collective image of death—what the larger society thinks and feels about death. In examining suicide, I provide an explanation congruent with the book's overall theoretical perspective. Suicide is a topic which fascinates many in the field of thanatology, which is a more formal title for the field of death and dying. It is fascinating in that the very act itself is often shrouded in mystery, and it is seemingly contrary to the vital image of existence which most people cherish. We will see that the suicidal act is influenced by the social context within which it takes place. Euthanasia, the subject of the final chapter, is an issue which, while intensely personal (in dealing with the termination of a person's existence), also reflects the image of death in the larger society.

This book looks at death, dying, and bereavement from within the context of the American experience. The American image of death is a unique one, as is the image of death in any society. Obviously, we cannot generalize from this study to other societies. It is not possible within the parameters of this book to thoroughly examine the entire range of cultural variations in the depth to which the American image is examined.

CHAPTER ONE

Death:
A Theoretical Perspective

THROUGHOUT THE HISTORY of humanity, and even in prehistoric times, people have sought to give meaning to death. The evidence of this surrounds us, whether it be an army of statues created to protect a Chinese emperor, the pyramids of Egypt, or the Tomb of the Unknown Soldier. All of these are statements about death, and the meaning that it has for people. Death is an event that everyone knows about, but about which little is known. We do know that at one point life as we know it ceases to be. Beyond that, we know little except what is told to us by seers, mystics, prophets, and those who claim to have returned from the dead. From the time that humanity first became aware, people have had to grapple with the question of their mortality. They have answered that question in many different ways, usually in response to many different experiences and reasonings. But the quest has always been there—the search for an answer to the question, "Why was I born, if just to die?"

To live and then die meaninglessly is a terrible fate. And so humanity struggles to find an answer which will make sense of existence. "Why death?" is and has been a fundamental question for all people. Answers to this question become infused in cultures and are passed on to succeeding generations. Most cultures are blendings of many different rationales and explanations of death, which means that the value and meaning of death within a particu-lar culture may be many-faceted.

1

In American society, which will be the focus of this book, death has many meanings. It may mean that one is to dwell in heaven or hell. To some, death is a state of nothingness. To others, death is a transitory state until one returns in another life or life form. These are some of the various explanations for the *state* of being dead. Being dead is very different from dying, which is a process of living.

The way in which one dies is an important part of death, and so it has its own meanings. For example in America, altruistic suicide—where one gives his or her life for another—is highly valued. Taking your life in the face of a painful and lingering fatal illness is not seen as a good act. Thousands of dollars will be spent by the state to keep a suicidal prison inmate alive, so that the state can then carry out the capital punishment verdict and kill him or her. The federal government will devote great energies to save the lone sailor and his foundering boat caught in a storm at sea; and at the same time support the toxic tobacco industry through large subsidies. In American society, a high number of automobile deaths is acceptable; a high number of crib deaths is not.

The dying process involves individuals who behave in ways contingent upon the situation in which they find themselves. Their behavior, in other words, is influenced by their understanding of the situation. "Understanding" is a subjective process. It involves the individual's internal symbolic constructs, which we will call images. Images are internal recreations of our unique experiences, which are combined with and influenced by our emotions and past experiences. However, images are not simply static, emotionally-tinged visual impressions. The human mind is such that we can internally influence the images that we hold. We can both act on and react to our internalized images.

We are assuming that the individual is born with some elementary drives toward biological survival, which Boulding calls a biological value system.[1] Lifton posits the existence of what he calls an inchoate image: "a vital or controlling image, which determines the direction of the organism's activity."[2] The society into which we are born teaches us through the socialization process the commonly held values of the larger social organization. These acquired images, which come to dominate the inchoate biological image, are what Boulding calls the "public image." Every public or collective image begins in the mind of some single individual, and only becomes public as it is shared and incorporated within the images held by others. Society is involved in the process of transmitting, legitimizing, and enforcing images. Cassirer states that "a glance at the development of the various symbolic forms shows us that their essential achievement is not that they copy the outward world in the inward world or that they simply project a finished inner world outward, but rather that the two factors of 'inside' and 'outside,' of 'I' and 'reality' are *determined* and delimited from one another only in these symbolic forms and through their mediation."[3]

The images held by individuals are strongly influenced by the social environment. Where the individual exists in a state of reduced awareness, public images can come to dominate his or her thinking to the point of determining the individual's behavior. Because consciousness (awareness of self) develops out of socialization, the influences of the external environment can be profound.

These two assumptions—that human beings are unique, internally-imaging animals, and that the environment strongly affects this process—form the basis for our discussion of thanatology, the study of death. The nature and function of imagery is such that to disregard either its psychological or social aspects would render our examination of the subject incomplete.

An example of the importance of internal imagery is its explanatory value in understanding the individual's reaction to the death of a loved person. Small children, not yet having a complete and accurate image of death, often will not grieve as adults might expect. This is because of the child's inability fully to "imagine," or comprehend, what has taken place. The importance of considering the social environment's effect on our image and hence our behavior is seen in understanding mourning behavior. In mourning behavior, which is the social aspect of the grief process, the inchoate feelings of the griever are channeled into socially appropriate ways of behaving on the basis of social custom. Social custom is another term for normative behavior—the valued ways of acting which represent in action the person's internalized image of the world.

Because images serve as inner schema upon which behavior is based, we have to understand the internalized image—the frame of reference—which precedes and determines behavior if we are to understand human behavior itself. This internal representation of the world and the self's relationship to the world will determine behavior; external stimuli which impinge upon the individual will not. Herbert Blumer speaks to this point when he argues that hu-

man beings act toward things on the basis of the meanings that
things have for them.[4] For example, the message, "The medical
tests show that you have cancer" will produce very different reactions among people. Those who have seen others die painfully
and whose images of cancer include such things as fear, hopelessness, and pain might react differently from those whose images
contain a belief in medicine, a determination to survive, or a strong
religious belief system.

Sheehan describes the functioning of the image as providing
a basis for action in this manner:

> It structures and creates some order that is meaningful and rele-
> vant to our physical and to our psychological needs out of the
> terrifying chaos that is the world of sight, sound, smell, taste,
> touch and movement. Through the image we sift, select and
> render down to a manageable scale both the world of the objects
> and our own human experience. Furthermore, with the help
> of images we learn to span time and so relate the objects and
> experiences in the present; this then assists abstraction and clas-
> sification. Again, by using images of the past as a bridge to
> the present, man is better able to tolerate discomforts and frus-
> trations in the present for the sake of a future satisfaction.
> Thus, when an infant manages to survive the mother's tempo-
> rary absence without panic he is probably enabled to do this
> because images of the mother's face and body have begun to
> form themselves and thus he can comfort himself while she
> is not actually present. The image also "fixes" an experience
> and so helps to preserve this experience for future use and
> reference. In the form of an image, experience retains some of
> the original vivacity and effect.[5]

How do these images develop? Blumer believes that the images
we hold (he uses the term "meanings that things have") are derived
from the messages in social interaction.[6] In other words, our images
are the products of our social interactions. Blumer does not deny
the internal dynamics of symbol formulations—the psychoformative process—for he acknowledges the importance of interpretation
as a formative process in which meanings are used and revised
as instruments for the production of action. Symbolic interaction-
ism is, according to Blumer, grounded in the root, or basic images
which all of us have of the self and the world. The process of
social interaction is the development of a shared image of the world.
People agree to interpret the world and themselves in certain shared

ways. These regularities allow for the smooth functioning of social groups. Examples of our shared, or collective, images are such concepts as "fair play," our belief in the importance of progress, and in the goodness of the democratic political system.

Parsons likewise acknowledges the importance of the image in understanding human behavior when he writes that "the major structure of the ego is a precipitate of the object-relations which the individual has experienced in his life history" and that the internalization of the social environment provides the core of human personality.[7] Parsons acknowledges the ability of the human being to act upon his or her own images, and states, "While the main content of the structure of the personality is derived from social systems and culture through socialization, the personality becomes an independent system through its relations to its own organism and the uniqueness of its life experience; it is not a mere epiphenomenon of the structure of society."[8] Parsons, like a great many other sociologists, opted for an investigation of social life—focusing on the structure and functioning of the larger social system—and paid comparatively little attention to the individual.

According to the social psychological paradigm that I have just described, both the individual and the social organization are necessary parts of any explanation of human behavior. The individual learns to symbolize from the social environment. The social environment retains and passes on to the individual shared meanings about the world. Some of these meanings (images) concern death and dying, and are central to all other images that are held by individuals and the larger social group (society or culture). In our approach to thanatology, we will take a social psychological perspective which allows us to examine images of mortality from the perspective of both the individual and the larger society.

Individual Meanings of Death

Each of us holds an image of death. That image is the sum of all our thoughts, feelings, and experiences concerning death. For example, someone may have had a traumatic encounter with death as a child, which resulted in an overwhelming sense of vulnerability. This becomes an important part of that person's image of death. Our image may include fears of the unknown, or a theologically based conviction that death leads to a better life. Many of us retain as a part of our image of death the belief that to die a hero's death battling for one's country is a good death. Some people's image of death has been influenced through reading popular books on death and dying. Common experiences can have a long-lasting effect upon a society's image of death; an example is the impact of nuclear bombing upon the Japanese psyche. Our individual images of death, while having some content similar to the collective image, are also the products of our own unique experiences and thoughts. But what about personal death? Can we really know of it, and fully accept our mortality? Sigmund Freud believed not, for he saw death in a unique way.

The Drive Toward Death

Freud built his theory of human behavior upon the premise that the actions of individuals were influenced by the pleasure principle. The basic drive possessed by all human beings, according to Freud, is a drive toward physical pleasure. As a child, the pleasure is found in various parts of the body, but successful maturing finds the individual receiving the greatest physical pleasure from heterosexual intercourse.[9]

This theory, for the most part, served Freud well. But there were some human behaviors that he was unable to explain in terms of his theory. One of these behaviors was what Freud termed the repetition compulsion. This is the urge to repeat painful and sometimes traumatic experiences in such forms as dreams and children's games. The repetition compulsion is also seen in the behaviors of individuals who act in ways that lead them into repeated unpleasurable experiences, thus appearing to be cursed by tragedy. Clearly these experiences which are repeated over time "include no possibility of pleasure."[10] How, then, to account for such actions?

In order to explain these behaviors, as well as providing a better understanding of masochistic behavior in general, Freud postulated the metapsychological concept of a drive toward destruction, which competes with the pleasure principle. This was a major shift in Freud's thinking. Prior to the development of the death instinct theory, which took place late in Freud's life, he had argued that the pleasure principle—the instinctual drive toward pleasure manifested in sexual activity—was the primary force in the individual's life.

Freud was, at this point, thinking and writing on more and more abstract levels. This metapsychological inquiry concerned itself with questions in psychology which deal with the philosophical significance of mental processes. Being metapsychological in its construction, Freud's death instinct theory is not as clinically well grounded as his earlier work. Also, the postulation of a death instinct shifted Freud's theory from a unipolar to a dualistic perspective. Now the mind was not only at war with the environment (as civilization imposed restraints on the pleasure seeking individual), but the mind was also at war with itself because it contained not only life instinct (pleasure, reproduction) but also an instinct to move toward death (pain, destruction). This urge to become inorganic again—to return to an earlier entropic state—led Freud to his famous statement, "the aim of all life is death."[11] Clearly this was a major reformulation of Freud's theory. Interestingly, it has received little recognition among Freud's followers through the years, a group known for its adherence to orthodoxy. (To wax analytic for a moment, we might ask if the well-known high fear of death among physicians has been a factor in Freud's followers defending against the acceptance of the death instinct.)[12]

Some years prior to the publication of *Beyond the Pleasure Principle,* in which he postulated the existence of a death instinct, Freud wrote an influential paper entitled "Thoughts for the Times of War and Death."[13] In this paper, Freud asserts that no one really believes in his or her own death. We all think of ourselves as immortal because in our unconscious we are, in fact, unable to conceive of ourselves as dead.[14] Because our unconscious has always existed—that is, we did not "think" before we "were"—it is impossible for us to fully imagine a state of not being. One cannot imagine one's own death without becoming a spectator to the event, thereby in a sense removing oneself from death's full dominion. But if we can't really imagine our own deaths, what about the fears of death which people do experience? Since Freud was writing about unconscious immortality prior to his development of the death instinct, he turned to his sexual theory to explain people's fear of death. Accordingly, the fear of death became a secondary fear; what is primary is a sense of guilt, according to Freud.[15] Later this was elaborated upon as a product of fear of castration.[16] By subsuming the fear of death under the fear of castration, Freud was able to keep his sexual instinct as primary in his theory. However, one could argue that fears of both castration and death are representative of a symbolic loss of power and autonomy, two concepts integral to people's images of life. Further, Freud's fear of castration is a masculine and sexist concept, which requires quite a stretch of the imagination to make it applicable to females.

The fear of death has been extensively investigated by those in the psychoanalytic field. This fear, often thought to have its roots in sexuality as Freud postulated, has not suffered the same fate as Freud's more abstract and pessimistic concept of the death instinct itself. However, recent ethological studies by Lorenz and others which focus on the functions of aggression in animal behavior have renewed interest in Freud's death instinct.[17]

Gifford and Shor provide overviews of the issues surrounding psychoanalytic theories of death.[18] Working independently, these authors point out that the nature of Freudian theory is such as to make it scientifically untestable. Shor notes that Freud himself admitted that his death instinct theory was speculative, and far beyond empirical testing.[19] The concept of the immortal unconscious, when investigated from outside the Freudian conceptual framework, appears as something one can never directly know. The unconscious can only be understood by an interpretation of symbolic representations that are manifested in various human behaviors. Since the unconscious cannot be known, whether or not it is involved in immortal fantasy cannot be subjected to scientific scrutiny. One is left with unprovable, although fascinating, conjecture.

The impact of Freud's writing has been tremendous. His work has influenced many fields such as anthropology, ethology, sociology, and psychology. His concepts of defense mechanisms such as denial and projection, and his arguments for the importance of the developmental process in human growth are but a few of his contributions to our knowledge of human behavior. His death instinct theory, however, has enjoyed little popularity.

Ernest Becker: The Knight of Faith

In his book, *The Denial of Death*, Ernest Becker attempts to reconcile Freud's psychoanalytic thought and existential philosophy.[20] By reinterpreting Freud's examples and findings, Becker argues that the fear of death, and not the sexual instinct, is the primary force governing human behavior.

Initially, Becker states that the fear of death is a natural fear and is present in all people. This fear is healthy, according to Becker, because it serves our need for self-preservation.[21] It is present in all of us, and is the basic fear behind all other fears. Becker's position differs markedly from that of Freud, who believed that the fear of death is not a real fear, but rather masks a deeper fear of castration.

According to Becker, a human being is a creature of paradoxical nature. He or she is a symbolizing thinker, possessing a mind that "soars out to speculate about atoms and infinity" and yet that mind is trapped in a body which is subject to decay and death.[22] As a result, people exist in a dilemma. A fine writer, Becker describes the paradoxical nature of man's existence:

> Man is literally split in two: He has an awareness of his own splendid uniqueness in that he sticks out of nature with a towering majesty, and yet he goes back into the ground a few feet in order blindly and dumbly to rot and disappear forever. It is a terrifying dilemma to be in and to have to live with.[23]

This, then, is humanity's existential position. While our minds can dwell on thoughts of perfection and immortality, our bodies constantly remind us of our inevitable death.

Existential philosophy is concerned with the meaning that death assumes for the individual. As one becomes aware that he or she exists, one also becomes aware that that existence is limited. The full realization of the temporality of life—of our mortal condition—brings to question the very meanings (images) of life itself.

According to Becker, an individual who fully confronts the nature of his or her own existence comes face to face with the horror of unknown death; the hell of a terminal existence while just waiting to die. Here the existentialists make an important distinction: Abstract death, as it is often considered in the more classical philosophies, is not of great concern. What is important is *my* death—that personal, emotion-laden, one-to-a-customer ending. Carl Jung was also aware of the differences between abstract and personal death when he wrote:

> But when one is alone and it is night and so dark and still that one hears nothing and sees nothing but the thoughts which add and subtract the years, and the long row of disagreeable facts which remorselessly indicate how far the hand of the clock has moved forward, and the slow, irresistable approach of the

wall of darkness which will eventually engulf everything you love, possess, wish, strive, and hope for—then all our profundities about life slink off to some undiscoverable hiding place, and fear envelops the sleepless one like a smothering blanket.[24]

We shall see in our discussion of grief that these concepts of abstract and personal death serve as very different motivations for grieving. Our mortal condition is something over which we have no control. There is no way of our avoiding death, and in this way death differs from all other human situations. As a result, when one faces death, one faces total failure. This leads to a questioning of the meaning of existence itself. Becker sees this existential confrontation with death as unbearable. To truly confront one's own mortality will drive one mad. "Mad because," Becker states, ". . . everything that man does in his symbolic world is an attempt to deny and overcome his grotesque fate."[25] In other words, Becker would say that our image of the world and ourselves is based to a large extent upon our denial of death. This is not, according to Becker, necessarily a bad motive. In fact, in order to be protected from the awfulness of death, one should use the defense mechanism of denial. For Becker, it is exactly this that makes life bearable: our ability to deny the terror of our existence. This is the reason for people's desire to treat death as a taboo subject. The only way to live well is to deny death.

Becker argues that Freud can be reinterpreted in such a way as to reinforce his argument. Such Freudian concepts as anality, the Oedipus project, the primal scene, penis envy, and the fear of castration are reinterpreted by Becker to show that the fear of death is the basic issue with which the child is contending. Becker claims that the body "is one's animal fate that has to be struggled against in some ways." Sex becomes a "screen for terror," blocking out the fear of death.[26] Developing sexually means coming to a realization of one's sexual potential, but also one's bodily mortality. As Becker puts it, "Sex is an inevitable component of man's confusion over the meaning of his life, a meaning split hopelessly into two realms—symbols (freedom) and body (fate)."[27]

Relying heavily on the work of Otto Rank, Becker claims that all forms of sexual behaviors can best be understood in terms of the individual's desire to control his or her body and thereby his or her own mortality. "It is as though one tried to transcend the body by depriving it entirely of its given character, to make sport and new invention in place of what nature 'intended.' "[28] What

Becker attempts to do is to replace Freud's primacy of sex with the primacy of death. According to Becker, the developmental struggles of the individual basically are not concerned with his sexuality, but only in learning to control that sexuality which is to grapple with death issues. To master one's sexual urges is to control one's mortal body, to have mastery over death.

In the works of the existential philosopher Soren Kierkegaard, Becker found an existential perspective which he uses to further strengthen his own argument. Kierkegaard argues that if man did not lie about the nature of his condition—if he didn't spend his life fleeing from his mortality—he would be able to transcend himself and to "open himself to new possibility."[29] Most often, mankind chooses not to face up to the reality of his existence. As Becker describes Kierkegaard's position:

> In the prison of one's character one can pretend and feel that he *is somebody,* that the world is manageable, that there is a reason for one's life, a ready justification for one's actions. To live automatically and uncritically is to be assured of at least a minimum share of the programmed cultural heroics—what we might call "prison heroism": The smugness of the insiders who "know."[30]

If one leads this kind of existence, one must deny those indicators of mortality, one must ignore one's body and its functioning, and one must ignore death itself. Becker could be describing our contemporary American society, which works so hard to avoid the reality of death lest the entire facade of our death denial should crumble before us, leaving us to the ravages of our mortal anxieties. But Becker argues that the acceptance of anxiety, of the reality of our existential position, is the only way to discover an authentic life. And leading an authentic life allows one to develop faith.[31]

Drawing the psychoanalytic theories of Freud and Rank together with Kierkegaard's existentialism, Becker argues that sexual activity is not a response to a basic instinctive drive, but is a struggle to deal with the reality of our mortal creatureliness. Through sexual expression we seek to transcend our fears of death, to escape from its terror. Of course, this human activity, like all human endeavors, meets with failure, and ultimately we are confronted by the reality of death. However, Becker sees a solution to our predicament. By living our lives heroically—that is with honesty and dignity—we can give meaning to our existence. This is not the altruistic heroism of the everyday world, but the heroism in which one is an exemplary member of society. Becker's heroism means allegiance to honesty and dignity, which transcends the social control programming of society.

Here, then, is Becker's knight of faith: the heroic individual. Through the concept of the heroic life Becker offers us a solution to the dilemma in which he has placed us. His romantic, almost quixotic solution is to become the tragic hero. Doomed to ultimate failure (death), surrounded by maddening terror (knowledge and fear of death), the individual can make sense out of life by denying death and transcending mortality through living an honest and dignified existence. This act gives life meaning and makes it all worthwhile.

Becker challenges us to take responsibility for our lives. In a sense Becker is telling us to throw off the shackles (or scapegoats) of Freudian instinct theory and to take charge of our lives. Yes, we ultimately die. But this does not mean that existence is fruitless. For now what we must do is put death out of our minds and focus upon living a meaningful life. This calls for heroics, Becker tells us, because one must carry on in spite of a knowledge of the reality of death.

If we take a moment to separate Becker from his romantic image of the tragic individual questing for his impossible dream, there are criticisms of his position. Becker maintains throughout that if we were to confront our mortality, it would surely drive us crazy. Is this, in fact, true? While Becker's argument appeals to Americans who have been steeped in a culture that denies death, there is no proof for Becker's claim. If one examines other cultures where death is confronted more directly, there is no evidence of this awareness leading to madness. On the contrary, some Eastern traditions would hold that such confrontation and resolution around the issue of one's mortality can ultimately lead to a more peaceful mental state.

Freud argued that the individual could never really "know" his own death. Becker stated that it was possible to develop such an awareness of death, but that it would drive us crazy to constantly do so. Neither of these positions seems to carry much weight when examined outside Becker's argument. This criticism does not necessarily have to be seen as destroying Becker's entire contribution to the field. Like Freud, Becker has made substantial contributions to thanatology. He challenges modern humanity to acknowledge the reality of death. Further, he argues strongly for the responsibility that we each have to examine our lives and to bring meaning to our existence.

One does not have to accept Becker's tragic project or his monocausal explanation of human behavior in order to appreciate *The Denial of Death*. Becker's work is a brilliant attempt to synthesize psychoanalytic and existential thought. The real tragedy lies in his inability to move beyond the confines of his own romantic imagery. One does not have to accept Becker's tragic hero in order to lead an authentic life. The tragic hero of which Becker writes appears to be an image in which he was personally caught up. One may accept the existential reality of death and still be triumphant in living a meaningful existence.

Robert Jay Lifton

While Becker leaves us with a dramatic plea for heroics, Robert Jay Lifton presents us with a more studied perspective, but one that in its own way is no less impassioned.

According to Lifton, the newborn is endowed with a psychological plan that allows for the development of internal images which represent, give meaning, and attach feelings to the external world.[32] The psychoformative process is the symbolic internalizing of experience.[33] This is fundamental to man's psychological life. It is through symbolization that we understand, feel, and attribute meaning to our world and ourselves.

Lifton leans heavily upon the psychoanalytic tradition. Like Becker, however, Lifton sees Freud's perspective in need of reworking in light of contemporary philosophic and psychological thought. Lifton develops the concept of the image as having primary significance for understanding human motivation and behavior. This conceptualization is similar to that developed earlier in this chapter, although it is more psychological in its emphasis.

Confronting the question of our ability to truly know our own mortality, Lifton states that we both have knowledge of our own mortality and refuse to act upon that knowledge. We know and yet we resist knowing. In order to deal with death, we develop a "symbolization of continuity" which allows us to assign meanings and act on our understanding of the world in ways that allow us to accept the inevitability of death, but not necessarily the absurdity of it.[34] Lifton argues that we have the conceptual ability both to realize our death and to counteract that chilling fact by becoming aware of continuities—"imaginative forms of transcending death"—that exist in our world. In other words, we can develop a sense of immortality.[35]

But why do we develop modes of immortality (ways of transcending the reality of death)? We do so in order to cope with the reality of our own finiteness—that maddening destiny of which Becker spoke. Lifton states that the development of a sense of immortality reflects a "compelling and universal" inner quest to establish a relationship to history and the future.[36] This effort is not made in order to compensate for the reality of death as Freud might suggest, nor is it a form of Becker's denial. Rather, it is an image which attempts to relate to the individual's existential condition.

Modes of Immortality

According to Lifton, our struggle for symbolic immortality is at the core of our mental processes. This need to reconcile oneself to the reality of death can be met by finding meaning in one of several modes of immortality—ways in which a person seeks to establish a sense of continuity in the world which lasts longer than his or her own mere life-span.[37] Since we have the ability to contemplate the meaning of our existence, we also have the ability to develop images which extend beyond our own lives.

The biological mode of immortality, according to Lifton, is "the sense of living on through and in one's sons and daughters and their sons and daughters."[38] This mode extends beyond the biological, to include living on in one's "tribe, organization, nation, or even species."[39] With these images in mind, the individual feels that even if he or she must die, he or she will live on in offspring, namesake, cause, or country. Ernest Becker was aware of the immortalizing aspect of thought; he spoke of passing on one's belief system to others. People do this, Becker argues, because one's beliefs are more than just a way of viewing the world; they are a formula for immortality.[40]

The theological mode consists of images of an existence of some sort after death. This mode, represented in the many religions of the world, provides an immortal image for many people. The spiritual power to transcend death is a theme in every major religion. By believing in a life after death, one finds a meaning that mutes the finality of death.[41]

A third mode of symbolic immortality is through one's creative works. This mode takes the form of expressions in the arts or in any form of endeavor that the individual believes to have some lasting value—to live on after the individual. Lifton points out that the scientist accomplishes this by working within a "framework of larger connectedness" as a part of the larger scientific process. This is a form of the creative mode, as one scientific work becomes part of the larger body of knowledge which will continue to exist after the individual's death.[42]

Being survived by nature—finding a sense of permanence in the natural world—is a fourth mode. This mode, Lifton points out, is stronger in other cultures, such as the Japanese, than in American culture. Still, it is evident in America to some extent in the concern among Americans for the natural environment.[43]

Lifton's fifth mode is called experiential transcendence. This mode of symbolic immortality differs from the others, all of which rely to some degree upon external realities and experiences. Experiential transcendence is primarily a psychological process. It is the state of mental awareness at which point there is an experience of transcending time and space. This kind of mystical, ecstatic experience is similar to what Arnold Toynbee calls "merging oneself with ultimate reality."[44] It may take many forms, from LSD to a religious revelation. The experience of such a transcending state leaves the individual with the awareness of an existence beyond death:

> One summer morning I stood for some time by an estuary, enthralled by the flying clouds and gulls and the sunlight on blue water; then I turned up the sleepy village street towards an ancient church which guarded its end. Flowers were rampant in the cottage gardens, and at the sight of one splendidly flaming rose bush my little consciousness broke out of its shell as a chicken breaks out of its egg, into awed awareness of a Supreme Consciousness within whose ambience all that rejoicing beauty was held in love. (None of these poor sloppy little words are any good.)[45]

The author, Rosaline Heywood, thus describes a moment of experiential transcendence, adding a commonly held feeling of frustration in trying to express her feelings in words.

Death and the Developmental Process

In examining the psychoformative process, whereby the individual forms images of the world, Lifton takes a developmental approach. Early in life, the child is confronted with death. Not death as an abstract concept, but the idea of death becomes real for the child as he or she becomes aware of threats to the self. These symbolic death-threats to the child's being are forms of separation, disintegration, and stasis (confinement, lack of mobility). These images also have polar opposites: connection, integrity (wholeness), and movement.[46] Descriptions of children working to master these issues have often been considered in developmental psychology, sometimes in a different terminology. The issues of separation involve the fear of separation from a nurturing mother; disintegration—similar to Melanie Klein's annihilation—originates in the child's fear of physical disintegration; and stasis refers to the deathlike state of an inability to move, the stopping of all activity.[47] The polar opposites of these death-related images are the vital images which represent continuity and life. Connection, the polar opposite of separation, begins with the child's seeking attachment to the nurturing mother. Later in life this becomes highly symbolized in connection with other persons, ideas, or organizations. When this connection is lost, the polar image of separation is present— one of those images Lifton terms "precursors for the idea of death."[48]

Integrity and its polar opposite, disintegration, have a developmental basis also. The infant is threatened with losing control; of losing physical intactness. Early in development, the child has no sense of self, of physical definition. Developing a sense of integrity (wholeness) combats such threats of dissolution of self. In the mature person, integrity takes on a more ethical meaning. However the biological aspect is still a part of the basic meaning of the word.

Finally, the polar issues of movement and stasis must be mastered by the child. An inability to move (stasis) is a deathlike state, and bodily movement is an indication of a vital existence. As adults, we enjoy a sense of progress, development, and change. The opposites of these movement-images are associated with death: total inactivity and a lack of energy.

It is, then, through connection, integration, and movement that the individual comes to terms with the death threats of separation, disintegration, and stasis. These death images are not destroyed or totally negated by this process, but the development of the polar vital images, "associated with vitality and affirmation," provide life-affirming alternatives to the death-related images.[49]

In the development of vital images, the individual begins the psychoformative process which at the adult (more abstract) level becomes the personal basis of the quest for immortality. The modes (ways of connecting with immortality) provide a linkage with that which will live on after the death of an individual. They provide an answer to the threat of an absurd death. For example, one of my students wrote of an experience in Vietnam, where he found himself staring at a village animal which he was about to destroy. The animal returned his stare just prior to its death. The awareness of death so frightened the young soldier that he found himself running back to his buddies to try to surround himself with life, in order to somehow blunt his confrontation with death. Coming face to face with the reality of death brought about a tremendous urge to counteract that image by immersing himself in life images. By developing an image of life which has within it a transcendence of our own mortality, life becomes not only bearable but also meaningful. Something will live on after we die—perhaps in our children, a cause we fought for, a song we wrote. Something will be here after we are gone, which will be evidence that we existed, that we *mattered*. Through one of the modes of immortality, Lifton suggests that we can find a way to transcend absurd death.

Conclusion

In our examination of the social psychological perspective, and in the theories of Freud, Becker, and Lifton, we have seen varied interpretations of the meaning and importance of death. In studying death, dying, and grief, we need to keep in mind that the images of death pervade many levels of social and individual existence.

Freud was unable to account for human behavior with his monistic pleasure principle, and so he had to develop the concept of the death instinct to explain human behavior adequately. Freud postulated a powerful drive toward death. So powerful was this concept, that Freud found himself revising his work in order to incorporate the death instinct as a factor which, along with the drive toward pleasure, determined human behavior. Becker, in reinterpreting psychoanalytic theory, argued for the supremacy of the fear of death to the point of becoming almost as dogmatic as Freud had been in his early writings about the drive toward pleasure. In Robert Jay Lifton's work there is a more balanced approach, synthesizing social, historical, and psychological explanations into a perspective that includes the image of death within the psychological and social processes of life. Lifton states that "we must open ourselves to the full impact of death in order to rediscover and reinterpret the movement and sequence of life."[50]

In the following chapters we will seek to do just that. As we examine the structures of society and social groups, and the individual strivings to cope with death-related social issues that confront humanity today, we will do so from a perspective that includes both social and psychological levels of explanation. The human being is a symbolizing creature who creates internal images of external experience. Commonly held images are necessary in order for social organization to exist. Within a social context, collective images are retained and transmitted which represent the ways in which people make sense of the world.

Collective images are those which are held in common by members of a particular society. Some images held by Americans are fairly well crystallized, such as our belief in the primacy of the nuclear family. Other social images, such as current fashions or trends, tend to be more fluid. In the study of thanatology, we will see that our understanding and experience of death is shaped by our images of the world on many levels, from the deepest values to the most superficial styles of the times. By understanding what death means to us as a society and as individuals, we can come to understand our feelings and behaviors when confronted with the reality of death.

In this study we will examine both individual and social responses to death and dying, keeping in mind the interplay between the individual and society. The issue of man's mortality is central to an understanding of the world on both the individual and the social levels. Both aspects influence, and are in turn influenced by, the death-related images held by individuals, groups, and larger social structures.

Notes

1. Kenneth E. Boulding, *The Image* (Ann Arbor: University of Michigan Press, 1961), p. 72.

2. Robert Jay Lifton, *The Broken Connection* (New York: Simon & Schuster, 1979), p. 40.

3. Ernst Cassirer, *The Philosophy of Symbolic Forms*, Vol. 2, *Mythical Thought* (New Haven: Yale University Press, 1955), pp. 155–56.

4. Herbert Blumer, *Symbolic Interaction* (New York: Prentice-Hall, 1969), pp. 2–5.

5. P. W. Sheehan, ed., *The Function and Nature of Imagery* (New York: Academic Press, 1972), p. 75.

6. Blumer, p. 6.

7. Talcott Parsons, *Social Structure and Personality* (New York: The Free Press, 1964), p. 80.

8. Ibid., p. 82.

9. Sigmund Freud, *An Outline of Psychoanalysis* (New York: W. W. Norton, 1949), Chapter 3.

10. Sigmund Freud, *Beyond the Pleasure Principle*, Vol. 18 of *Standard Ed. of the Complete Psychological Works of S. Freud* (London: Hogarth, 1955), p. 20.

11. Ibid., p. 38.

12. Herman Feifel, et al., "Physicians Consider Death," *Proceedings, 75th Annual Convention, American Psychological Association* (1967): 201–202.

13. Sigmund Freud, *Thoughts for the Times of War and Death*, Vol. 14 of *Standard Ed. of the Complete Psychological Works of S. Freud* (London: Hogarth, 1957), pp. 275–300.

14. Ibid., p. 289.

15. Ibid., p. 297.

16. Ibid., p. 297 (footnote).

17. Lifton, *The Broken Connection*, p. 156.

18. Sanford Gifford, "Freud's Theories of Unconscious Immortality and the Death Instinct," *Journal of Thanatology*, 1 (March-April 1971): 109–127; Ronald E. Shor, "A Survey of Representative Literature on Freud's Death-Instinct Hypothesis, *Journal of Humanistic Psychology* 1, (1961): 73–83.

19. Shor, p. 75; cf. Frank J. Sulloway, *Freud, Biologist of the Mind.* (New York: Basic Books, 1979), pp. 404–415.

20. Ernest Becker, *The Denial of Death* (New York: The Free Press, 1973).

21. Ibid., p. 17.

22. Ibid., p. 26.

23. Ibid.

24. Carl G. Jung, "The Soul and Death," in Herman Feifel, ed., *The Meaning of Death* (New York: McGraw-Hill, 1959), p. 4.

25. Becker, p. 27.

26. Ibid., p. 45.
27. Ibid., p. 44.
28. Ibid., p. 45.
29. Ibid., p. 80.
30. Ibid., p. 87.
31. Ibid., p. 90.
32. Lifton, *The Broken Connection*, p. 40.
33. Ibid., pp. 36–40.
34. Ibid., p. 17.
35. Ibid., p. 18.
36. Ibid., p. 17.
37. Acknowledgement is also due Arnold Toynbee, whose earlier work covered much the same material as Lifton's modes of immortality. See Arnold Toynbee, "Various Ways in which Human Beings Have Sought to Reconcile Themselves to the Fact of Death," in Edwin S. Shneidman, ed., *Death: Current Perspectives* (Palo Alto: Mayfield, 1984), pp. 73–96.
38. Robert Jay Lifton, *Death in Life* (New York: Touchstone, 1976), p. 32.
39. Ibid.
40. Lifton, *The Broken Connection*, p. 255.
41. Lifton, *Death in Life*, p. 32.
42. Lifton, *The Broken Connection*, p. 21.
43. Arnold Toynbee, *Man's Concern with Death* (New York: McGraw-Hill, 1969).
44. Ibid.
45. Ibid., p. 250.
46. Lifton, *Death in Life*, pp. 37–40; *The Broken Connection*, pp. 57–59.
47. Lifton, *Death in Life*, p. 38.
48. Ibid., p. 58.
49. Lifton, *The Broken Connection*, p. 53.
50. Ibid., p. 52.

CHAPTER TWO

Death in America

HUMAN DEATH is not simply the cessation of biological functioning, nor is it merely a state of non-life. While certainly an intensely personal event, most dying takes place within a social milieu. The individual's image of the world, of himself or herself, of dying, are all greatly influenced by the social milieu within which he or she exists. The Roman senator died differently from the Egyptian pharoah. The medieval serf died differently from the contemporary corporate executive. Of course there are some similarities. All face the unknown; all must deal with losing that which they have known in life. But to each person, death means different things depending upon his or her social reality. As a result, the process of dying requires different behaviors on the part of the dying person and the bereaved. An understanding of how a biological process (dying) can take on very different social meanings can be gained by examining the ways in which some Americans have approached death in past times as well as the present.

The Puritans exerted a powerful influence on American history but they should not be seen as completely determining later attitudes and behaviors. Rather, the following examples are to be viewed as case histories, detailing a specific response to death characteristic of a particular time.

The Sacred Death of Early New England

The Puritans who colonized New England in the seventeenth century held an image of the world which differed sharply from that of Americans today. The everyday world of the Pilgrim had within it witches, devils, magic, and hell. The hell of the Puritan was a place of fire and brimstone, and of horrors and torments difficult for us to conceive of or to take seriously. But these things were real for the Puritan. It was

> a world that saw divine perfection, purpose, and design in every detail of nature; a world that accepted the everyday reality of witches and demons and fought back against them with a magic and astrology; a world that was helpless before the devastation of disease, starvation, and neglect. It was a world in which the nights were blacker, the days more silent, and the winters more terrifying and cold than most of the men of the Twentieth Century can even begin to imagine.[1]

The eschatology of the Puritans—that branch of their theology concerned with death—placed the individual in a terrifying position at the end of life. The Puritan belief structure held that the fate of almost all men and women (as well as children) was to burn forever in hell. A very few, selected by God and known only to Him, would enter into Heaven. There was little that the individual could do except to lead as good a life as he or she could, and to pray to be one of the chosen few to go to heaven.

As a result of their beliefs, the act of dying was not one of calm acceptance and peacefulness. Since there was no way of gaining assurance of one's salvation—even for the most devout leaders of the religious community—dying was a time of fear and anguish. To add to the suffering of the dying Puritan, any self-confidence on his or her part that he or she might be saved was interpreted as pride and, therefore, a sure sign that one was destined for eternal damnation. In fact, if one ceased to be fearful of approaching death and damnation, this was a sure sign that one was "either spiritually lost, or stupid, or both."[2] And so the Puritan arrived at death's door armed with nothing but doubt. The Puritan was helpless to do anything about his or her condition, a condition best described as one of sinful depravity. Consequently, dying was a time of fearful suffering and torment, as the individual fought to avoid death and almost certain damnation. The dying Puritan's prayers and acknowledgment of his or her depravity were mixed with an awful fear of an almost inevitable condemnation to hell.

Thomas Shepard, writing of the death of his wife, exemplified the Puritan image of death. He stated first that his wife was a devout Puritan and "had a spirit of prayer beyond ordinary of her time and experiences. She was fit to die long before she did die. . . ." She died because of complications of childbirth, and Shepard spoke of her last hours as spent in "a most heavenly, heart-breaking prayer, after Christ, her Redeemer, for the spirit of life, and so continued praying until the last hour of her death, 'Lord, though I unworthy, Lord, one word, one word, etc.: and so gave up the ghost. Thus God hath visited and scourged me for sins, and sought to wean me from this world."[3]

We see in Shepard's writing that death even permeated the loving description this Puritan gave of his wife (she was so fine a person that she was ready for death long before it occurred). He described her fear of condemnation when death was near as so acute that she begged Christ to intercede and save her from hell.

The Puritan's preoccupation with death and hell can also be seen in Michael Wigglesworth's 224-stanza poem, *The Day of Doom*. Printed in 1662, the poem was so popular that it sold one copy for every twenty-five people in New England. Nine printings followed over the next century. The book was praised by Cotton Mather as destined to be the Book of the Ages, and many a Puritan strove to memorize such lines as the following, which describe hell as a place where:

> With iron bands they bind their hands
> and cursed feet together,
> And cast them all, both great and small,
> into the lake forever,
> Where day and night, without respite,
> they wail, and cry and howl,
> For tort'ring pain which they sustain
> in Body and in soul.[4]

The belief system of the Puritans, which maintained that rewards were only possible in the next life, was reinforced by the prevalence of death. The typical life span in the seventeenth century was thirty years, and deaths were four times as common as they are today.[5] People lived in small, highly interdependent communities, and each adult death represented a threat to the entire community. Children had an especially high death rate, and it was not at all uncommon for a family to experience the deaths of more than half of their children. Since a high infant death rate was the normative expectation, parents did not make the emotional investment in their children that they do today. Plagues were quite common, and in early New England graveyards one can find entire families whose members died within a few months of each other. For example, in Boston in 1677 and 1678, smallpox combined with the normal mortality rate to kill over 20 percent of the population.[6]

In the age of sacred death, death was everywhere, and could not be avoided. But by the same token, death had a meaning for the Puritans, albeit an unpleasant one. As Shepard described it above, death was an act of God: the price that humanity must pay for its depravity. Death did not obliterate the person, but only removed him or her from this life to await the final judgment day. There was a reality beyond the grave for the Puritan as well as a rationale for death itself. Both of these beliefs were a part of the Puritan's theological belief structure.

One of the functions of a belief structure is to provide an explanation of what happens to the dead. The Puritans knew where the dead were, and why they were dead. Simply put, the wages of sin were death. A gloomy view of the end of life, perhaps. Nonetheless, the Puritan was provided with an explanation; a way of understanding what was going on about him. While the Puritans were surely no more fond of death than we are today, they understood it. Death was a result of humanity's fall from grace. Also, the Puritan eschatology was not isolated in a one-hour segment each Sunday; it permeated every aspect of life. The amalgam of belief and community, reinforced by a harsh existence, dominated the mind of the Puritan. Death was everywhere, and it served as a constant reminder of God's power over people.

Gradually, as the eighteenth century wore on, the Puritan belief system lost its hold on the people, although earlier a desolate existence had reinforced Puritan beliefs. As life got better and material rewards increased, a tension was steadily growing. The double bind of attempting to lead a saintly life while at the same time knowing that one was most likely predestined to a hellish fate became more and more untenable. The only recourse was to reject the premises of such a belief system, and this was the option chosen by most of the population. As a result of this change in people's image of the world, behavior associated with death and dying changed as well. A sacred image of death was no longer predominant by the time of the American Revolution. By 1800, the sacred death of the Puritan had been replaced in the public image by a more naturalistic outlook on mortality, and the focus had shifted away from the dead person, and onto the bereaved survivors.

Secular Death

By the beginning of the nineteenth century, several changes in American life and thinking had combined to produce a radical shift in the image of death that the people commonly held. This changed image was to last until the time of World War II. The period of the rise of the image of secular death, with its intense focusing upon the bereaved, is also associated with a blurring of the lines between the worlds of the living and the dead.[7] Clearly, in the previous age of sacred death, there was a sharp distinction between the two spheres of the living and the dead. During the period of the secularization of death, however, contact with the dead became a topic of popular interest. For example, over a million people were involved in the spiritualism movement. Spirit photographs, accounts of life in Heaven (which tended to be very middle class), and actual contact with spirits of the dead became a part of the popular culture. The result was a blurring of the distinction between the two worlds, separated only by some mysterious dimension that served as a barrier between them.

It may well be that the intensity of grieving during this period was due in part to the closeness of the worlds of the living and the dead. The proximity of the dead may require an extensive grieving process on the part of society's members in order to differentiate clearly the living from the dead. In contemporary society, as a contrasting example, the worlds of the living and the dead are seen as clearly separate entities. The grieving process has diminished in importance as these worlds are seen as further apart.

The rise of science also affected society's image of death. Charles Darwin's *Origin of Species,* published in 1859, challenged the concept of God as creator and destroyer. Evolutionists argued that human beings and present-day animals evolved from lower life forms. Those who were successful in this process did not do so by the grace of God, but by being the most fit to survive. The scientists involved in studying nature were not concerned with humanity's ultimate destination, but rather the process of its development to its current position in the world. Natural selection, the process used to explain evolution, depended upon death. Death was a necessary event in order for new life to survive and for evolution to occur. As a result of popular acceptance of evolutionary theory, death was no longer considered a sacred encounter between the individual and God. Death became a collective process, a natural event, as a secular understanding of death replaced the sacred image of the earlier age.

A powerful implication of evolutionary theory is that life is constantly improving; that progress is an important aspect of life. This is certainly not the long-suffering and fatalistic philosophy of the Puritan. Instead, people of this secular period believed that life could be made better, and not just endured. And life *was* getting better. Science was beginning to combat diseases that had decimated populations in the past. The germ theory stated that germs cause death, not God. In the minds of the people, God was displaced from his position as ruler of all nature. Death is not caused by original sin; it is caused by disease. Disease is subject to the laws of nature. Therefore, as humanity learns to control nature, it will ultimately control death as well. Pain, earlier interpreted as suffering for sin, was also becoming controllable. This is another example of the displacement of God. What had once been His sole province was now being controlled by people. We should understand that these changes in people's image of the world did not take place all that easily. Some people objected to the introduction of pain relievers as an unnatural interfering with the sacred process of suffering, and evolutionary theory is still being fought by creationists who wish to see the Biblical theory of the origin of life given at least equal representation in the schools.

During this period, no longer was God to be relied upon to provide for this sectarian population. Instead, people were relying on their own abilities to provide for themselves. And that included providing for one's survivors after one's death. This new image of death required a change from a reliance on "divine providence to human prudence," as the good life here on earth became something that could be passed on.[8] More and more people were living in heterogeneous urban areas, and they began to rely upon amassed capital, rather than upon their family or community. The security of family and community was replaced with financial security. Death was less of a spiritual matter, and became an event which one met in an organized and rational manner. For example, the life insurance business, almost unknown prior to 1800, boomed after 1830. Life's worth became something quantifiable in terms of dollars and cents. Life had become convertible to money, and in the process human life had lost some of its sacred and priceless qualities.[9]

The nineteenth century was a time of disenfranchisement for the Protestant churches. An aftermath of the American revolution was a severing of the church from the state, and a concomitant diminishing of power of religious leaders. Historian Ann Douglas sees this as a time of the feminization of religion, as the powerful and dominating clergy of an earlier period were replaced by passive, emotionally oriented men.[10]

The rise of science threatened the more conservative aspects of Christian theology which had been popular in the past. The more liberal Protestant groups responded by questioning and attacking many of the religious tenets which were parts of the foundation of earlier Christian theology. The just and terrible God of the earlier age was reinterpreted as being all-forgiving and compassionate. Hell became either a temporary diversion along what would ultimately be the road to Heaven or, less concretely, a temporary spiritual suffering which prepared the sinner for paradise. Eternal damnation was no longer a probable outcome of death. As the threat of damnation became less and less potent, converting the unbeliever became less important than assuaging his or her sorrow. The minister, therefore, shifted his emphasis from jeremiad hell-fire-and-damnation preaching to helping the bereaved to cope with their loss.

Even though life was getting better in comparison with past generations, the popular literature abounded with stories and poems that dwelt on death and grieving. Books were published with such titles as *Agnes, and the Key to Her Little Grave,* and *The Empty Crib.* It sounds melodramatic, and that is exactly what it was. But while today we view the melodrama for amusement, we should remember that in its time it was considered to be a serious art form. Poetry seeking to console the grief-stricken was published in newspapers and popular magazines. The following, written by an English-woman, is a typical poetic piece of the time.

THE LITTLE SHROUD
LETITIA E. LANDON
She put him on a snow-white shroud,
A chaplet on his head;

And gathered early primroses
    To scatter o'er the dead.

She laid him in his little grave,
    'Twas hard to lay him there
When spring was putting forth its flowers,
    and everything was fair.

She had lost many children—now
    The last of them was gone,
And day and night she sat and wept
    Beside the funeral stone.

One midnight, while her constant tears
    Were falling with the dew,
She heard a voice, and lo! her child
    stood by her, weeping too!

His shroud was damp, his face was white,
    He said, "I cannot sleep,
Your tears have made my shroud so wet,
    Oh, mother, do not weep!"

Oh, love is strong!—the mother's heart
    Was filled with tender fears;
Oh, love is strong!—and for her child,
    Her grief restrained its tears.

One eve a light shone round her bed,
    And there she saw him stand
Her infant in his little shroud,
    A taper in his hand.

"Lo! mother, see my shroud is dry,
    And I can sleep once more!"
And beautiful the parting smile
    The little infant wore!

And down within the silent grave
    He laid his weary head,
And soon the early violets,
    Grew o'er his grassy bed.

The mother went her household ways
    Again she knelt in prayer,
And only asked of heaven its aid
    Her heavy lot to bear.

The emphasis in the poem is not upon the dead child as much as it is upon the unconsolable mother, whose tears were extensive enough to wake the dead. This example of the popular poetry of the time raises two questions: Why were the women of this era not finding support for their bereavement in family and society, and if death had become thought of only as a natural evolution to a better heavenly state, why was there such an extensive focusing upon grief?

The answer lies in part in the fact that consolation literature was written for a female audience whose position in society had shifted dramatically from earlier times. This literature, which abounded during the later nineteenth century, sought to ease the burden of the griever (most usually the mother), whose feelings were apparently not shared nor understood by others.

The identity and power of women as central figures in the self-sustaining family had disappeared. Women of the seventeenth century were not only producers and caretakers of the children. They were providers who produced homespun clothing, gave medical care, and performed many functions necessary for surviving in a harsh environment. Later in Colonial times, women might produce some income through a cottage industry. But in the Victorian world of growing technology and industrialization, woman as provider became woman as consumer. The cooperative theocratic community had given way to the anonymity and competition of urban life. Jobs that were once her sole province were being taken over by craftsmen and professionals. Men were finding a meaning for their lives in the world of commerce, and wife and family took a back seat to the battle of competition in order to survive. All that was left for a great many women was to love their children. The world of emotions became foreign to the Victorian gentleman, and women received no emotional support from their husbands.

Douglas argues that women were seeking in their church affiliations meaning for life and emotional support which was not to be found in their marriages.[12] One of the predominant messages in the sentimental literature of this period is that the true goodness of womanhood was fated to endure suffering at the hands of their unfeeling husbands. The combination of women and emotionally-oriented ministers served to produce an outpouring of sentimental literature that focused a great deal of its attention upon the griever. Perhaps, as Douglas suggests, the intense emphasis upon grieving which was so much in vogue during the time of secular death was in part a grieving over a loss of an image of life and a concomitant set of values which was fading from existence.

For hundreds of years, the dying individual had been at the center of the image of death.[13] In the nineteenth century this changed, as death became a part of the natural process. This view has continued into the twentieth century, and science and technology now heavily influence our contemporary image of death. At the same time that death was losing its sacred meanings, the more emotionally based nature of community living was being eclipsed by the heterogeneous life in cities and towns. Competition and contract were beginning to replace cooperation and kinship, and material goods were pursued in order to provide the emotional comfort and security once found in the community and religion. The death of a loved one found the individual, especially the woman, bereft of any support. The intense grieving of that sentimental period may have been for a lost set of values as well as for the death of a particular person.

In addition to sorrowing over the loss of a set of values and a way of life, the extensive grief may have also been triggered by a sense of the loss of the image of a sacred death. Recall that the Puritan had a meaning for death: it was God's will. It was not for believers to question or understand God's ways, according to Puritan thinking. Death might not have made sense to the Puritan, but that would be because of his or her inability to understand how God works. Still, there was a solace there, which existed in the Puritan's knowing that God had willed the death to occur. No such solace was available to the individual living in the age of secular death. "God's will" had been replaced by an actuarial table.

Not since Job had humanity in the Western world been without the support of a religious explanation for mortality. The one recourse left was for people to engage in extensive mourning, which became popular during this period. Ornate funerals, cemetery statuary, and a long mourning period provided some solace, as well as an opportunity to display one's wealth and social standing.

One other factor may have contributed to the over-reaction to loss which seems to have predominated during this period: Recall that during this age the worlds of the living and the dead had become closely connected in the popular mind. Spiritualism, spirit photographs, and literature which purported to describe the world of the dead were all extremely popular. It may be that the proximity of the world of the dead necessitated a longer and more extreme reaction to death. As Blauner points out, extensive mourning rituals tend to exist in cultures where spirits are held to have power to affect this world.[14] Perhaps when the world of the dead is seen as close by and able to affect the world of the living, extensive grieving and mourning are necessary in order to emotionally separate from the deceased.

The Avoidance of Death in Contemporary America

Philippe Aries claims that the last thirty years have seen the beginnings of another phase in our attitudes toward death. Death has become forbidden, a taboo topic.[15] While I do not disagree with Aries's observation, I do not think that the changes he notes constitute a total redefinition of the image of death. Death is still a secular event; a natural process. Our basic image of death is similar to that which predominated a century ago. If anything has changed, it has been the way in which we seek to defend against death and the grief that may follow.

After World War II, an event commonly used as a mark for the shift in our attitude toward death, the extensive mourning process and the sentimental approach to grief of the past were seen as old-fashioned and a waste of time. Perhaps the extensive killing in World War II, both on the battlefield and in the concentration camps, following as it did so soon after the inglorious deaths suffered during World War I, combined to produce a kind of "death overload." As a result, the multiple losses families and individuals experienced led to a desire to rid reality of extensive grieving and mourning rituals, and a desire to seek out the good life free from death and sorrow. And thus the old ways of feeling and behaving no longer provided meaning for people.

Also, the materialistic world, which had captured the hearts of the men of an earlier era, was now becoming available to women and children as well. Women were finding meaning in work and as consumers, and the sexist educational barriers common in the past were fading. Children also began to benefit from the wealth of society and soon became as adept at consumerism as their parents. Thus a new, meaningful role for women came into being.

Death has also become less of an everyday reality, and we have now reached the point where we have what is termed the first "death-free generation."[16] Statistically, a family can reasonably expect that a death will not occur within it for twenty years. Also, death has been institutionalized—hospitals, hospices, and nursing homes serve to keep the dying out of sight. Death is thus more avoidable than it was in the past. Since it is also contrary to many of our values, we can begin to understand why it is not a subject that we wish to discuss openly. Indeed, a great many people find the subject an intolerable one to deal with, and try to avoid any mention of it.

Part of this avoidance of death lies in the fact that death is, in a sense, un-American. In the following section, we will examine the values which we hold in our society that are antithetical to the secular definition of death as a natural event.

The Image of Death in Contemporary America

Howard and Scott studied American values and the reality of death.[17] Their study gives us a better understanding of just why we prefer to avoid the subject of death as much as we do. First, they point out that death implies separation. Whether one believes that the dead person is existing in another state (i.e., heaven) or no longer exists in any form, death involves separation from the world as we know it. Existing relationships, both emotional and social, are severed by death. Those relationships will never exist in the same ways again.

Death is also unknown. Every sacred explanation of death requires belief on the part of those accepting it as valid. Whether appealing to the authority of the Bible or the logic of a particular theological argument, at some point the individual must make a "leap of faith." We have no proof of what it is like to be dead. Death is as much an unknown today as it has ever been, popular claims of those "brought back to life" notwithstanding.

Another fact of death is that people die. Human beings do not live forever, in spite of our efforts to escape this reality by denying our own mortality. The death of anyone is a reminder to us that the bell will someday toll for us. Death tells us that mortality exists in all human beings.

Another aspect of death is that it signifies the end of all activity as we know it. There is a lack of movement associated with death: one is "dead as a doornail." Also death as a natural event may be meaningless. This implies that death may be absurd; without obvious import in the larger scheme of things. Devoid of religious interpretation, death may be seen as a-rational. It occurs when it occurs. Although we have the ability to make death happen by means of murder and suicide, we may also die before we can fulfill our life's intention. Humanity's secular image of the world can only take it so far and explain so much. While scientific knowledge and technology may grow tremendously, there is little psychological comfort to be found in germ theory.

An examination of some of our contemporary values will show that a conflict exists between these values and the realities of death that we have just examined. For example, Americans believe in progress. We view time as linear, and believe that life has a particular direction to it. Time has become important to us, and we measure ourselves in terms of it. We admire those who reach high goals at a young age. We describe ourselves in terms of our careers. One of our major corporations had a motto which proclaimed that progress was their most important product. We ask our children what they want to be when they grow up. All of these examples point to our strong emphasis upon linear direction, or progress. Getting ahead is a part of our image of the successful American.

This image of progress as a valued part of the American ethos is closely associated with an action-orientation among Americans. Social status may hinge upon what one does, both in terms of occupation and leisure activities. Moreover, Americans are pragmatic. The world around us is a problem to be solved; to be acted upon with "American know-how." Passivity, intellectual pursuits, and inward contemplation are not dominant values in the American image. Some would argue that these are considered negatively; as un-American.[18] But action, as exemplified in an emphasis upon youth and activity, is highly valued in our collective image of the good life. Howard and Scott point out the converse of this: guilt is assigned to idleness. From Ben Franklin on, Americans have been reminded that if you are doing nothing, you must be up to no good.

Materialism is another powerful value in American life. One's success is often measured in terms of the accumulation of wealth and goods. In other times and cultures it was possible to be poor and yet highly respected by society. In today's America that is no longer the case. Personal worth is more often judged in terms of one's conspicuous consumption than of expertise, education, or family. This has led to an increased valuation on things of this world: on one's possessions and wealth. To some—if not most—Americans, the kingdom of heaven is available right here on earth if they can just swing the down payment.

Along with materialism has come our instrumental orientation toward life. We have produced a technology that is expanding at a tremendous rate. With its roots going back to the Biblical admonition to "subdue the earth," Americans today place great value upon science and technology. Our image is one of the world as controllable by the application of scientific information, a result of a progression of scientific philosophy dating back over the past century. For example, one hears television fund raisers explain that this or that particular disease can be cured, given enough time and, of course, your money. (As an aside, it is interesting to note that if we accept the legitimacy of this argument—often reinforced by pleas from the victims themselves—then the guilt for the deaths *not* prevented lies with us for not having provided enough money.)

It seems as though the human condition itself has become a solvable problem in the current American image. Millions of dollars are spent by Americans to learn how to solve what are often self-determined problems. Workshops, therapies, popular books, and tape recordings are ready to show the individual how to solve problems in life, including facing death. This exalted view of science and technology has led to the establishing of the business of cryogenics, whereby people are frozen at the time of death, to be thawed out later when science finds a cure for whatever killed them (as well as a method to thaw them out). American faith in technology has brought us to a belief that the individual can beat death—that science may find a cure for the major diseases before he or she develops one of them. This belief may not be too logical, but it is comforting nonetheless, especially when one wants to continue an unhealthy activity such as smoking.

It is obvious that the notion of death is antithetical to the American image of what is important in life. Death represents failure; failure of science to keep the person alive. Death also represents the failure of the individual who is, after all, master of his fate. Death represents stasis (a lack of movement). This is not only opposite to the American notion of progress and activity; it is downright sinful. There is, as a result, a tinge of guilt upon the state of being dead in America.

The meaninglessness which may accompany death—often explained in other cultural images as outside of knowing—runs counter to the American belief in pragmatic rationality. One can find this aspect of our image of the world deeply threatened by what we will discuss later as inappropriate loss: the deaths that shouldn't have happened; those that don't make sense. The value Americans place on materialism requires an emphasis upon meaning and pleasure derived from this world. Death, which separates the individual from the material world, threatens the meanings we have established by placing a value on material possessions.

Another way in which death threatens the American image is by its ultimate triumph over science. No matter how long the battle or what the cost (in terms of continued suffering), death ultimately wins. (This raises many important questions that will be discussed later in the context of extending the life of the terminally ill.) On a more abstract level, the ultimate triumph of death (Emily Dickinson notwithstanding) may leave the American intellectually challenged as to the validity of his or her belief in science, and emotionally despairing in the face of ultimate helplessness. Like the hedonist who flees from death by pursuing pleasure, the contemporary American is confronted with an even greater despair when his or her defense against mortality—a belief in the omnipotence of science—fails.

The separation that death signifies runs counter to the American image, which holds to the value of a few intimate relationships to meet our emotional needs. Death threatens those relationships, exposing us to the dangers of a cold, impersonal, and competitive world. The helplessness and despair that are so much a part of our grieving process assert themselves when death arrives and we find ourselves with no one to turn to for support.

And so we react to the reality of death with dread. The subject is obscene; it is pornographic. It is not polite to speak easily of death. We are too uncomfortable with it. It doesn't fit into our image of life. Institutions are created to contain death, and emphasis is placed upon youth, for to grow old is to exemplify the decay of the body. Anxiety often accompanies a confrontation with death. Where there is a lack of definition in the individual's image, anxiety will be felt. As the reality of death impinges upon our consciousness, we respond to our growing anxiety by repressing the subject. The cognitive dissonance is too great, and so we shunt death out of our awareness by avoiding the subject as much as possible.

We have seen from Howard and Scott's analysis that the reality of death often runs counter to values in American society. We have organized ourselves in such a way as to be immune from individual death as much as possible. Bureaucracy, our dominant form of organization, has replaced the interdependent community. Death is dealt with by substitution in a bureaucracy, where ideally no one is indispensible. The organization itself has become, in a sense, immortal. Taking a lesson from bureaucracy, on an everyday level we tend to deal with death and other forms of loss by substituting one pet for another, and a new love for the old. Often this is done without a complete working through of the grief process, leading to complications at a later date.

The institutionalization of American society, the process whereby we have become more and more dependent upon large-scale organizations to meet our daily needs, also performs the function of taking care of the dead and dying. As a result, the problem of death is banished to the hospital or nursing home. Out of sight, out of mind.

Often death is avoided by placing the institution between ourselves and the dying. Recently, for example, the parents of a retarded new-born chose to deny the doctors permission to perform simple lifesaving surgery. The baby remained in the hospital and slowly starved to death because of an intestinal blockage that could easily have been removed. The father would call the institution every day to inquire about the child's condition. The hospital, in this case, became death caretakers, while the parents went on with their lives, avoiding any contact with their dying child. Many times families will stop visiting dying relatives, instructing the hospital to notify them when the death occurs.

Religious rites which once focused our attention, however briefly, upon the significance of death fade in popularity as we seek to avoid the reality of death. Embalming and other techniques used by the funeral director to blunt the reality of death are in demand as a means of sanitizing death into an acceptable (nonemotional) event. Again, the intent is to avoid the reality of death and hence not have to confront its meaning.

While striving to avoid the reality of death, American society seems to value violence. As we have sought to repress from our conscious minds the reality of death, it re-emerges in violent forms to fascinate and horrify us. This preoccupation with violence does not take place solely in the media.

Many sports such as ice hockey, football, and boxing have

violent components. Hunting (which some have trouble categorizing as "sport"), is a major source of recreation for many. Children often engage in violent or violence-simulating games, encouraged by toy guns, war toys and dolls, and violence-prone media heroes.

Violence is not restricted to witnessed experiences such as spectator sports or simulated violence in play. In the American image, taking the law into one's own hands and righting a wrong is acceptable behavior. In fact, we could go so far as to say that one who refuses to act violently in response to certain aggressive acts by another would be held in contempt. A recent popular song described "The Coward of the County," who endured ridicule and shame because of his refusal to engage in violence. He redeemed himself in the last verse by beating to a pulp the three brothers who had attacked his wife. The moral is that in America by acting violently one can prove one's masculinity.

One might ask if violence is ever justified. Defending one's family against a violent intruder is widely accepted as a situation in which a violent response is justified. American society does not restrict acceptable violent behavior to such a narrow definition. Americans tend not only to see violence as acceptable behavior in a wide range of situations, but often glorify the violence in the process. Military heroes are held in high esteem, and may build political careers on the basis of their military records. Murderers are often featured in the press and write popular books about themselves. Violence as a means to an end is often condoned on television.

Capital punishment is violent behavior. At its root, it is a form of revenge. It affirms that violence is an acceptable form of behavior when used in the name of the state and justice. The state uses violence to punish the offender, and thereby right a wrong.

One argument used in favor of capital punishment is that it serves as a deterrant to those who might consider a crime which would possibly bring about such a penalty. If this were the motive behind the death penalty, then why aren't executions held in public, where maximum publicity would certainly strengthen the deterrence factor?[19] When one does find accounts of executions in the popular press, the event is usually played up in lurid tones in order to appeal to people's more prurient interests.

I would argue that violent revenge is at the heart of our motivation to impose the death penalty. Evidence of this lies in our belief that a person who goes insane while awaiting the death penalty (but who was sane at the time of the crime) cannot be executed. The reasoning is that the person should be sane in order to fully realize what is occurring. In other words, the death sentence is not effective unless the person is aware of what is happening. Then it is appropriate. If the motive were primarily deterrance, the mental state of the person being executed would be irrelevant. But since retribution and punishment are at the heart of the matter, the person must be able to experience his or her punishment. (As an aside, this results in the criminal justice system encouraging one to become insane, as that holds a sure way to avoid death.)[20]

It is not a fear of punishment that deters one from committing a crime which might bring about the perpetrator's own death. Most capital offenses are either crimes of passion or impulsive acts. In sanctioning capital punishment, the state is promoting a policy that devalues life and places a premium upon violence as a response to a problem. At the same time that the execution itself must be seen as sanctioning violence, the process leading up to the execution is also cruel and dehumanizing. Recently a stay of execution was granted only sixteen minutes before the appointed time, with the man already strapped to the table and the intravenous tube attached. This after years of isolation and waiting to die.

One function of the death penalty is to divert attention from the underlying problems that tend to encourage violent behavior. Rather than come to grips with these issues, which would call into question the values that underpin the American social structure, the legal system responds in violent ways, thus giving the citizenry a false sense of security. The reality of the situation is that until the United States deals with the problems of poverty, injustice, and discrimination, violence will continue to prosper.

The death penalty is a part of America's romance with violence. As we have seen above, Americans embrace violence as a valid response; it is a virile act in a masculine society. The imposition of capital punishment is a legitimization of violence as an acceptable means of solving human problems.

A violent response to a problem or threatening situation is likely to be met with acceptance if not approval by many Americans.[21] If we were to conduct a poll of Americans, it is probable that most people would voice their disapproval of violence. What is extraordinary about Americans, notes Richard Hofstadter, is not so much the amount of violence in our society as "our ability to believe that we are a peace-loving and law-abiding people."[22]

Perhaps we can gain an understanding of this paradox by look-ing at our culture's values concerning violence. "Thou shalt not kill" certainly takes a strong stand against violence, as does the precept of turning the other cheek. The Golden Rule makes clear to all but the masochistic that violence is not to be condoned. On the other hand, the law of talion and Jesus' actions in ejecting the money-lenders from the temple give us acceptable views of violent behavior. Thus we hold a contradictory view of ourselves: a peaceful and lawful people who live in a world full of violent acts and images, who jealously hold on to our handguns and extol the manly virtues of acting violently in the pursuit of valued ends. "Violence," said the black leader Rap Brown, "is necessary and it's as American as cherry pie."[23]

America has entered into a romanticization of violence. The outlaws of the Old West are portrayed as Robin Hoods; Indians are seen as barbaric savages; mob actions are memorialized as brave citizens reacting to intolerable repressive British rule.[24] The image of violence as acceptable behavior easily became enshrined in suc-ceeding generations of Americans. The American image of the noble frontiersman persists today: handguns are found in many homes. Not only do these weapons provide a sense of personal well-being; they serve to enhance their owners' image as tough and virile. One of the results of this proliferation of arms has been an increase in accidental injuries and killings.[25]

We have spoken of American values, social organization, and avoidance behaviors used to keep the reality of death from invading our consciousness. There has been a debate among social scientists over the extent to which Americans deny death, if they do so at all. And if we do deny that death exists, is this pathological? In the following section, we will review the issue of denial of death in American society.

The "Denial of Death" Controversy

One of the early writers on the attitudes people hold toward death was Geoffrey Gorer. In his article entitled "The Pornography of Death," Gorer argues that death is treated today much as sexuality was in Victorian times.[26] The subject has become unmentionable in polite society. The process of the decay of the body and death itself has become a subject that will produce shudders of revulsion among people. Natural death, a basic and necessary part of life, has been removed from people's conversation, in the hope of keep—ing it out of consciousness.

Gorer goes on to discuss some interesting parallels between the Victorian treatment of sexuality and contemporary death atti-tudes. The repression of sexuality brought with it a flourishing of pornography. The attempt to deny the existence of death by repressing the subject has brought about a popular fascination with violence. The similarities go further. As with sexual pornography, the pornography of violent death de-emphasizes feelings. Sociolo-gist Ellen Zinner refers to violent pornography by the apt title of "necrography," which combines the rotting, decaying aspect of death and its display in sensationalistic ways.[27] In sexual pornogra-phy there is little or no caring, tenderness, or love. In necrography, people are "wasted" or "blown away." The emphasis in both cases is upon the sensational. Necrography serves as a form of substitute gratification, allowing us to meet death and remain unscathed, and our feelings of grief and mourning are replaced by the thrill of pseudo-terror at the violent act. Thus our repressed fears of death are vented through our love affair with necrography, now available through the medium of television in every home to viewers of all ages.

Another parallel in our approaches to death and sexuality lies in our acceptance of substitute gratification while denying depic-tions that are genuine. "Jiggle shows" and sexual jokes are accepta-ble television fare, but portrayals of people making love are forbidden. Likewise, nonemotional violent acts are permitted on television, but a recent documentary chronicling a woman's deci-sion to take her own life was refused airing by some local stations. Authentic presentations of taboo subjects are prohibited, but more indirect (and perhaps perverse) representations are acceptable. An-other example of our concern about "real" death was an advertise-ment I recently received in the mail. On the envelope, in purple script, was a warning that the contents contained information about funerals. The only other mail I have received with warnings on the envelope has contained sexually explicit advertisements.

Death is banished from our everyday reality in other ways than by simply refusing to talk about it. Elizabeth Kubler-Ross reported that when she first asked to visit with dying patients in a Chicago hospital, she was informed that there were no dying patients in the hospital.[28] Feifel also reported that his proposal to study dying patients was met by strong resistance from the hospital doctors and staff.[29] Even medical people who work intimately with the dying prefer to avoid the reality of death.

The lack of open observance of mourning and the individualization of grief have aided in banishing references to death from everyday living. No longer are those who are grieving easily identified. Any public display of strong feelings is considered inappropriate today, further excluding death from our awareness. The relegating of death to institutions has removed death from the home, and hidden it behind institutional walls.

As death has become more secularized, it has become more deritualized. The symbols of death are no longer as prevalent as they once were, when they stood as constant reminders of the omnipresence of death. For example, a suburban church, wanting to build a small columbarium wall to hold the ashes of its deceased members, had to convince upset community members and zoning officials that no clue as to the nature of the wall would be evident from the street. One of the chief complaints of neighbors petitioning against the building of the wall was that children walking to and from school would have to pass by a place where death was present. An ironic twist to this complaint, which reinforces Gorer's contention that death is considered pornographic, was that one parent freely admitted to permitting his children to watch violent movies on television. Apparently the violent destruction of mobsters and police is acceptable television fare, but the proximity of ashes would somehow harm his children.

The sociologist Talcott Parsons attempted to argue against the denial of death position.[30] He built his case on the contention that American society has institutionalized the values of science, and this requires that we be realistic in facing the facts of life. It seems implausible to Parsons that our realistic society would deny such a basic fact as death. At the same time that society has been internalizing the scientific ethos, science and medicine have mitigated suffering and gained more control over adventitious death. While death may be inevitable at the end of the life cycle, premature death (preventable disease, war, accidents, etc.) is the responsibility of man. Dealing with premature death is what man has difficulty with, according to Parsons.

To explain this difficulty, Parsons introduces the concept of "apathy." This is not the apathy of indifference; it arises from a conflicted mind that does not know what to say or do in the face of the reality of death. As a result, we tend to downplay our reactions to adventitious death. This apathy, when combined with our value of individualism renders death a personal issue which is not open to public display.

Parson's position does not hold up under scrutiny, however. While the abstract values of science may have impacted heavily upon American values, studies of the behaviors of doctors and nurses reveal that they tend to have an aversion to the reality of death that can hardly be called "apathy." Also, it would be difficult to argue that people today are any more comforted by the triumphs of science than they have been in the past. The mass media reflects our growing concern with dangers in the air, water, and food we consume. Just as the Puritan faithfully searched for sin and wickedness in his world, contemporary America seeks out the carcinogens and non-nutrients which beset us. The popular phrase from the comic strip "Pogo" could easily have been attributed to an orthodox Puritan: "we have met the enemy, and they are us." Parsons's description of a people who rely on a scientific ethos has not shown that Americans are more comforted by the advances of technology.

I also question whether Parsons's use of the term "apathy" contributes to our understanding of the situation. It seems to be used more to deal with the implications that the denial hypothesis has upon Parsons's grand scheme of the social system. In effect, Parsons is arguing that denial does not exist because it does not fit into his view of the instrumental nature of American society. However, the bulk of empirical evidence indicates that far from simply being confused about death, people actively seek to avoid any manifestation of death, be it conversational, symbolic, or directly present. Parsons is on valid ground when he speaks of more acceptance of the death of the elderly among Americans. In American society such a death is considered appropriate; as such it is anticipated and not completely denied. Inappropriate death (for example the death of a younger member of society), is never totally denied either, but such a death is not as easily accepted, as we shall see when we examine the grief process.

In an article that considers the position that Parsons takes on the denial of death issue, Peter J. Donaldson points out two basic problems in Parsons's reasoning which need to be resolved.[31] First, there is the question of what denial means; second, the problem of measuring denial. Given an operational definition, an empirical examination can be undertaken to measure "the extent, correlates, and causes" of the existence of a denial process in American society. But Parsons is not considering denial on a psychological level. Instead, he limits his discussion to social systems and normative patterns. As a result, his argument could be valid on a societal level, yet not hold true on an individual level. Donaldson points out that it may be possible for some people to deny that death exists, but that social systems do not do so. Obviously, the concept of denial needs further refinement and investigation. The overwhelming majority of investigators argue that Americans seek to evade death, and to regard the subject with some dread.

Dumont and Foss argue that it is socially necessary for us to remain somewhat ambivalent toward death.[32] They argue that if our culture attempted to teach us totally to deny the existence of death, it would result in total chaos when death occurred. On the other hand, they argue that total acceptance of death would also be disastrous, producing mass suicide and a breakdown of social order. Therefore, society must maintain both positions simultaneously. Taking such a middle position, Dumont and Foss are able to reconcile the contradictory ways in which the same information is used by both sides of the denial argument. For example, aspects of the funeral can be seen as denial mechanisms on the one hand, and as ways of helping the individual to accept the reality of the death on the other.

Lifton, using a concept developed by Avery Weisman, offers a similar resolution of the controversy, by pointing out that we have a sort of "middle knowledge" of death: partial awareness and partial denial both characterize our approach to death.[33] This provides a way out of the dilemma by acknowledging that we both deny and accept death—we deny when we can, and accept when we must.

I would also like to point out that not only is the term "denial" a very general concept, but also we have to ask for a better definition of "death." If, for example, we divide death into two distinct categories, the issue of how we react to it becomes clearer. Extrinsic death—the death represented by mortality tables and statements such as "all living things must die"—is conceived of very differently from existential death, which refers to our own personal death. We have seen that as death has become more secularized, the earlier meanings of personal death which were embodied in religion have diminished. The result has left contemporary men and women bereft of any symbolic or theological armament against the awfulness of their own deaths. From earliest childhood on we are taught not to think of death; to do so is morbid and unacceptable. As a result, we numb ourselves to death's existence, allowing it into our consciousness only as distant, nonthreatening, abstract death. When we are forced to confront personal death, we often find ourselves unable to imagine that reality. Our internal confusion and lack of symbolic referents for the reality of personal death leads us to defensive actions, such as avoidance, in order to deal with it.

In the psychological literature "denial" refers to a massive negation of reality. It is obvious that on some levels extrinsic death is affirmed by Americans. Evidence of this is the growth of life insurance sales and pre-need funeral plans. The reality of existential death, however, seems to be the avoided aspect of mortality. This dualistic nature of our reactions to death makes the use of the term "denial" that much more confusing. In order to describe adequately the American attitude toward death, we will adopt Lifton's description of middle knowledge and modify it to include both extrinsic and existential death: Americans accept the notion of abstract death, but avoid dealing with the reality of their own personal mortality. With this understanding in mind, we will use the term "avoidance" when referring to the ways in which Americans deal with the fact of death, rather than the more clinical and imprecise term "denial."

We have seen that people's feelings and behavior are affected by the image of death that they hold. The Puritan image of death, itself a product of many factors, meant that dying was a fearful and anguished process. Yet death was neither mysterious nor avoidable to the Puritan. Instead, death was an everyday occurrence, and a manifestation of the sinfulness of humanity. People of the secular age which followed saw death as a natural reality. This rationalization of death also included an emphasis upon the grieving survivors. Several factors were suggested as effecting this shift in emphasis from the dying to the bereaved, including the social and religious tenor of the times.

Today, we live in an age that is a continuation of the age of secular death. Death, especially existential death, has become a subject to be avoided to the extent of being a socially taboo topic. The reality of death is antithetical to America's values. As a result, the subject is avoided, rather than accepted. To accept the reality of death openly implies a confrontation with many cherished values in the American collective image.

Notes

1. David Stannard, *The Puritan Way of Death* (New York: Oxford University Press, 1977), pp. 38–39.
2. David Stannard, ed., *Death in America* (Philadelphia: University of Pennsylvania Press, 1976), p. 69.
3. Reprinted in Larzer Ziff, *Puritanism in America* (New York: Viking Press, 1973), p. 119.
4. Reprinted in S. E. Morison, *The Intellectual Life of Colonial New England* (New York: New York University Press, 1956), p. 214.
5. Charles O. Jackson, *Passing* (Westport, Conn.: Greenwood Press, 1977), p. 7.
6. Stannard, *Death in America,* p. 53.
7. Charles O. Jackson, "Death Shall Have No Dominion," *Omega* 8, no. 3 (1977): 195–203.
8. James J. Farrell, *Inventing the American Way of Death: 1830–1920* (Philadelphia: Temple University Press, 1980), p. 70.
9. Ibid., p. 71.
10. Ann Douglas, *The Feminization of America* (New York: Alfred A. Knopf), 1977.
11. Letitia E. Landon, "The Little Shroud," in Michael R. Turner, ed., *Parlor Poetry* (New York: Viking Press, 1967), p. 24.
12. Douglas, pp. 97–103.
13. Philippe Aries, *Western Attitudes Toward Death* (Baltimore: The Johns Hopkins University Press, 1974).
14. Robert Blauner, "Death and Social Structure," in Robert Fulton, ed., *Death and Identity* (Bowie, Md.: The Charles Press, 1976), pp. 35–58.
15. Aries, pp. 85–107.
16. Robert Fulton, "Death, Grief, and the Funeral in Contemporary Society," *The Director,* November 1976 and March 1977.
17. Alan Howard and Robert Scott, "Cultural Values and Attitudes toward Death," *Journal of Existentialism* 6 (Winter 1965–66): 161–74.
18. Richard Hofstadter, *Social Darwinism in American Thought,* rev. ed. (Boston: Beacon Press, 1955).
19. John Lofland, "Open and Concealed Dramaturgic Strategies: The Case of State Execution," *Urban Life* 5, no. 3 (1975): 272–295. Also, Louis J. West, "Psychiatric Reflections on the Death Penalty," in Phillip E. Mackey, ed., *Voices Against Death* (New York: Burt Franklin, 1976), p. 293.
20. West, p. 292.
21. Monica D. Blumenthal, Robert C. Kahn, Frank M. Andrews, and

Kendra B. Head, *Justifying Violence: Attitudes of American Men* (Ann Arbor: University of Michigan Press, 1972).

22. Richard Hofstadter, "Reflections on Violence in the United States," in Richard Hofstadter and Michael Wallace, eds., *American Violence* (New York: Alfred A. Knopf, 1970), p. 6.

23. Hofstadter, p. 6.

24. Richard Maxwell Brown, "Historical Patterns of American Violence," in Hugh Davis Graham and Ted Robert Gurr, Eds., *Violence in America* (Beverly Hills: Sage, 1979), p. 20.

25. Robert Brent Toplin, *Unchallenged Violence* (Westport, Conn.: Greenwood Press, 1975), p. 225.

26. Geoffrey Gorer, "The Pornography of Death," in Edwin S. Shneidman, ed., *Death: Current Perspectives* (Palo Alto: Mayfield, 1984), pp. 26–30.

27. Ellen Zinner, personal communication.

28. Elizabeth Kubler-Ross, *On Death and Dying* (New York: MacMillan, 1969), pp. 22–23.

29. Herman Feifel, "Scientific Research in Taboo Areas—Death," *American Behavioral Scientist* 5 (March 1962): 28–30.

30. Talcott Parsons, "Death in American Society—A Brief Working Paper," *American Behavioral Scientist* 6 (May 1963): 61–65. Also, Talcott Parsons, et al., "The Gift of Life and Its Reciprocation," in Arien Mack, ed., *Death in American Experience* (New York: Schocken Books, 1973), pp. 1–49.

31. Peter J. Donaldson, "Denying Death," *Omega* 3, no. 4 (November 1977): 285–290.

32. Richard Dumont and Dennis Foss, *The American View of Death* (Cambridge, Mass.: Schenkman, 1972).

33. Robert Jay Lifton, *The Broken Connection* (New York: Simon & Schuster, 1979), p. 79.

CHAPTER THREE

Institutions for Dying

$\mathbf{A}$s our society has become more technological, functions once performed by the primary group—the family—have been transferred to large-scale bureaucratic organizations. This process is quite evident in the study of death and dying. Dying now takes place in hospitals, hospices, or nursing homes, and death is the province of the morgue and the mortuary. Clearly, this shift in responsibilities has had many ramifications. For example, family members take care of each other for affective (emotional) reasons. Organizations provide a service primarily as an economic endeavor. Obviously such a shift in motivations can produce a change in the approach to the basic problem of how best to care for the dying. Expertise may replace caring, and the priorities of the system may come to be more important than the needs of the patients.

In this chapter we are going to examine the three organizational systems in our society that most commonly deal with death and dying: the hospital, the nursing home, and, more recently, the hospice. Each one of these organizations has developed a system for dealing with the process of dying. The hospital deals with dying within its system of medical care, and the nursing home within its system of caretaking for the elderly. The hospice considers the needs of the dying person and his or her family to be paramount and has organized itself around meeting those needs. The hospice is the newest concept in patient care; it endeavors to keep the dying person as free as possible from pain while ministering to the person's social, psychological, and spiritual needs.

The Hospital

If we examine the development of large scale organizations in the United States, the importance of the modern, efficient hospital as a bureaucratic institution becomes more understandable. With the growth of knowledge concerning medicine and medical technology, there developed a need to coordinate increasing amounts of information. The increasing size of hospitals requires formal organization as well. In order to meet these requirements, the hospital is divided into specialized units, each with a hierarchy of power and a specific task. The activities of these specialized units are controlled and coordinated through a central administration. A large hospital is now made up of departments such as oncology, obstetrics, neurology, and radiology.

The United States is served by nearly 7000 hospitals that contain 1.36 million beds. Two and one-half million people are employed by these institutions; they serve 33 million inpatients and more than 200 million outpatients in the course of a year. Hospitals vary in size from those with less than a 200-bed capacity to those which may have thousands of beds. They may be profit or nonprofit organizations, operated by private corporations, churches, or government agencies. Most hospital stays are of short duration (eight days), and most hospital expenses involve short-term care.[1]

The goal of a hospital is to provide health care for members of the community. In order to do this in the most efficient way possible, the contemporary hospital is bureaucratically organized. This form of organization has ramifications for patient care and management. This rational system can be highly beneficial, as experts can bring the latest medical knowledge to bear in the fight against disease, but oftentimes the *person* becomes lost in the maze of technology and bureaucracy. Hospital patients report feelings of loneliness and being less than human, and can become angered at being referred to as "the peptic ulcer" or "the broken leg." The hospital staff, immersed in the world of medicine, combating disease, and helping in the healing process, may lose sight of the individual person and see only the symptoms.

A bureaucracy is an organization that is developed to satisfy the requirements of efficiency and effective goal attainment.[2] The demands of complex medical technology require a formal organizational context. If we consider the hospital as a bureaucratically organized medical delivery system, we can see that, like every other form of social organization, bureaucracy has its advantages and disadvantages. The system has the advantage of providing the patient with highly technical and specialized treatment. Experts in particular aspects of a disease or treatment can be called in when needed. This care is available both speedily and economically. "Economically" refers, in this case, to what it would cost the individual to pay the complete cost of his or her medical needs. By procuring equipment and other medical necessities for use by many of its patients, the total cost is spread out among all of the hospital's many patients. For example, comparatively few people could afford to retain a personal physician and all the medical equipment they might need during their lives. On the other hand, a disadvantage of this process is that the purchase of expensive and sometimes exotic equipment is one of the factors contributing to increasing hospital costs.

The hierarchical organization of the hospital provides for accountability. The hospital may be held responsible for the actions of its employees. As a result, the hospital may require of its staff high standards of patient care. These standards of care are spelled out in the hospital's requirements for employment, job descriptions, policies, and procedures. The disadvantages of such a form of organization arise out of the employees' concern about their accountability to the system. The employee may become more involved in protecting his or her position than in meeting patient needs. As a result, patients may find themselves of lesser importance than schedules, protocols, or other demands of the medical bureaucracy.

A further disadvantage of bureaucratic organization lies in the nature of the goals of the hospital bureaucracy. We spoke earlier of the hospital's emphasis upon efficiency and expertise. These criteria may become of greater importance than the goal of providing health care. As a result, the individual may find himself receiving categorical treatment: a bureaucratic response to the rules without regard for the uniqueness of the individual. The client can easily become objectified and lose all sense of being a unique individual while within the bureaucratic organization. As Robert Merton states, "The structure is one which approaches the complete elimination of personal lives, relationships, and nonrational considerations."[3]

Of further importance for our particular interests is the fact that hospitals are committed to curing sick people, and this does not necessarily include helping people to die well. The hospital staff has been trained to cure; to defeat death. They often do not know how to cope with the "failures"—the hopelessly ill and dying.[4]

The following description of an eighty-year-old terminally ill woman's experience in a hospital is typical of many such accounts:

> She was isolated behind drawn curtains, and when the interviewer intruded, she pleaded, "Please come talk to me." During her 35 day stay in the hospital she was cared for by 38 different nurses. Except for three days in July, Miss R was never cared for by the same nurse on two consecutive days. Of the 105 nursing shifts during her hospital stay, the nurses recorded her status only for 66 shifts, and only nine of the nurse's notes mentioned her psychological pain, that she was very lonely, crying all day, depressed, asking to die, afraid of everything. Because she was continually calling for a nurse to rectify her isolation, nurses responded to her call bell with increasing delay, avoiding her as much as possible. The resident physicians on ward rounds were found to spend only an average of one minute in Miss R's room, none got close enough to touch her, and only rarely did anyone speak to her. She begged the student observer to stay with her, after he held her hand and listened to her talk. She pleaded: "Help me, you are not like the others, help me." The staff laughed nervously in discussing the fact that she once called the police for help. She voiced suicidal thoughts of trying to jump out the window, and the staff reaction was an expressed wish to get her moved out of the ward to a nursing home, because they found her care so troublesome.[5]

Hospitals are often reluctant to define a patient as dying, at least on a formal basis. This is in part reinforced by the insurance industry, which may not pay for the care of a dying patient. This attitude, when combined with a dedication to the medical model which views death as pathological and unnatural, leads to anecdotes such as the following:

> One of the family members interviewed was a nurse whose mother was dying. She repeatedly asked doctors to let her mother die, but they insisted on aggressive treatments which only increased her pain. Her mother at one point said, "When all this flesh is gone, maybe then they'll let me die." Family members stayed with her mother at all times because they felt the care she was receiving was inadequate. One evening, they

overheard a nurse comment, in a very disapproving and contemptuous tone, "They've been having a wake in there for a week."[6]

The hospital remains the institution which most often accommodates the dying, with over 70 percent of all deaths taking place in hospitals.[7] The ways in which people are classified as dying was one of the interests of David Sudnow, who reported on fifteen months of participant observation at two hospitals.[8] "Cohen Hospital" is a private institution serving a middle class population. "County Hospital" where Sudnow did most of his field work, is "very much a lower class establishment."[9]

In his now classic study, Sudnow took the position that death and dying are social as much as biological events.[10] Often the staff, without consulting the attending physician, will decide that a patient is dying. Once this decision has been made, there are very definite ramifications in the ways in which the staff members define their own roles in interacting with the patients. The status of "dying" or "dead" requires different services from the bureaucratized staff than the status of "living."

Although Sudnow did not write in terms of the hospital as a bureaucracy, some of his observations will serve well to highlight the characteristics of bureaucracy. For example, the doctor at County Hospital must wait for prescheduled medical services to be available in order to have his or her patient treated. If an EKG machine and operator are scheduled to be on a particular ward on a certain day of the week, the patient and the doctor must wait until that appointed time to have the service performed.[11] Here we see an example of strictly defined rules of procedure operating within a bureaucracy.

It is interesting to note the differences in the way the two hospitals that Sudnow studied operated. The private hospital (Cohen Hospital) is oriented much more toward the needs or desires of its clients (doctors or patients) than is the public hospital (County Hospital). Medical services are available at Cohen on the demand of the medical staff. In other words, at the private hospital the needs of the patient, as determined by the physician, are paramount. At the public institution, both doctor and patient have to accommodate themselves to the scheduling. The coordination of technologies took precedence over patient needs at County Hospital.[12]

In examining routines within the hospital, Sudnow described

the social processes that are important in determining the ways in which a patient will be treated by the hospital organization. There is, as Max Weber pointed out, a tendency for bureaucracies to deal with the public on an emotionless, impersonal level.[13] The management of the patient's feelings is a part of the hospital's way of dealing with patients. As an example of this desire to control, Sudnow described the effort made by the staff to disguise the death of a patient from other patients nearby. Nurses and interns would talk to the corpse, use their bodies as visual barriers, and wheel the dead patient "off to X-ray." This process allowed the staff to go about their assigned duties without having to deal with the feelings of the surviving ward members. Also, it allowed the hospital members to avoid dealing with their own feelings or becoming emotionally involved with patients. Again we see demands of the bureaucracy for efficient, economical use of time by employees. Those demands may supercede the needs of the patients.[14]

When investigating the dying process, Sudnow found that "dying" is a predictive term. That is, it defines "the likelihood of death within some temporal perspective."[15] Usually some employee on the ward is seen as having the ability to predict when a patient can be classified as dying, and is thus allowed to determine the status of the patient and, as a result, the kinds of service or lack of service that the patient will receive. This is an informal process more likely to be used at night when the doctors and relatives are not likely to be present. Once the status of "dying" has been achieved, the staff will act in ways customary for treating the dying—even to the point of leaving newly admitted patients in a laboratory or storeroom to die so that the staff will not have to remake the bed and clean the room that would have been occupied had the patient been admitted to the ward. If the patient survives the night, he or she is quickly moved into a room the first thing in the morning, before relatives and doctors arrive.[16]

Sudnow observed that when the staff had determined that a patient would die very soon, they would perform such tasks as forcing the patient's eyes shut, inserting dentures, diapering the patient, changing the bed, and binding the patient's legs together, all prior to biological death. Dealing with a dead body is not liked by the staff, and so it becomes more acceptable as well as efficient to start the necessary processes on the still living body.

To make their tasks easier, nurses were known to work actively to separate the patient from relatives. If the relatives were about, Sudnow noted, the nursing staff would be required to have a nurse constantly with the patient. When the family was absent, the nurses were free to perform their other duties, leaving the patient to die alone.[17] Another function of the separation of relatives from the dying deals with the problem of accountability. One does not have to be accountable to a dead person, but the presence of others who could possibly make the employee accountable for his or her actions may be threatening to the bureaucratic employee. This may be the reason for more patient-centered activity at the private Cohen Hospital, where the patients were better educated and more socially powerful.[18]

Another more official process to determine dying is to have the decision made by the medical staff.[19] From the doctor's standpoint, once the patients have been labeled "dying" they become medically uninteresting. Moreover, their deaths may represent failure on the part of the doctor. Although this kind of failure is supposed to be acceptable within the medical world, it may not be so to the individual doctor.[20] By locating the cause of death, Sudnow points out, the doctor is freed from personal accountability for the process of dying. The doctor explains to the family what is happening in ways that will justify the doctor's actions: "We did all we could."[21]

In an effort to maintain the legitimacy of the hospital, it is important that the dying status be applied judiciously. Often relatives are forewarned of the danger of dying, so that when it actually occurs it is not a complete shock to the family. If it has been hinted at, but not proclaimed, then the failure to achieve a dying status can be seen as a success for the institution. There is always a danger in conveying the status of "dying" too soon:

> On several occasions premature proclamations of inevitable death resulted in embarrassing situations. An intern informed a group of sons and daughters that their father was "dying" and the father continued to live for over a week. Each day, a large number of sons, daughters, grandchildren, nieces, and nephews came to visit the patient, and each member of the family took turns going into his room to have a last look at "Papa." A son served as the ritual leader each evening, standing outside the door to the room and scheduling the visits so that each member of the family would have his turn. This went on for several days, and, as time progressed, the finality of their visits

became questionable. Those relatives who had made what they thought to be a final farewell found themselves returning to the hospital and reentering the room again and again; soon the ritual seemed to degenerate through the lack of closure. On the sixth day, the son asked to see another physician and, it was reported, offered a cautiously voiced complaint because it seemed to him that his father was indeed not dying, yet apparently was being treated as though he were. The intern was advised by his superiors of the tactlessness of his premature announcement to the family. Because things had stretched out a bit too long, he had provided for the relevance of predeath bereavement when it wasn't apparently relevant.

"Fortunately," perhaps, for the intern, the man died on the seventh night in the hospital.[22]

We have seen that the status of "dying" has effects upon the patients and the relatives. The patient begins to experience a withdrawal of interest from the doctor and the staff and essentially a lessening of relatives' visits and in a sense the patient becomes a social object to which the bureaucratic hospital has no direct accountability. The patient becomes a non-person.[23]

"Social death" is a term Sudnow employs to describe that time when "socially relevant attributes of the patient begin permanently to cease to be operative for treating him. . . ."[24] This appears to be an extension of the dying status described above. In social death, for all intents and purposes the person has ceased to exist. The heart still beats within the body, but the world has begun to act as if the person were no longer alive. Sudnow gives the following example of one who returns from social death:

A typical instance of "social death" involved a male patient who was admitted to the Emergency Unit with a sudden perforation of a duodenal ulcer. He was operated upon, and, for a period of six days, remained in quite critical condition. His wife was informed that his chances for survival were poor, whereupon she stopped her visits to the hospital. After two weeks, the man's condition improved markedly and he was discharged in ambulatory condition. The next day he was readmitted to the hospital with a severe coronary. Before he died, he recounted his experience upon returning home. His wife had removed all his clothing and personal effects from the house, had made preliminary arrangements for his burial with a mortuary establishment (she had written a letter which he had discovered on his bureau, requesting a brochure on their rates), she no longer wore his wedding ring, and was found with another man, no doubt quite shocked at her husband's return. He reported that he left the house, began to drink heavily, and had a heart attack.[25]

While social death refers to the cessation of social attributes, to what extent do social attributes affect being classified as dying? In observing emergency room behaviors, Sudnow learned that the patient's social attributes might influence the treatment received.[26] Criteria such as age, social status, and the perceived moral worth of the individual were seen as important determinants as to the amount of effort made to sustain the life of the individual. For example, Sudnow observed that an older indigent would receive minimal care, where a middle class child would receive heroic efforts by the staff.

Two persons in "similar" physical condition may be differentially designated as dead or not. For example, a young child was brought into the ER with no registering heartbeat, respiration, or pulse and was, through a rather dramatic stimulation procedure involving the coordinated work of a large team of doctors and nurses, revived for a period of eleven hours. On the same evening, shortly after the child's arrival, an elderly person who presented the same physical signs, with what a doctor later stated, in conversation, to be no discernible differences from the child in skin color, warmth, etc., "arrived" in the ER and was almost immediately pronounced dead, with no attempts at stimulation instituted. A nurse remarked later in the evening: "They [the doctors] would never have done that to the old lady [attempt heart stimulation] even though I've seen it work on them too." During the period when emergency resuscitation equipment was being readied for the child, an intern instituted mouth-to-mouth resuscitation. This same intern was shortly relieved by oxygen machinery and when the woman "arrived" he was the one who pronounced her dead. He reported shortly afterwards that he could never bring himself to put his mouth to "an old lady's like that."[27]

Michael Simpson replicated Sudnow's study, and confirms that different treatments were applied to people of various social classes.[28] The biases of the physicians were seen by both researchers to negate the established hospital policies, as decisions were made about the amount of effort to be made to save a patient's life. Individual biases and prejudices override the authority of the system, but even at that the older woman received minimal treatment; she was not totally rejected. The bureaucracy responded, and was not necessarily negligent in responding to that kind of patient, but the response to the child shows the minimal nature of the response to the older woman. We see here a paradox: while we can applaud the fact that we have established at least minimal standards by which all people must be treated, we can also become horrified at the obvious bias in the doctor's refusal to use the same efforts on one patient as upon another.

In Sudnow's description of hospital functions he notes the conflict between bureaucratic functions and human needs. The patient becomes a depersonalized object being processed through an unconcerned system. The imperatives of the bureaucracy may become more important than the patient's needs. The dying or dead cannot demand accountability, as Sudnow points out in describing the County Hospital routine.

Sudnow presents us with a study that shows workers responding to the system and to its values, and humanistic treatment of the dying is not a high priority in the bureaucratic system.

In assessing Sudnow's work we must be aware of some of the pitfalls of participant observation. The study's findings are accounts of certain situations as perceived by Sudnow. The findings may be affected by Sudnow's particular biases, and the situations being observed may be influenced by the very presence of an observer. However, even with these caveats in mind, Sudnow presents us with the stark reality: dying is affected by the social context in which it occurs. The hospital staff, often acting upon nonmedical criteria, make decisions which can adversely affect the lives of the patients.

The findings of a team of sociologists, Barney Glaser and Anselm Strauss, tend to reinforce a great many of Sudnow's findings. In *The Awareness of Dying,* and *Time for Dying,* they report on the interactions between the hospital staff and patients at six hospitals.[29] In *The Awareness of Dying,* Glaser and Strauss present material concerning the context of awareness held by the patient and staff concerning the severity of the patient's illness. There are four awareness contexts, according to Glaser and Strauss: Closed awareness exists when the staff is aware of the patient's condition, but the patient is not told the truth. A suspicion context comes about as the patient begins to question what he or she has been told. In open awareness, everyone knows and speaks openly concerning the patient's condition. Sometimes, rather than an open awareness context, the patient and the staff or family will enter into a mutual pretense context, where everyone knows the truth about the patient's condition, but no one speaks of it.[30]

Glaser and Strauss point out that hospitals are arranged in such a way as to withhold medical information from patients. This gives the doctor and staff more control over the patient. Treatments, medications, and the like do not have to be justified to the patient. In order to be trusted and to better manage the patient, the staff and physicians often feel they have to convince the patients that they will live. So, in a sense, the staff will conspire to convince patients that they are not dying. Conversations with the patient are controlled by the staff in order to avoid lying as much as possible. Benoliel reports that nurses, caught up in the unrealistic closed context situation, will often minimize their contact with the patient.[31] The result is greater social isolation for the patient. This might involve refusals to answer ("You'll have to ask your doctor"), or keeping the conversation away from future-oriented subjects such as when the patient might expect to go home. The conversations are "managed" so as to avoid having to deal directly with the question of the patient's condition. The staff and doctors work to minimize the impact of any actions which the patient might question such as new treatment, being moved to a private area, and so forth. If necessary, "reasonable" lies are told in order to keep the situation "manageable." Glaser and Strauss point out that this rationale of the importance of "manageability" is reinforced by the misbeliefs by doctors that patients will go to pieces if made aware of the fact that they are dying, and that they really don't want to know anyway.[32]

It may be that "manageability" extends not only to the patient but to the emotions of the staff and doctors as well. By not having to deal with the emotions of the patient, staff members can avoid dealing with their own fears about death. We will have more to say about this when we look at specific occupations dealing with the dying. At this point it is enough to indicate that there may be personal as well as bureaucratic motives behind the decision to keep the patient manageable.

The effort needed to maintain a closed awareness context is very great. Veatch and Tai point out that the modern hospital bureaucracy involves "a bewildering array of physicians, nurses, orderlies, technicians, interns, residents, students, and secretaries all having contact with the patient."[33] A "confusion of fictions" may arise, leading the patient to suspect he is not being dealt with openly. Often the signs of oncoming death become too obvious to be denied easily or explained away. At this point a suspicion context arises, wherein the staff is aware but the patient only suspects his true condition.[34] In the following passage, we see John Gunther's description of the context in which he learned of his son's terminal illness, and how the context failed to keep the author unaware of his son's true condition:

> Five minutes after I got there I knew Johnny was going to die. I cannot explain this except by saying that I saw it on the faces of the three doctors, particularly Hahn's. I never met this good doctor again, but I will never forget the way he kept his face averted while he talked, then another glimpse of his blank averted face as he said good bye, dark with all that he was sparing us, all that he knew would happen to Johnny, and that I didn't know and Frances didn't know and that neither of us should know for as long as possible.[35]

Glaser and Strauss point out that a suspicion context is an unstable condition, for the patient may often work actively to resolve his or her newly awakened fears. Any subtle cues given by the staff may confirm what the patient already suspects. One of the unfortunate consequences of a suspicion awareness context is that "patients can be made frantic by the evasiveness of physicians and nurses."[36] Obviously, there is a psychological strain on the family and staff to maintain the pretense as there was in the closed awareness context, but now the patient is suspicious, adding to the burden of those involved in the pretense. The suspicion context is an unstable condition, as the patient works to confirm his fears. The situation will usually resolve itself into one of two possibilities: a mutual pretense context or an open awareness context.

In the mutual pretense context, both the patient and staff know that the patient is dying, but both pretend that the patient is not. There are several reasons why this situation may develop. First, the patient may need the pretense because of his inability to deal with the awful reality of the fact that he is dying. Also, it may serve to protect the family from too much grief. Family members who are not able to express themselves easily or who need to defend against strong emotions may need to "play out" the death scene under this kind of a pretense in order to be able to function at all. Another result of the mutual pretense context is that the staff can do their jobs better (and perhaps more impersonally) knowing that they will not have to face an emotional involvement with the dying patient. This impersonal aspect of the interaction between staff and patient is an important part of the formal bureaucratic functioning of the hospital. A staff member tells of the tremendous emotional strain felt by staff members of an intensive care unit who "got too close" to a patient:

> We found Richard to be very interesting, intelligent, and a likeable person. He had worked in a hospital previously and therefore understood much of what was happening to him and what his prognosis was. His attitude was one of kindness, concern, and warmth, all which was easy to return. He had a wife and family that were very concerned about him and were equally considerate and kind to the staff. Because of these qualities in Richard and his family, it became very easy to become involved in them. Richard became not just a patient, but also a person. His care was made more emotionally difficult by the fact that, unlike most patients, everything he asked for was preceded and followed by "please" and "thank you." He sincerely appreciated everything we did for him. We found it difficult to care for him because we knew he was going to die. We tried to be cheerful to him, despite the fact that most of us felt quite depressed concerning him and his condition. Many of us who took care of him often wished he would stop being so nice, so considerate, and be the opposite—almost as though it would be easier for us to adjust to his death if we could be angry at him. Even now, many years after his death, we find ourselves remembering him and the emotional difficulties concerned in his care.[37]

One of the interesting observations made by Glaser and Strauss is that the pretense context may also give the patient more dignity and privacy.[38] With the immense onslaught of bureaucratic controls stripping away the patient's autonomy, he may be able to combat this attack on himself by developing a kind of pretense awareness. By doing this, the patient at least has something left in his life which he controls. This need to control our lives is an important part of the individual's sense of wholeness and well-being. We can see in this account how those who deal constantly with dying would perhaps find that keeping matters on an impersonal level is to their advantage. It allows the staff to go about their duties efficiently and to minimize their own emotional investment in the dying patient. One of the characteristics of a total bureaucratic institution such as the hospital is that it is an organization which is responsible for its inmates 24 hours a day. This means that there is the potential for interpersonal relationships between the staff and patients. The depersonalization of the patients allows the hospital organization to maintain an emotional distance between patient and staff.

There is another possible consequence of a mutual pretense context. Often the patient will, as a result of taking part in the denial, find himself or herself without any real relationships. The patient is left with a feeling of being isolated. For example, a woman recounted to me the death of her uncle. She was the only member of the family with whom the dying man was open about his condition. When his friends would stop in for brief visits, a rather surreal drama would be acted out. His friends would dominate the conversation, saying how good he looked, and that he'd be back on his feet in no time flat. All this to a man who was wasting away in a cancer-wracked body. The patient, low on physical and emotional energy, would passively go along with the charade. Only after his friends had left would the man turn to his niece, take her hand, and with tears in his eyes ask, "Why can't they be honest with me?"

The final context described by Glaser and Strauss is that of open awareness. In this type of situation both the patient and the staff are aware of the patient's true condition and openly acknowledge the fact that the patient is dying. While the staff may keep the patient unaware as to how soon they expect the patient to die or the extent of possible deterioration prior to death, the fact that the patient is terminally ill is known to all. The advantage of open awareness is that it allows the patient "an opportunity to close his life in accordance with his own ideas about proper dying."[39] The patient may choose to write a will or to develop a pretense context, but he will at least have the opportunity to choose his own style of dying. An open awareness of the condition of the patient may also reduce the strain on the family. Everything can be out in the open now, and there is no longer a need for elaborate pretensions or avoidances. It may relieve or increase the strain on the staff, as was discussed earlier. The open awareness context may put pressure on the staff to interact with the patient about his oncoming death, which may place a greater emotional strain on the hospital staff members.[40]

In summary, Glaser and Strauss have observed different contexts in which dying patients and staff members interact. There are differing consequences for each. Today, as hospital staff members become better educated in dealing with the dying, the open awareness context is becoming more popular. At the same time, the characteristics of the dying patient are changing. More and more patients are entering the dying phase after suffering from a chronic illness for some period of time. This allows them to become knowledgeable about their illness, its treatment, and workings of the medical bureaucracy. Being aware of their condition, they are able to become actively involved in their own treatment.

It is important within the context of our investigation of these various systems to keep in mind that we are examining the behavior of individuals caught up in the values and priorities of a larger social system. It is not my contention that individuals working in large bureaucratic organizations are less responsive to the human needs of their patients. What is important is that we become aware of the subtle ways in which the demands of the bureaucracy force bureaucratic personnel to act in ways which are perhaps counter to the human needs of the dying patient. For example, efforts by nurses and doctors to eliminate family members from the deathbed scene may not be strictly in response to their own selfish desires, but may be influenced by the fact that the ward is so heavily understaffed that to respond fully to the needs of the dying patient would severely limit the functioning of the hospital staff in other areas of their work responsibilities. A hospital is basically an economic institution. If it does not operate efficiently or at a profit it could be shut down. Therefore, in the context of a hospital, efficiency, profit, and money motive can tend to become more important than human needs of the patient. This becomes evident in the studies by both Sudnow and Glaser and Strauss, where we see members of the bureaucracy acting in ways that will meet with approval from the bureaucracy but not necessarily benefit the human needs of the patients.[42] Wolf Heyderbrand, in his book *Hospital Bureaucracy*, stated that the hospital "must provide the setting or framework in which the principles and practices of modern business and technology can be successfully related to the standards and imagery of 'helping people' as derived from ethical precepts, social and psychological insights, and medical practice."[43]

Heyderbrand's statement is an idealistic one, for the values of business and those of helping people may often be in conflict.

When those values of business and technology supersede the more
humanistic ones, the patient may suffer as a result. The human
needs of the patient become subordinate to the bureaucratic demands of the hospital system, leaving the patient feeling depersonalized and alienated from the very system which, ironically, was
designed to help him.

William F. May, in an analysis of the hospital, states that
the institution is more a symbol of death than of life:

> Psychologically, it assaults—with its alien machines, rhythms,
> language, and routines—that identity which a person previously
> maintained in the outside world. The patient's customary con-
> trol of his world must be surrendered not only to the disease
> but to those who fight against it. His capacity for savoring
> his world is also numbered, once again, not only by the disease,
> but by those procedures imposed upon him in the fight against
> it—diet, drugs, X-rays, surgery, nausea-inducing therapy, and
> sleeping potions. Finally, his capacity for communicating with
> his world is unsettled by his loss of social role. Just at the
> moment that disease rips him out of his usual place in the
> community and makes him feel less secure in his dealings with
> fellows, the procedures of the hospital remind him acutely of
> this loss, by placing him in the hands of professionals—the
> nurse and the doctor—precisely those who seem unassailably
> secure in their own identities.[44]

The combination of the bureaucratic needs of the hospital
organization and the biomedical model which sees death as pathological and not natural, often supersedes the care needs of the
patient. The "cure goal" has become institutionalized in the hospital, and is more important than the "goal of care."[45] This is not
to imply that hospital physicians and staff are uncaring, but rather
that the organization in which they work is not oriented primarily
toward patient care as much as it is to saving lives and controlling
death. The result has been the depersonalization and objectification
of the patient in the cause of bureaucratic efficiency and improved
medical technology.

The Nursing Home

For an hour, the hour just before the bubble music of Lawrence
Welk, the two delicate looking women sat in the television
room and cried—quietly.

For an hour before that, they had tried to get a nurse to take them to the bathroom. Neither could walk.

"I'm too busy, we don't have enough people around here," said a nurse.

So, blushing and looking down, the two women relieved themselves where they sat.

The above description was part of a newspaper reporter's experience as a patient in a nursing home.[46] In order to report accurately on life in a nursing home, the reporter had himself admitted as a patient in three separate care facilities. He was shocked not only by the substandard care he witnessed, but by the ease with which an "aunt" (actually another reporter) was able to get a young person admitted to a nursing home. No legal or medical authorization was necessary to get him locked up in three homes. In the nursing homes where he was admitted, the reporter was questioned only superficially, mainly about financial responsibility. While his "aunt" described him as depressed, the reporter sat passively. The reporter, in articles that followed his stays in the various homes, described the conditions within the homes where patient abuse, filth, terrible food, and the misuse of drugs were common.

The function of the nursing home is to provide a caring environment for those too old or too ill to care for themselves. Over 80 percent of the nursing homes are privately run businesses; therefore, producing a profit is a major concern.[47] These two goals of profit and care can be mutually exclusive. Improving the patient's diet or the nursing home facility will lessen the profits of the business.

A recent study by the California Health Facilities Commission for the State Legislature found that the state's nursing homes were showing a 34 percent profit based upon equity.[48] Of the 973 homes in California, 5 percent had profits of 297 percent or more, while 14 percent had profits of over 165 percent, based on a return on investment formula. At the same time, most of the homes were providing insufficient care for their patients. The State Commission drew up a list of quality standards for nursing homes. Only 34, or 3 percent, of the 973 homes rated favorably on all ten criteria. Over a third failed four or more of the standards.

There are over 23,000 nursing homes in the United States, which care for over 1.2 million senior Americans. A conservative judgment is that 50 percent of the homes are substandard.[49] Though only 5 percent of the elderly are in nursing homes at any one time, one out of five of the elderly population in the United States will spend time in a nursing home.[50]

The Social Security Act of 1935 provided funds for the elderly in need of care. Entrepreneurs, realizing the large profit potential in this legislation, began the business of nursing homes. Federal funds have also been made available for mortgages, loan guarantees, and direct loans for the construction and expansion of nursing homes. Medicare and Medicaid have provided further economic incentives by providing funds for extended care for the impoverished elderly. Due to the lack of regulation and lack of enforcement of the regulations that do exist, the nursing home industry, for the most part, is allowed to maximize profits while minimizing care.[51]

In a powerful study of a typical American nursing home, Gubrium describes the horrible waste of human potential and the destruction of the incentive to live that take place within American nursing homes.[52] *Living and Dying at Murray Manor* describes the caretaking, as opposed to care giving, attitude which pervades the nursing home system. To quote Gubrium, "Making peace with hopelessness is a difficult task, and it is the one that people encounter in breaking up a home to take up life at Manor."[53]

Gubrium describes the destructive forces at work within the nursing home environment to take away from the patient those last vestiges of control of his or her own life. The patient's activities are highly regulated, his or her opinions, wants, and needs are met only insofar as they are provided for within the structure of the organization. In this sense we find that the nursing home resembles more Erving Goffman's total institution than a bureaucracy.[54] Within the medical context of a hospital there are at least goal-directed activities—the goal of providing adequate health care. Within the context of the nursing home there is only the performance of duties that will enable the individual to keep functioning biologically. Studies have shown that once one enters a nursing home his or her life expectancy drops drastically.

Upon entering such a system the individual gives up or has taken away the last vestiges of self-control. The person's autonomy and special needs, his or her ways of behaving, quickly become subordinated to the routine of the institution. The individual's sexuality is totally denied. For example, one gerontologist told me:

I discovered in a nursing home a couple who had very little chance to be alone together. I went to the women's section, picked up Mrs. X and wheeled her in her wheelchair to her husband's room in the male section. I wheeled her wheelchair up next to his bed and left the room, saying I would return in an hour. I put a "Do Not Disturb" sign on the door. In about an hour I returned to the room, knocked on the door and entered when they asked me to come in. I returned Mrs. X to the women's section and stopped by to visit with Mr. X. With tears in his eyes he took my hand and said, "Thank you. That was the first time I've had a chance to kiss my wife in ten years."

This is an example of the powerful ways in which the caretaking modes of the nursing home tend to rob individuals of their only reasons for living. Put another way, Gubrium points out that the floor staff at Murray Manor were mainly concerned with "bed and body" work. When this kind of activity is completed the staff feel that they have done their jobs. They have administered to the needs of the patient population.[55]

The Daily Functioning of the Nursing Home

Contrary to the more formal functioning of the hospital, the nursing home is so organized as to allow for nonacountability for activities on the part of the employees.

In a participant observation study of a sixty-five-bed proprietary nursing home, Stannard describes the processes and attitudes which lead to nonaccountability.[56] The staff at a nursing home can be divided into three subgroups: administrators, nurses, and aides. The administrators, while legally responsible for the home, generally leave the responsibilities for the day-to-day functioning of the home to the nurses. Nursing home employment is considered a low status job for a registered nurse. As a result, many of them have attitudes that Stannard terms "bitter cynicism and adamant custodialism."[57] They tend to interact in minimal and disinterested ways with the patients. Gottesman and Bourestom state that in the nursing homes that they observed, only 2 percent of the patients' time was spent interacting with professional staff members.[58]

One step below the nurses in the hierarchy are the aides. Poorly paid and untrained, the aides are often hired off the street.[59] (The

California Commission study described earlier found that the employee turnover rate in nursing homes was 283%, or three people for each position over the course of a year.)[60] Several aides were judged by Stannard to be alcoholics or to be displaying bizarre behavior. The nurses generally view the aides with contempt and mistrust. Absenteeism is high for aides, and the institution rarely attempts to fill the vacancy with temporary help. One former aide told me that "good aides" were discouraged from continuing their employment. He stated that an aide who might care more about the welfare of the patient would be seen as a potential threat by the higher level staff members of the nursing home.

Stannard observed that nursing home patients are often judged by the nurses to be "crazies" or "complainers."[61] The same contempt and mistrust which is a part of nurses' attitudes toward the aides holds true for the patients as well. The nurse, as a result of these perceptions, is unwilling to decide matters of accountability when patients receive minimal or abusive care. By distrusting the veracity of both groups, the nurse is able to escape responsibility for the actions of his or her subordinates and patients on the basis of a lack of information upon which to make a decision. The patients, aware of the nonaccountability of the system and the retaliatory powers of the staff, are reluctant to voice their complaints.

In the nursing home, the extreme objectification of the patients often results in a rapid mental and/or physical decline. A patient rapidly learns of his or her powerlessness and the patients' commonly held knowledge that they have come to the nursing home to die. What supports the elderly person did have in the world, both social and emotional, have been taken away. Jules Henry, in *Culture Against Man*, states, "routinization, inattention, carelessness, and the deprivation of communication—a chance to talk, to respond, to read, to see pictures on the wall, to be called by one's name rather than 'you' or no name at all—are ways in which millions of once useful but now obsolete human beings are detached from their selves long before they are lowered into the grave."[62]

While the nursing home is organized along bureaucratic lines, most often the functions of the staff members are oriented toward the profit motive, and not the needs of the patient. The organization, with little accountability to the greater society, cares little about the welfare of its patients, and this in turn produces a sense of hopelessness and helplessness among its patients.[63]

As a result of the profit motive, lack of adequate regulation, low staff morale, and minimal public concern, the nursing home situation in the United States is a national disgrace. Accounts of patient abuse and even patient murder, filth, malnutrition bordering on starvation, and wholesale neglect of the patients are not unusual. These accounts, documented by a United States Senate Subcommittee, come from patients, staff members, experts, and reporters.[64] Many nursing homes more closely resemble an eighteenth-century poorhouse than a contemporary United States institution. Why do we tolerate such inhumane abuses of our elderly? The answer to this question is complex. Many reasons are given for the national disgrace of our nursing homes. Abdication of physician responsibilities is cited, for often the nursing home patient is under a doctor's care when admitted to a nursing home. A lack of enforcement of state and federal regulations is well documented. There are suspicions, as a result of federal and state investigations, that organized crime is involved in the operation of many nursing homes.

It is my contention that the root cause of such a situation is twofold: first, the aged, like the poor and criminals, are judged by most Americans to be worthless. They are not valued in any real sense, save those few who may be powerful by virtue of the money that they still control. Our society, with its emphasis on the values of youth and technology, tends to view the elderly as having nothing of value to contribute to society. Rather, the elderly are often seen as making demands upon us which may deprive us of some of our personal pursuits of happiness. Second, the old, by their very presence, may represent death to us. In their deterioration, they are living examples of the inevitable deterioration of our bodies. Their loss of control disturbs us by reminding us of our own inevitable loss. They remind us of the reality of death we have been working so hard to deny.

Contrast the lack of care we allow for the elderly to the standards we insist upon in our public schools. Generally, the socially worthy and emotionally nonthreatening child is treated well. The elderly, representing worthlessness and being living reminders of our own mortality, are pushed aside to be victimized by less ethical members of our society.

In the process of discarding the elderly, we throw away a great national resource. The aged can teach about that which we fear, about growing old and dying. The elderly have the wisdom gained from living that can be valuable to all. Unfortunately, our nursing homes are a societal response to our avoidance of death.

As is often the case in a society, the weak and poor suffer the most for the "crime" of being old in America.

We may ask if the only difference between a hospital and a nursing home is one of medical expertise. In a sense, yes. But what is embodied in the notion of expertise is the professional value of medical care. Where these values are sometimes overpowered by other demands of the hospital bureaucracy, in the nursing home they are nonexistent. As a result, the nursing home becomes a dumping ground for the ill and aged who are unable to afford better care.

The economic factor in determining the quality of care received in both hospitals and nursing homes cannot be overlooked. There are fine hospitals within which the dying can receive the best of care, as well as those at which one finds appalling conditions. To a more extreme degree, the major factor that determines the care one receives depends on the kind of institution one can afford to die in. After spending time observing life in Rosemont, a privately run nursing home, Jules Henry wrote the following passage which accurately describes the conditions that we have been examining:

> Given the commitment of Rosemont to profit, the laughable social security checks of the inmates, and the cost of food, comfort, and a high standard of living, certain consequences have to follow. In order for Mrs. Dis (the owner) to be comfortable and make a good profit, according to her lights, she has no choice but to extract as much as she can from the pensions of the inmates and the salaries of her help and to limit the standard of living of both. That of the inmates is cut to a level just above starvation but below that of a good prison. In order to do this a fundamental transformation has to be brought in the mode of life and the self-conception of the inmates and in the staff's way of perceiving them. In short, Mrs. Dis makes it necessary for her institution, as personified in her staff, to conceptualize the inmates as child-animals, and to treat them accordingly. This in turn is made possible because in our culture a personality exists to the extent of ability to pay, and in terms of performance of the culturally necessary tasks of production, reproduction, and consumption.[65]

The Hospice

The concept of the hospice originally developed in Ireland, where the Sisters of Charity organized homes for the dying poor. Today, the ideal hospice has three components: 1) a staff devoted to home care for those patients who are able to stay in their homes, 2) outpatient services, and 3) an inpatient facility. Those forming teams to care for the dying in their homes are available twenty-four hours a day, so that the patients do not feel that they are alone or without others who care about them. The teams are just that, and lack a rigid, hierarchical authority structure.

In New Haven, Connecticut, a group of interested clergy, professionals, and lay people have established what is probably the best known hospice in the United States, following the model set forth by St. Christopher's Hospice in London.[66] The "hospice movement" is spreading across the United States, as people organize themselves to seek better care for the dying.[67]

The goals of the hospice are the management of pain symptoms and meeting the social, psychological, and spiritual needs of the dying person. Also, many hospices treat the aged and infirm. DuBois lists sixteen characteristics of a hospice program, among which are:

> Expert, multiple disciplinary management of pain and other symptoms.
> Easily available personnel and other services of comfort whenever needed.
> Reasonable fulfillment of individual lifestyles.
> The provision of care and consideration to all those affected by the patient's death, including the incorporation of family members into the decision-making process, even when special education may be required.
> Continuing follow-up care for the bereaved.
> Special care and concern for the staff.[68]

There are well over 1500 active groups around the nation that are involved in establishing a hospice in their communities. Most hospice groups focus upon setting up teams to care for the dying in their own homes; few have been able to afford their own free-standing facilities. In the ideal form, with its own building, the full meaning of hospice can be seen in action.[69] In the ideal hospice, the patient is treated with personal care and empathy from the moment he or she arrives. The patient is given a bed and a space on the ward which remains his or hers as long as the person is in the hospice. Hospital gowns are not used, and each patient is encouraged to bring his or her personal belongings. Visiting hours are liberal, and children of all ages are allowed to visit. Family celebrations of birthdays and other events are recognized, and both staff and other patients join in.

While a community atmosphere is encouraged in a hospice, the privacy of the patient is observed where necessary. Whatever causes distress for the dying patient is of concern to the hospice staff, and this concern extends itself to the grieving family. Families may receive the services of the hospice staff in dealing with their grief for as long as is necessary.

By committing themselves to the alleviation of suffering in the patient, the hospice staff reduces the anxiety and tenseness so often a part of the pain process. The emphasis is not upon cure, but upon helping the individual to die with a certain amount of dignity—something many have come to feel is not possible in a hospital.[70] Ideally, pain killers are available on demand, and not on a schedule set up by someone not experiencing the pain. Polypharmacy, the use of drugs in combination, is aimed at reducing pain while allowing the patient to be alert. The myth that this will produce addicts among the patients simply is not true, as the patients tend not to develop the psychological dependency of an addict.[71]

There is an emphasis upon the spiritual needs of the dying, although this is not a required part of hospice life. Obviously, the environment is one that produces emotional strains among the staff. There is a strong sense of cooperation among the staff, families, and other patients as they support each other in the daily confrontation with death. Nursing staff members work fewer days each week and have more vacation time than typical nurses. This helps to avoid "burn-out" among the staff. Staff members are chosen not only for their expertise, but also on the basis of their emotional strength.[72] As one hospice worker put it, "we need humanists with professional skills."[73]

Kenneth Cohen, after surveying many of the existing hospice programs in the United States, summarizes his findings as follows:

> The typical hospice model represented by this survey is a non-profit corporation offering home palliative care, inpatient palliative care (either through their own facility's beds or through an arrangement with a local hospital or convalescent home), consulting and referral, bereavement follow-up, medical and nursing, counseling, spiritual, teaching and social services. Visiting hours and days are unlimited, with no age restrictions for visitors. The patient and family are the unit of care. The great

bulk of the patients come from within a thirty mile radius, and the population they serve is about five hundred thousand. Home care services are provided seven days a week, twenty-four hours per day for about thirty-five patients. The average length of stay for inpatients is about fourteen days. There are about thirty volunteers in the program, who each contribute about four hours' service per week after about twenty hours of orientation and in-service training. The numbers of personnel are extremely varied, and no generalization can be made; however, usually a team is used consisting of the following disciplines: registered nurse, licensed vocational/practical nurse, social worker, physician, clergy, administrative personnel, and nursing assistants. The overwhelming number of patients are admitted with cancer diagnoses. More than half the patients are sixty-five years or older; only about five percent are under eighteen years of age. Most of the inpatient beds are classified as acute hospital beds. Funding and revenues come from foundations, federal grants, state government, philanthropy, commercial insurance, Medicare, and Medicaid. Some accommodations are provided for overnight stay of patients' families.[74]

It should be noted, however, that most programs in the United States have yet to reach such an advanced stage, and vary greatly in the degree to which they fulfill all the functions Cohen describes.[75]

While the hospice is organized around a hierarchy, the team approach to the tasks at hand tends to mitigate the negative effects of specialization and a rigid authority structure. With the team approach can go a more democratic form of organization, as opposed to a more bureaucratic structure.

In the hospice, there is a concern for the staff members' emotional well-being. At the same time, there is no evidence that the lack of formality interferes with the staff's functioning. Efficiency is evident in the hospice organization, yet it differs from that of the hospital and the nursing home. Efficiency does not refer strictly to producing for less. The term refers to competency and performance as well. Given the task of caring for the needs of the dying and their families, the hospice performs the task much better than either the hospital or nursing home. It is questionable whether or not hospitals and nursing homes even see treating the dying as their concern:

. . . The right sort of nursing home to take care of the terminally ill person may not exist in a community. It is apparently the policy of the best nursing homes in the area not to accept terminally ill people, and to send their own patients to hospitals when they become terminally ill. At the same time the hospitals in the community had a policy of dismissing terminally ill people in order to provide beds for persons who could be cured. To families who felt they could not take care of a dying patient at home these hospitals recommended that they look for a nursing home. When this contradiction was pointed out to them, the hospital and nursing home officials all expressed surprise at learning the policy of the other.[76]

If this is indeed the situation, then the hospice, in meeting the needs of the dying, is extremely efficient.

In sum, in the hospice, medical systems and caretaking functions give way to concern for the total needs of the dying person and those around him. While recognizing professional competencies, the hospice replaces the impersonal goals of medical science (hospitals) and profit making (nursing homes) with a humanistic concern for the quality of life of the dying.

A caveat is necessary here: For the most part, the hospice movement is still in its formative stage. Few organizations have reached a point of achieving all three of the goals mentioned earlier. A recently released study by Robert Kane demonstrates no greater relief of patient pain, symptom relief, or psychological distress for hospice patients than for those in hospitals.[77]

Whether the hospice concept can survive in its pure form is a matter of conjecture. Already the demands of funding agencies have forced changes in the organizational structures of some hospices which may be seen as pushing the organizations toward a closer approximation of bureaucracy.[78]

In looking at the history of the hospice movement in the United States, one finds indications that the movement arose in protest to the treatment of the dying in hospitals and nursing homes. Experiencing such treatment, professionals who sought better care for the dying found the hospice model offered a better solution than hospitals and nursing homes. However, as is so often the case in American society, feasibility is measured in dollars and cents. For many in the hospice movement, the success of the hospice seems to be measured in terms of the ability of the particular group to raise funds. Because 95 percent of Americans are insured by some form of medical insurance, the fledgling hospice organizations have had to contend with a lack of recognition by health insurance companies.[79] Insurance companies do not, as a rule, pay for "bereavement care or many of the social work functions" that are carried out by hospices.[80] Other factors, such as rival service providers, licensing boards, and special interest groups, have put pressure upon the hospice movement to legitimize itself in terms of bureaucratic standards and the medical model. As a result, it may be that the hospice model will not survive in its present form.

One alternative form being implemented in several places is the formation of a hospice within a hospital. Objections to this include differences in philosophies, placing the dying in the same environment as those recovering from illness, the different training required by the two organizations, and the negative views of the hospice concept held by many hospital staff members.[81] Arguments in favor state that there are many hospitals with extra space available, the hospital's vast resources could be available for the hospice staff, and that the hospice approach can bring about changes in the attitudes of the entire hospital staff.[82]

From a sociological perspective, it seems naive to expect that an organization so radically different from the larger parent organization is going to survive intact. Attempts at innovation within organizations, when those innovations imply changes in roles or values, often meet with both resistance and efforts to bring about conformity to the goals and values of the parent organization.[83] Without financial independence, it is doubtful that the hospice concept will be able to survive intact.

The hospice idea is often characterized by those involved as a "movement." This term implies a certain amount of idealism and ideology, as well as an orientation toward action.[84] The implementation of the hospice ideology, whose humanistic values run counter to many of the dominant American values, will face many challenges both directly (opposition from interest groups such as professional organizations and governmental bureaucracies) and indirectly (competition within the larger hospital organization). The success or failure of the movement will depend not only on the leadership ability of those involved in the hospice movement, but also on the ability of the larger society to accept or at least tolerate an organization whose humanistic and death-accepting values are so opposed to the dominant values in American life. Kane, whose study of the effectiveness of hospice versus hospital care is described above, believes that the hospice may have achieved the important goal of sensitizing the medical world to the need for humanistic care for the dying.[85]

An alternative to institutionalization, and a basic part of the hospice concept, is allowing the patient to remain in his own home for the last days of his life. As the focus of hospice care, the patient remains at home, unless physical problems require hospitalization. The dying person who is not receiving hospice care, however, is not necessarily better off than those institutionalized in a hospital. Often the burden placed upon the family, the lack of adequate care, as well as feelings of being a burden to one's relatives will combine to make the dying person more unhappy than he would be if hospitalized. However, if proper care such as that offered by a hospice is available, and the family is capable and willing to meet the needs of the dying, passing one's final days in familiar and loving surroundings far outweighs the benefits of the hospital's medical technology.

In the hospital, nursing home, and hospice we have seen three varying responses to the dying in America. The hospital, while seeking to serve the community's health needs, must also pay homage to economic realities. The nursing home does not display this conflict in its objectives, as it is committed primarily to making money. The hospice, on the other hand, holds to the value of "service." Each of these organizations, as we have seen, has developed its own systematic organizational responses to meet its goals.

Notes

1. Mary Castles and Ruth Murray, *Dying in an Institution* (New York: Appleton-Century-Crofts, 1979), pp. 47–48.

2. Marvin E. Olsen, *The Process of Social Organization.* (New York: Holt, Rinehart & Winston, 1968), p. 297.

3. Robert K. Merton, *Reader in Bureaucracy* (New York: The Free Press, 1952), p. 368.

4. Castles and Murray, p. 52.

5. Parker Rossman, *Hospice* (New York: Association Press, 1977), p. 133.

6. Paul DuBois, *The Hospice Way of Death* (New York: Human Sciences Press, 1980), p. 119.

7. Robert M. Veatch and Ernest Tai, "Talking about Death: Patterns of Lay and Professional Change," *The Annals of the American Academy of Political and Social Science* 447 (January 1980): 29–45.

8. David Sudnow, *Passing On* (Englewood Cliffs, N.J.: Prentice-Hall, 1967).

9. Ibid., p. 5.

10. Ibid., p. 8.

11. Ibid., p. 21.

12. Ibid., p. 21.

13. Peter Blau, *Bureaucracy in Modern Society* (New York: Random House, 1956), p. 32.

14. Sudnow, pg 62. Cf. Marcia Millman, *The Unkindest Cut* (New York: William Morrow, 1977).

15. Sudnow, p. 64.

16. Ibid., p. 83.

17. Ibid., pp. 84–86.

18. Ibid., pp. 99–100.

19. Ibid., pp. 90–95.

20. See Millman, Chapters 4, 5, 6.

21. Sudnow, pp. 87–88.

22. Ibid., pp. 93–94.

23. Ibid., p. 98.

24. Ibid., p. 74.

25. Ibid., p. 77.

26. Ibid., p. 100.

27. Ibid., pp. 97–98.

28. Michael Simpson, "Brought in Dead," *Omega* 7, no. 3 (1976):243–248.

29. Barney G. Glaser and Anselm L. Strauss, *Awareness of Dying* (Chicago: Aldine, 1965); *Time for Dying* (Chicago: Aldine, 1968).

30. Glaser and Strauss, *Awareness of Dying,* p. 29.

31. Jeanne Quint Benoliel, "Dying in an Institution," in Hannelore Wass, ed., *Dying: Facing the Facts* (Washington, D.C.: Hemisphere, 1979).

32. Ibid., p. 29.

33. Veatch and Tai, p. 142.

34. Glaser and Strauss, *Awareness of Dying,* p. 47.

35. John Gunther, *Death Be Not Proud* (New York: Harper & Row, 1949), pp. 39–40.

36. Glaser and Strauss, *Awareness of Dying,* p. 62.

37. E. Mansell Pattison, *The Experience of Dying* (Englewood Cliffs, N.J.: Prentice-Hall, 1977), p. 218.

38. Glaser and Strauss, *Awareness of Dying,* p. 77.

39. Ibid., p. 103.

40. Ibid.

41. Veatch and Tai, p. 42.

42. Glaser and Strauss; Sudnow.

43. Wolf V. Heydebrand, *Hospital Bureaucracy* (New York: Dunellen Publishing, 1973), p. 14.

44. William F. May, "Institutions as Symbols of Death," in James P. Carse and Arlene B. Dallery, eds., *Death and Society* (New York: Harcourt Brace Jovanovich, 1979), pp. 413–414.

45. Benoliel, p. 148.

46. *San Diego Union,* 12 September 1971.

47. Ibid., p. 9.

48. *Los Angeles Times,* "Excessive Profits by Nursing Homes Cited in Task Force Study," 31 July 1981.

49. Subcommittee on Long Term Care of the Special Committee on Aging, United States Senate, *Nursing Home Care in the United States: Failure in Public Policy* (Washington, D.C.: U.S. Government Printing Office, 1974), p. 3.

50. Linda Horn and Elma Griesel, *Nursing Homes: A Citizen's Action Guide* (Boston: Beacon Press, 1977).

51. Elizabeth S. Johnson and John R. Williamson, *Growing Old* (New York: Holt, Rinehart & Winston, 1980), pp. 136–141.

52. Jaber F. Gubrium, *Living and Dying at Murray Manor.* (New York: St. Martin's Press, 1975).

53. Ibid., p. 84.

54. Erving Goffman, *Asylums* (Garden City, N.Y.: Doubleday, 1961), pp. 3–124.

55. Ibid., p. 124.

56. Charles I. Stannard, "Old Folks and Dirty Work," *Social Problems* 20, no. 3 (1973): 329–342. See also Diana K. Harris and William E. Cole, *Sociology of Aging* (Boston: Houghton Mifflin, 1980), pp. 351–359.

57. Ibid., p. 332.

58. Leonard E. Gottesman and Norman C. Bourestom, "Why Nursing Homes Do What They Do." *The Gerontologist* 14 (December 1974): 501–506. See also Joseph N. Henderson, "Chronic Life: An Anthropological View of an American Nursing Home" (Ph.D. dissertation, The University of Florida (Gainesville), 1979), pp. 64–72.

59. Stannard, p. 330.

60. *Los Angeles Times,* 31 July 1981.

61. Stannard, p. 335.

62. Jules Henry, *Culture Against Man* (New York: Random House, 1963), p. 393.

63. Ibid., pp. 440–442.

64. Subcommittee on Long Term Care.

65. Henry, pp. 440–442.

66. Rossman, pp. 81–84.

67. Ibid.

68. DuBois, p. 68. (Author's paraphrase)

69. Leonard M. Liegner, "St. Christopher's Hospice, 1974," *Journal of the American Medical Association* 234, no. 10 (8 December 1975): 1047–1048.

70. Elizabeth G. McNulty and Robert A. Holderby, *Hospice: A Caring Challenge* (Springfield, Ill: Charles C Thomas, 1983), p. 13.

71. Liegner, p. 1048.

72. DuBois, p. 63.

73. Ibid., p. 96.

74. Kenneth Cohen, *Hospice: Prescription for Terminal Care* (Germantown, Md.: Aspen Systems Corp., 1979), p. 173.

75. McNulty, pp. 13–15.

76. Rossman, p. 23.

77. Robert L. Kane, et al., "A Random Controlled Trial of Hospice Care," *The Lancet* 1, no. 8382 (1984): 890–894.

78. Glen Davidson, "In Search of Models of Care," in Glen Davidson, ed., *The Hospice* (Washington, D.C.: Hemisphere, 1978).

79. Cohen, p. 101.

80. Ibid., pp. 101, 104.

81. Ibid., p. 69.

82. Rossman, pp. 146–150.

83. John Stephenson, "Professionalism and Innovation Acceptance among Teachers" (Ph.D. Dissertation, The Ohio State University, 1972), pp. 120–124.

84. Ian Robertson, *Sociology* (New York: Worth Publishers, 1981), p. 584.

85. *Los Angeles Times*, "Hospices Rated Only on Par with Hospitals," 1 May 1984.

CHAPTER FOUR

The Dying Process

T HE INDIVIDUAL who is dying is in a state of transition between the living and the dead. Being in the stage of life known as "dying" has ramifications for both the individual and the larger society. In studying the dying process, we will focus on both the psychological and sociological dimensions of dying. Historical studies of dying provide us with an understanding of the social and psychological meanings placed upon dying at different times and in different social contexts.

Normative ways of behaving not only demonstrate a society's values, but in turn reinforce those values through traditional legitimation. Dying is a human activity which is carried out in a normative manner. The individual learns the meaning of death and what are considered to be proper or "good" ways of dying from the larger society. One hopes to die what one's society considers a good death. At the same time, dying "well" reinforces certain values within the society itself.

The historian Philippe Aries, in his study, *Western Attitudes Toward Death,* describes dying as it existed for 1000 years before the twelfth century in Western civilization as being "tamed."[1] One had a foreknowledge of his own death, and was therefore able to prepare himself for death.[2] There were ritual gestures and customs which the individual was ideally supposed to act out. The person who was aware of his imminent death first took it upon himself to express his regrets over the end of his life. This was followed by a pardoning of those who were important to him for any wrongs that they might have committed against him. At that point, the individual shifted his attention away from this world, and onto his God. He confessed his sins, and gave his soul over to God. If possible, he received absolution from a priest, and then waited in silence for death.

Note that the individual who was dying was the center of the process. He organized it, decided what was important, and carried it out in a public ceremony. It was not a theatrical, maudlin, or emotional act, but was instead a simple, meaningful ritual. Aries states that death, which was "both familiar and near, evoking no great fear or awe," was met as "a familiar resignation to the collective destiny."[3]

Beginning in the eleventh and twelfth centuries, Aries sees a shift from the former "tamed death" to a style of dying he calls "One's Own Death."[4] The gathering at the death bed became an emotional scene, as the judgment of the individual by God took place at this time. Still, the individual controlled his dying. No longer the passive, fatalistic person of the former style of dying, the individual now cherished his life. Individual existence was becoming more important. As we saw in our examination of the history of American attitudes toward death, this judgmental dying was predominant among the early settlers of New England.

Aries's work describes the influence of society upon what was considered the proper way to die at various times throughout history. Earlier, we examined the attitudes and values which have affected the changing American image of death. In this chapter, we will examine contemporary American thinking and research on the dying process.

The Living-Dying and Terminal Intervals

In contemporary times, one no longer relies upon an inner conviction such as Aries described that he or she is dying. Most usually, that definition is arrived at by a medical analysis of one's physical condition. One may enter the doctor's office with a minor complaint, only to learn that the condition is a symptom of a terminal illness. A person is considered to be dying when death is no longer the inevitable abstraction that it is to us all, but has become a very real, time-bound condition.[5] I would prefer to use Pattison's term, the "living-dying interval" for this period of time.[6] This term allows for the fact that a person may, at least at the time of entering the living-dying interval, be doing more living than dying, and that his or her physical debility or symptoms are not yet at a point where the individual is to be considered as being controlled by his or her ailment. For example, a friend of mine was told of his diagnosis of leukemia as a result of a blood test for his marriage license. The only difference in his condition initially was a psychological change when he was told of his illness. He had not consulted a doctor about any symptoms, nor did he feel ill. Suddenly, he was given information which was to drastically change his life and his social identity. However, he had no physical feelings of illness at that time, only information from his physician that he was not well. As the individual continues in the living-dying phase, eventually the term "dying" becomes a more apt description than does "living." Within the living-dying interval, Pattison describes three distinct phases: the acute crisis phase, where the person tries to cope with the knowledge of impending death; the chronic living-dying phase, during which the person works through the fears and anticipatory grief; and the terminal phase, wherein the individual begins to close off his or her emotional investment in life, and prepares for death.

As the individual enters the status of being in the living-dying interval, his or her status in society changes as well. Typically, when his or her condition is known to others his or her definition as a member of society is modified. The clarity of terminality produces marked changes in the ways in which the rest of society relates to the individual. Typically, the person in the living-dying interval is isolated from his or her everyday world and the people in it.

Ronald Preston uses an interesting analogy to describe the social plight of the dying.[8] He describes what he calls the Gregor effect, which is derived from Franz Kafka's story, *Metamorphosis*. In that story, Kafka describes Gregor's slow change from a person into a giant cockroach. As his physical condition changes, Gregor fights to retain his position as a social being among his family and friends. Society, however, is horrified by Gregor's condition, and he gradually withdraws from any social interaction. Ultimately rejected by those whom he loves, Gregor retreats to his room to die alone.

Note in Preston's description below the similarities between the ways in which the horrible creature Gregor was treated, and the ways in which we typically respond to the dying:

> From the onset of his affliction, Gregor cannot mingle with the general public. His position in the outer society is immediately forfeit. This situation, together with Gregor's presence, burden his family suddenly and crushingly. They must endure his appearance, compensate for his economic absence, seclude him from outsiders and suffer their grief at his fate and their own.
>
> Initially, though they are ambivalent, the family treats Gregor with some consideration. They are repulsed by his appearance. They imprison him in his room to be spared the sight of him. Yet they also maintain him as best they can. Gregor is fed regularly, his room is cleaned daily, and his furniture is removed so that he may have unrestricted movement. The family hope for his rejuvenation.
>
> The hope fades, the reality oppresses, and the family's perception of Gregor changes. Alternately, the family shrinks from and is angered with his presence. Financial matters are worked out: Gregor is no longer counted on for moral and financial support. The family busies itself with diversions so that it is spared attending to the son or reflecting on his ambiguity. Ultimately, Gregor's care is foisted onto a charwoman who neither fears Gregor nor sees his humanity.[9]

Whether still functioning in society or institutionalized, the social isolation of the dying person often leaves him or her bereft of emotional and social support at a time when he or she may need the support the most. Society's reactions to the dying are reflected Richard Kalish's study of college students' attitudes toward the dying, which found that a third of the respondents would not willingly allow a dying person to "live within a few doors" of them.[10] Only half of the sample would willingly become close friends with a dying person. A death-avoiding society such as the contemporary United States has no categorical response, no normative behaviors which serve to guide our interactions with the dying. As a result, most people avoid the dying as they do the grieving, often with a rationalizations such as "I just don't know what to say." This is not, I believe, merely an excuse to avoid an unpleasant situation, but it is a real explanation of the public's dilemma when confronted with death. Death and the dying are not avoided simply because they do not fit into the world of the contemporary death-denying pleasure seeker. It may be that a lack of experience and/ or learning about interacting with the dying leaves the individual with no understanding of how he or she is supposed to behave. A lack of normative expectations for a situation, coupled with a death avoiding mentality, leads to the tendency of others to withdraw from or avoid the dying.[11]

At the same time that the dying person is being avoided by others, and as a result becomes isolated from the everyday world, medical technology is increasing the length of time he or she may spend in the living-dying interval. Once, dying was a status one usually entered and left rather quickly. Today, the diagnosis of a terminal condition may occur weeks, months, or even years prior to death. The prolongation of the living-dying interval has extended and compounded the problem of isolation for the dying.

Another result of the extension of the living-dying interval has been the increased strain that this places upon the dying person's relationships. The dying person has his own grief process to go through. Knowledge of his impending death can lead to a kind of preparatory grief, which entails not only reactive grieving over the coming loss of his relationships, but also the existential grief felt over the loss of his own existence, and its ultimate meaning.

Along with the social isolation may go a lack of normative expectations for the dying themselves. We have little or no knowledge in American society about how one should behave in the role of a dying person. Diana Crane cogently argues that the dying person is best described as a kind of marginal man.[12] There exists no clear understanding of what the newly imposed identity as dying entails, in terms of either feelings or behaviors. If there is any kind of definition of behavior, it is one that is imposed by the bureaucratic medical system within which most Americans spend time while in the living-dying interval.

The dying person is no longer expected to function as a "normal person;" for instance, he or she is no longer expected to be concerned with the everyday issues of making a living or caring for others. That person is expected to put all his or her energies during the living-dying interval into fighting death, and this generally implies a compliance with the directives of medical science.[13]

Noyes and Clancy, both medical doctors, argue that there is a difference between being in the sick role and in the dying role.[14] The sick role involves an exemption from social responsibilities and a right to be cared for. The person should want to get better, because being sick is negatively valued. Also, the sick person is supposed to cooperate with what is deemed proper medical procedure. Noyes and Clancy point out several differences between that kind of behavior and what is expected of the dying. Most obviously, the dying are not going to get better. This fact alone challenges the assumption that the patient should fight to stay alive. However, by fighting to stay alive, the authors point out, the patient demonstrates to others that he or she is not responsible for his or her own death. We expect a person in the dying role to retain the will to live in spite of what dying really means.

Another aspect of the dying role described by Noyes and Clancy is that the dying person is expected to arrange to pass on any responsibilities and property that he or she possesses. This is not only a responsible act, but one which promotes the dying to disengage from society.

Notice the double-bind implicit in the Noyes and Clancy description. One should continue to want to live, but should at the same time give up many of the things that make life worthwhile in being an active and autonomous member of society. Implicit also in both roles is a passivity, a giving of one's self over to medical caretakers.

The individual in the living-dying interval of life must also contend with becoming a burden on family and friends. A great many dying persons report that their greatest concern is with the ability of their relatives to carry on after they are dead. This is especially true when younger children will be affected by the death.[15] Socialized to value independence and self-mastery, dealing with the helplessness of dying adds to the dying person's concerns. Becoming a burden may take the form of being a financial drain, a source of emotional distress, or of being a living example to people of their own mortality—a fact not well accepted in our society. These strains may lead to the termination of relationships prior to death, when the pressure becomes too great for the individuals involved.

The individual in an extended living-dying interval may find that a good deal of that time can be of good quality, with the person still functioning at a high percentage of his or her former activity level. This lengthening of the living-dying time period can also allow the dying person to gain a sense of closure around his or her life by settling affairs and bringing an appropriate end to relationships.

The nature of the illness and its treatment protocol can also be a factor in the way the individual will behave during the living-dying interval. Martocchio describes four major patterns of physical dying, each associated with different types of diseases and their treatments.[16] "Peaks and valleys" is a pattern of exacerbations and remissions. The "hopeful highs" and the "depressing lows" of this pattern produce an emotional roller-coaster effect. The typical illness in this pattern is leukemia, where the remissions are seen as dramatic resurgences of health, and the reoccurrence of the illness becomes a fight for life. The overall pattern, however, is usually a declining path, as the remissions usually do not fully return the individual to his or her state of health prior to the last exacerbation.

"Descending plateaus," Martocchio's second category, refers to an illness pattern where, at best, the illness is held in check at a certain level for a period of time. This stepwise descension, typical of such diseases as multiple sclerosis, always has an element of uncertainty about it, as the length of time the person may stay on any one plateau is unknown. Martocchio notes that feelings of anger, depression, and futility are typical of this pattern.[17] These people are likely to be hospitalized less than those in other patterns of dying, but will spend more time in chronic care or nursing care centers.

The third pattern is one of the "downward slope"—a steady, relatively steep and unremitting decline in health. The degree of slope will, of course, vary in a great many cases depending upon the disease, the condition of the patient, and the medical interventions used. Due to the inexorable downward trend, this dying pattern tends to evoke a sense of urgency among the victim and those surrounding him or her.

Finally, there is a pattern of a gradual slant, in which life is continually, perhaps almost imperceptably, declining. Often this pattern of dying is associated with physical trauma such as accidents, where the individual continues to exist, often dependent upon machines. Questions arise concerning the rightness or wrongness of continuing to maintain biological life in such cases.

Each of these patterns will affect the behaviors of the dying person. For example, the gradual slant pattern often promotes resignation on the part of the person. The peaks and valleys pattern may often, according to Martoccio, lead to some form of resignation as the person becomes fatalistic or relies upon God to get through each crisis. Hope is high in this pattern, as each remission may rekindle the person's interest and involvement in living.[18]

Chandler suggests yet another pattern of dying, when he describes those individuals in whom the *presentiment* of death is a factor. By this term, Chandler refers to "patients whose illnesses are such as to lead them to expect to die at any moment, that is chronic cardiovascular and cerebrovascular patients with a history of many crises."[19] Chandler describes these people as manifesting a great deal of anger, in the form of hostility, aggressiveness, and negativism. Being, in a sense, living time bombs, the stress on both the patient and his caretakers leads to a great deal of anger being acted out between them.

In addition to the nature and treatment of the illness, the psychological make up of the person, his or her history, age, and sex, as well as the social context in which the dying takes place will all contribute to shaping the individual's behavior.[20] Let us look at an example of these factors at work: In *The Death of Ivan Ilych,* Tolstoy describes the suffering of a man who, finding himself entering the living-dying interval at the age of forty-three, discovers his life to be without meaning.[21] Ivan Ilych's dying takes a long time; over four months. Steadily declining in health, kept in ignorance of the seriousness of his condition, Ilych is finally bedridden with only two constant companions; the servant boy Gerasim who cares for him, and his own pain. The last four weeks of his life are times of physical and emotional stress, as Ilych struggles both with pain and the knowledge of his dying. His last three days are spent in screaming; a screaming which expresses his emotional as well as physical pain. Through this time of agony, Ilych is able to work through his emotional torment over his life, and finally to "give up the ghost" with little struggle, having resolved the issues surrounding the meaning of his life.

Ivan Ilych died in Russia in 1880. How would his dying in America today be different? He most certainly would not die at home, but would very likely be in a hospital. Nor would he be surrounded by familiar things, but would instead be in an institutional environment. His physical suffering would be controlled with drugs, and any screaming (Tolstoy states that Ilych's horrifying screams could be heard through two closed doors) would be silenced by medication. Most likely his screams would be considered a sign of physical suffering, and nothing more. The task of dying, which Tolstoy so vividly describes, would be taken away from Ivan Ilych today, to be replaced by a comatose state. Modern institutional dying is expected to be passive, nonemotional, and nondisruptive.

We have seen in this discussion that individual factors, social environment, disease, and treatment will all affect the individual's dying. As a result, dying remains a highly variable act, subject to many influences. One attempt to classify the responses of the individual to his or her dying has been the work of Elizabeth Kubler-Ross.

Kubler-Ross' Stages of Dying

Perhaps the best known study in thanatology is *On Death and Dying* by Elizabeth Kubler-Ross.[22] Her work is an important contribution to the study of dying. In addition, the popularity of her study among the general public has helped to bring the subject of death and dying out of its taboo status. In this section we will critically examine Kubler-Ross's study of dying people.

Trained as a psychiatrist, Kubler-Ross acknowledges the influence of Freud early in her book. As Freud stated, she believes that we cannot, in our unconscious minds, conceive of ourselves as dying of natural causes or old age. We can, she notes, only imagine ourselves being killed.[23] As a result, death becomes something of a "bad act," which demands revenge or punishment. In addition, our unconscious minds cannot discriminate between a wish and a deed. For example, if we wish for someone's death to occur and it does, we will feel guilt at somehow having caused the event by wishing for it to happen.

These basic tenents of Kubler-Ross's position are important, as they provide a theoretical justification for her findings. Let us look at two examples of this: Angry behavior on the part of the grief-stricken can be explained by Kubler-Ross as the individual's responses to unconscious demands for revenge. Since the unconscious by definition is not directly verifiable, there is no way of testing this assertion. Another tenent of this position is that the psychiatrist, as a result of his or her training, is capable of accurately interpreting the actions and thoughts of the individual in such a way as to become aware of the person's unconscious mind. As a result, the psychiatrist claims to be able to define inner reality better than the patient. From such a perspective, Kubler-Ross interprets the actions and conversations of dying patients. Kubler-Ross interviewed over two hundred dying patients for her study. These patients were hospitalized, and most suffered from cancer. She asserts that all of her subjects were aware (perhaps only subconsciously) of their dying status.

Ideally, Kubler-Ross states, there are five distinct stages through which the individual passes, each of which displays a predominant defense mechanism against what she considers to be the universal unconscious fear of death.[24] The use of the term "stages" may be inappropriate, as it implies an order, or a sense of a particular direction. A careful reading of Kubler-Ross's work reveals this is not an accurate assumption. She states clearly that the stages "will last for different periods of time and will replace each other or exist at one time side by side."[25]

The first stage that Kubler-Ross describes is that of denial. The initial response to the awareness that the person has entered the living-dying interval is to defend against that information by not accepting it as true. Usually, denial does not last through the entire living-dying interval, but exists initially so that the individual may defend against accepting into his or her inner symbolic system the fact that he or she is dying. After the shock of that information has passed—as the individual is better able to accept the new image of him- or herself—some denial may still be present. However, it does not dominate the individual's thinking.[26] Occasionally a patient will return to the denial stage, if only to avoid the reality of his or her impending death long enough to enjoy a brief respite from a constantly death-oriented existence.

Kubler-Ross's second stage is anger. Often, when the person is unable to continue to deny the fact that he or she is dying, he or she then becomes angry, looking for the cause of this unhappy fate. This anger may be projected out almost at random upon the environment. Kubler-Ross describes one such case which involved a young nun who displayed her anger at being terminally ill by visiting with other patients, soliciting their needs, and then demanding attentions for them from the nursing staff.[27] The staff referred her to Kubler-Ross. Since she would not become angry with fate, or God, or cancer, the nun vented her anger on the staff, according to Kubler-Ross.[28]

Bargaining, the third stage, comes about as the patient seeks to forstall or delay the terrible fate that awaits. Kubler-Ross believes that this may cover up an unconscious guilt. For example, people may attempt to bargain with God, stating that if they are allowed to live, they will dedicate themselves totally to a religious life. Bargaining with God for more time may indicate an underlying guilt at having become a religious backslider.[29]

The fourth stage, depression, comes about as the individual begins to acknowledge his or her impending loss. Kubler-Ross maintains that there are really two kinds of depression manifested. "Reactive depression" is the response to the losses one undergoes in progressing through the living-dying interval: the loss of such things as physical well-being, autonomy, and physical attractiveness. "Preparatory depression" refers to the emotional response to the impending loss of one's life.[30]

Finally, having worked through the depression, the individual enters the fifth stage of acceptance. In a sense, at this point the person is finished with life. This is far from a radiant, supernatural happiness. Instead, Kubler-Ross describes the patient as contemplating "his coming end with a certain degree of quiet expectation."[31] The patient is devoid of any feelings, and his interest in the rest of the world diminishes as he or she prepares for death. Later in this chapter we will discuss this stage in more detail as a part of the terminal interval.

Throughout the five stages of dying, Kubler-Ross maintains, hope is ever present.[32] The open acknowledgement of the patient's condition will not lead to a loss of will to live, because hope is present in all who deal openly with their dying. However, two conflicts can arise around the issue of hope: one is when the family gives up while the patient still needs to hold out some hope, and the other is when the family persists in being hopeful for a last-minute reprieve, although the patient has accepted his or her death and is preparing for it.[33]

A Critique of the Stage Theory

Criticism can be levied at Kubler-Ross's work on the basis of her data gathering techniques. First, all of the material was gathered by either Kubler-Ross herself, or seminary students who worked closely with her. There was not an independent gathering of data. In addition, one can question the underlying assumptions of her study. The definition of the unconscious and the role of the psychiatrist are both concepts that are not widely accepted by many scientists and researchers outside of the psychiatric community. Recall, for example, the nun who was described as acting out her anger by bothering the nurses. It is also quite possible that the nun was responding in appropriate ways to the lack of care of other patients which she observed. Her biggest "problem" may have been that she disrupted the normal routine of the hospital.

As a result of her behavior, she was referred to Kubler-Ross for psychiatric treatment. The underlying assumption in such a referral is that anyone who challenges the organization must have a personal (i.e., psychological) problem. This is dramatically seen in Ken Kesey's *One Flew Over the Cuckoo's Nest,* where challenges to the medical system are interpreted as further proof of psychosis, rather than as a healthy resistance to inhumane treatment.[34]

Throughout her work, one finds Kubler-Ross interpreting the actions and emotions of the patient. All these interpretations in turn reinforce her theory. It is possible that over time the five stages ceased to be hypothesis and became a self-fulfilling prophecy. New information, if it came about solely through the subjective interpretation of Kubler-Ross, would only serve to reinforce her theoretical perspective. This is an all-too-common problem for the psychoanalytic school.

In addition to the highly subjective nature of the data gathering technique that was used, the conditions under which the data were gathered may be questioned. We know that Kubler-Ross was working with patients who had been diagnosed as terminally ill and were hospitalized. In such a situation, the individual is experiencing a good deal of emotional turmoil. His or her life has been dramatically changed. He or she has been forced to give up a former identity, and to enter the foreign and alienating world of the hospital as a patient. Isolated from familiar things and people, he or she is left alone to contemplate death. The patient, I would contend, is in no position to debate the subjective interpretations of a visiting psychiatrist. Even if a patient did so, he or she could easily be labeled as exhibiting denial or anger. Alone and with no one to share his or her emotional pain, the patient may be reluctant to disturb the only sympathetic relationship that exists; that with the psychiatrist.

Similar to the victims of thought reform, the terminal patient may find it very difficult to reject the psychiatric interpretation of his or her behavior.[35] Perhaps this process becomes magnified when the patient is hospitalized with a terminal illness. The dying patient is subjected to the disruption of his or her routine existence, is isolated from others, and is socialized to become a passive and dependent hospital patient. These are the necessary emotional, social, and psychological prerequisites for effective psychological domination by another. This is not to accuse Kubler-Ross of any such activity, but to point out the high degree of vulnerability among her patients to her interpretation of their inner mental states.

The stages as described by Kubler-Ross also suffer from a lack of a clear observable behavior patterns for each stage. Bargaining exists, for example, but according to Kubler-Ross it is usually a secret process. How does one observe something done in secret? It can be argued that the individual is in a certain stage when Kubler-Ross says that he or she is there. This ambiguity has led to further doubt as to the overall credibility of the stage theory.

Kathy Charmaz, in an excellent critique of Kubler-Ross's work, points out that a great deal of her analysis deals with patient management—a point which reinforces my earlier concern about Kubler-Ross's interpretation of patient behavior. Charmaz argues that each stage can be reinterpreted from another reality to describe rational, direct, and purposeful responses to the hospital environment:

> Thus, while staff may feel that dying patients have had more ample cues about the nature of their diseases and their moribund course, these patients may not have correctly perceived or interpreted all the cues. Consequently, the patients may not have a clearly articulated prediction of death. Simultaneously, although patients may ultimately "know" that they are dying, it may take them much longer to piece together the cues that staff members anticipate. If they are not told directly, their behavior witnessed in the stages may reflect their process of discovering the truth. Denial may occur when the patients have not yet put together the cues, isolation follows when they realize that things are not quite right, anger when they learn that everyone else knew long before, depression when there is not much time and so much left unfinished, and acceptance when they realize that nothing more can be done.[36]

It is evident that Kubler-Ross's stage theory is the result of highly subjective data gathering, which has taken place under conditions in which the subjects are highly vulnerable to suggestion and manipulation. One finds in Kubler-Ross's writings a concern for the proper management of the dying process within the bureaucratic structure of the hospital. There is little reliance upon the patients' definition of reality, but a great deal of reliance upon Elizabeth Kubler-Ross's.

In addition to criticism of Kubler-Ross's data gathering and analysis, several researchers have produced data that questions some of her findings. Schulz and Aderman, in a review of the literature on the stage theory, determined that Kubler-Ross's theory is not supported by other research.[37] For example, they cite Hinton's study of seventy dying patients, in which the effects of medications upon patients is an important factor. Hinton, also a psychiatrist, using nondirected interviews similar to Kubler-Ross's, reports that depression was present in half the patients throughout the last eight weeks of their lives. Depression and anxiety tended to increase toward the end of the patients' lives, although anxiety was less prevalent. Schulz and Aderman state that this study raises some important questions: What effect did drugs have on the patients who were observed by Kubler-Ross? Although both researchers used the same data gathering techniques, how can we account for the differences in their results? In addition, Hinton claims that only 20 percent of his patients knew that they were dying, while another 20 percent thought that death was probable. Does this mean that 60 percent of Hinton's sample died in denial? Also, the two studies contradict each other in that Kubler-Ross describes a final state of acceptance, while Hinton speaks of an increase in depression and anxiety as his patients neared death.

Another study cited by Schulz and Aderman further substantiates their lack of confidence in Kubler-Ross's findings: Using objective testing measures, Lieberman describes a process of social withdrawal which results as the dying individual attempts to cope with the decline of his or her ability to control or interact meaningfully with the environment. What Lieberman labels withdrawal may have been interpreted by other, more clinically inclined observers as depression. Finally, Schulz and Aderman review the work of Weisman and Kastenbaum, who used the psychological autopsy technique to review eighty cases of patients with terminal illnesses. These patients were found to have adopted one pattern of behavior (usually either withdrawal and inactivity or energetically continuing living) which they maintained until death. The post hoc technique of the psychological autopsy may be viewed skeptically itself, but the results do cast additional doubt upon the stage theory.

Daniel Cappon, using a psychoanalytic approach, argues that people essentially die as they have lived.[38] He disputes the idea that hope is always present, a contention of Kubler-Ross. Instead, Cappon argues, the dying use denial, withdrawal, or repression to contend with the threat of impending death.

As one can see from the above discussion, the work of Kubler-Ross has been met with a good deal of skepticism among professionals in the field. Many would agree with Edwin Shneidman's observation:

> Rather than five definite stages discussed above, my experience
> leads me to posit a hive of affect, in which there is a constant
> coming and going. The emotional stages seem to include a con-
> stant interplay between disbelief and hope and, against these
> as background, a waxing and waning of anguish, terror, acquies-
> ence and surrender, rage and envy, disinterest and ennui, pre-
> tense, taunting and daring and even yearning for death—all
> these in the context of bewilderment and pain.[40]

If there has been a lack of professional approval for Kubler-Ross's findings, there has also been a strong popularity among the general public and many who care for the dying. Some of the criticisms raised about Kubler-Ross's work are not her fault; instead the problem lies with those who would put her findings to use.

Apparently Kubler-Ross's work has developed its own group of "true believers," who insist upon using the stage theory as incontestable dogma. As a result, many believe that the only "good death" is one in which the individual proceeds sequentially through the stages, arriving at acceptance and a successful death. While Kubler-Ross states that the stages are not necessarily sequential, it is unfortunate that this statement does not appear in a more forceful form earlier in her book.[41] As much as Kubler-Ross has been maligned for this, one cannot hold her totally responsible for the ways in which others attempt to use what she has written. She has worked to develop a fine conceptual instrument, which unfortunately has been used by some as a dogmatic sledge hammer. In considering what Kubler-Ross's followers have done with her work, the author is reminded of Freud's reply when asked by a reporter about his reaction to the popularization and vulgarization of his concepts: "I am not a Freudian." Freud realized that lay people were (and still are, for that matter) siezing upon his works and oversimplifying his conceptual scheme to meet their own needs. It is too bad that there are those who insist that Kubler-Ross's findings are the ultimate truth, and all dying behavior must be seen as manifestations of the stage theory.

Dictating emotional hoops through which the dying person must jump is a cruel "aid" to that person.[42] As psychiatrist Avery Weisman puts it, "To tell another person what he ought to do, think, or be is an affront at any time; but to do this when he nears the end of his life is sanctimonious cruelty."[43]

While one can criticize the misuse of Kubler-Ross's findings, it is difficult to deny that the popular acceptance of her work has had the effect of making a great many people more sensitive to the plight of the dying in America today. While one may fault the scientific rigor of her study and question the findings, there are few who are unwilling to acknowledge her contribution to a sympathetic approach to death and dying among the general public.

It may also be that the American public finds in Kubler-Ross's material a panacea for the fear of death so evident in society today. Perhaps Kubler-Ross provides, for some, a prescription for successful dying which allays their basic fears by providing a romantic view of acceptable death. If one works hard and achieves acceptance, then death itself is no longer nasty. In other words, there is a way out by which one can avoid the awfulness of death itself: Simply make your way through the five steps, and you too can avoid the ugliness of death. This pragmatic approach may appeal to many who are unable to deal with the grim realities of existential death; they may think that by carefully following the directions, they can achieve a successful death and will no longer have to fear such an end. While studies of the dying process are valuable to us, they should not be used to further a romantic denial of the realities of death and dying.

The Terminal Phase

As the individual proceeds through the living-dying phase, there is generally a decline in physical well-being to a point where he or she is indeed more dying than living. Usually, this is met with an institutional response, and the individual is either hospitalized or enters a facility such as a nursing home or hospice. When the individual reaches a point when he or she begins to turn inward, to withdraw from the external world, we can say that the terminal interval of existence has begun.

The grief that the individual had felt over the impending loss of his or her life is usually, though not always, left behind at this point. There is no love of life left in the person in the terminal interval. Hope, if it had existed, changes from hope as expection-of-cure to hope as desiring-of-cure.[44] In other words, a last-minute cure would be nice (desirable), but it is no longer expected. Kubler-Ross's stage of acceptance, described earlier, is similar to the terminal phase. The body's inability to cope becomes an imperative, and the world external to the dying person becomes a burden which cannot be managed. The terminal interval ends when biological death occurs.

On Fear, Pain, and Suffering

Throughout the struggle of the human race to make sense out of our awareness, the issue of the meaning of death appears and reappears. We are all aware that there are many ways of understanding the world. One can "know" through common sense, through experience, through mystical revelation, and through logical thinking. Humanity has always had to grapple with the issue of our humanness; of our subjection to fear, pain, and suffering. Great literature and art, from the early sagas to contemporary films, seek to explain the human condition; to understand our deaths as well as our lives. In examining the social and psychological aspects of dying, we can overanalyze to the point of losing the very humanness which is vital to our subject. One should not so rationalize and reduce the subject of dying as to lose sight of the mysterious and intensely human quality of a person's death. Being with the dying can be a humbling—and yet also an ennobling—experience. But whatever else it is, it is an intensely human event. Edwin Shneidman puts it this way:

> As I see a dying person moving from day to day toward that ultimate moment, I hope that perhaps I can learn something about how dying is done, something about the arcane mysteries of the magic moment of transition from life to nonlife, something about the components of an ideal death, and even, if the gods are gracious, some guidelines that will teach me how to die well when my own turn comes.[45]

An understanding of human dying entails not only the knowledge gained from social and psychological studies. It also entails a comprehension of the larger questions with which dying brings us face to face. The meaning of suffering is one such issue. In earlier times, suffering was explained by religion, which made human pain, both psychological and physical, understandable in terms of God's plan for humanity. In Christianity, for example, Jesus was the suffering son of God at Golgatha, and this suffering gave meaning to his life. Peace, as well as freedom from pain and fear, would be found in Heaven.

In *The Plague,* Camus uses the death of a young boy as a means of dramatizing these powerful issues. The boy has suffered terribly as his body fought the plague:

> The child, his eyes still closed, seemed to grow a little calmer. His clawlike fingers were feebly plucking at the sides of the bed. Then they rose, scratched at the blanket over his knees, and suddenly he doubled up his limbs, bringing his thighs above his stomach, and remained quite still. For the first time he opened his eyes and gazed at Rieux, who was standing immediately in front of him. In the small face, rigid as a mask of grayish clay, slowly the lips parted and from them rose a long, incessant scream, hardly varying with his respiration, and filling the ward with a fierce, indignant protest, so little childish that it seemed like a collective voice issuing from all the sufferers there. . . . Paneloux gazed down at the small mouth, fouled with the sores of the plague and pouring out the angry death-cry that has sounded through the ages of mankind. He sank on his knees, and all present found it natural to hear him say in a voice hoarse but clearly audible across that nameless, never ending wail:
>
> "My God, spare this child!"
>
> . . . His mouth still gaping, but silent now, the child was lying among the tumbled blankets, a small, shrunken form, with the tears still wet on his cheeks.
>
> Paneloux went up to the bed and made the sign of benediction. Then gathering up his cassock, he walked out by the passage between the beds. . . .
>
> Rieux was already on his way out, walking so quickly and with such a strange look on his face that Paneloux put out an arm to check him when he was about to pass him in the doorway.
>
> "Come, doctor," he began.
>
> Rieux swung round on him fiercely.
>
> "Ah! That child, anyhow, was innocent, and you know it as well as I do!"
>
> "I understand," Paneloux said in a low voice. "That sort of thing is revolting because it passes our human understanding. But perhaps we should love what we cannot understand."
>
> Rieux straightened up slowly. He gazed at Paneloux, sum-

moning to his gaze all the strength and fervor he could muster against his weariness. Then he shook his head.

"No, Father. I've a very different idea of love. And until my dying day I shall refuse to love a scheme of things in which children are put to torture."[46]

Powerless in the face of death, the doctor expresses the frustration and anger that are stirred up by the child's horrible dying. To him, there is no solace to be found in religion, no comfort in believing there is purpose behind such an act.

With the rise of science and the decline of traditional religion, suffering became meaningless. It may be, however, that technology, while being much more capable of controlling pain than in the past, has produced different forms of suffering. For example, while the cure rate for cancer has declined very little over the past forty years (which is especially shocking when one considers the amount of money and effort spent to fight cancer over that time), the ability to detect the disease has increased dramatically.[47] The result of this is that more and more people are now suffering the psychological (if not the physical) pain of prolonged terminal illness. When one considers the suffering of family members as well, then it becomes evident that technology, by detecting but not necessarily curing illnesses, provokes a great deal more suffering than was previously known. This is not to say that technology has not been of benefit to us. Obviously, it has contributed greatly to our lower mortality rates and longer life span. However, it has also contributed its own kind of suffering to our existence. While physical pain has been greatly reduced, psychological pain has been increased. That there is a great deal of psychological pain in contemporary America is evidenced by the fact that over four billion doses of tranquilizers are consumed in the country each year.[48]

Suffering has become meaningless, a misery that one should not have to endure. As a result, when people do find themselves in a suffering condition, it is often seen as a cruel trick of fate, for which one must hurriedly find a chemical or psychological analgesic. Many people die in such a state of chemical stupor as to have relinquished (or have had taken away from them) all humanness. At the same time, others surrounding the dying person may themselves be heavily tranquilized in order to avoid the pain of their grief. The fact of the person's dying, seen from the perspective of others, is not undone by drugs. Failure—be it to heap up a fortune or to live to a ripe old age—is often seen as having no intrinsic value. Frankl reminds us that lack of success does not necessarily mean lack of meaning.[49] And yet, all too often success is the god that is worshiped in American society. And so for many, death and dying are unavoidable yet meaningless events, best met with numbing drugs. Yet it may be that the meaninglessness that one imputes to suffering and death is that which is imposed by reality-distorting drugs, robbing both the dying and the survivors of their human feelings and awareness. While this discussion may seem too philosophical for a book of this nature, it is important to be aware of the effects of such abstract issues as the meaning of suffering within a society. Through the use of drugs, a human event, one which can be as meaningful as any other in life, may become a sedated happening, devoid of human dignity and import.

The strides made by medicine to overcome physical pain have not provided a panacea for suffering, nor does it seem possible within the foreseeable future to construct such a utopia. However, the reduction of physical suffering within American society has been so pronounced as to make it easy for the individual to shift from seeing death as inevitable and permanent, to a more simplistic and regressive view that death can somehow be avoided ("it happens to others, not me") through either applying the knowledge we have or by the "miracle cures" believed to be found almost daily. In this context, then, suffering is meaningless behavior, and meaning in life is found in the pursuit of happiness—a basic birthright of all Americans. The Biblical trials of Job become irrelevant, and handicaps become problems to be overcome. Dying—which cannot be beaten but which one must suffer through—finds the individual bereft of psychological defenses. The examples of dying in other times and societies, which were discussed earlier, were not merely empty behavior patterns. Meanings were given, values acted out, and purpose was assigned to the act of dying. Suffering itself took on meaning. Today, contemporary American society is bereft of any meaningful contexts for suffering and dying. As a result, the suffering or dying individual is in a state of alienation from his or her culture, involved in an activity which has no meaning or worth in society's image.

Harold Kushner's popular *When Bad Things Happen to Good People* speaks to our need to understand suffering and inappropriate death.[50] Kushner relies heavily upon the Book of Job. Unwilling to accept Job's solution of unfailing belief in an all-wise and all-powerful God, Kushner offers us a conception of God as limited;

as one who can provide courage and strength for us, but cannot solve all of our problems. More importantly, Kushner argues that we cannot seek solace from our grief and misery through intellectural understanding alone. A more traditionally religious explanation of suffering is Nathan Kollar's *Songs of Suffering*.[51] Both these books seek to provide modern humanity with an explanation for the existence of pain, fear, and suffering in a world that is seeking solutions through science and technology.

Fear, like pain and suffering, has been allayed by the growth of medical technology. Few would maintain that the contemporary American family has to contend with the threats to life and limb that existed in prior times. However, it is more difficult to argue that the fears that are present today, in their own insidiously malignant ways, are not taking their own toll on human life. Neurosis and stress-related illness are just two examples of the outcomes of the constant battle against contemporary fears such as nuclear holocaust, our vulnerability due to increased interdependence, alienation, and a lack of a sense of purpose and meaning in our daily lives. At times of dying, the spectre of having lived a meaningless existence may constantly haunt the individual.

The fears, suffering, and pain of terminal illness are magnified in our consciousness when the dying person is a child. In the following section, we shall examine how society's typical ways of coping with dying often isolate the terminally ill child from much needed support at a time of final crisis.

The Dying Child

Perhaps no topic in thanatology stirs the emotions more than that of dying children. Our culture glorifies youth, and to see a child struck down by death raises profound questions about the meaning of all existence.

The remarkable gains that have been made against diseases that commonly struck down children in the past have allowed us to increase our expectations that our children will live to adulthood. We seek to make the world a better place for them, and hope that they will have better lives than we have had. To lose a child today is often to lose a part of one's self-identity, as children are more and more seen as extensions of their parents. This emotional investment in children, combined with a comparatively low infant mortality rate and the isolation of the nuclear family, has made the death of a child an increasingly traumatic event. Also, as we have seen, religion no longer provides an explanation for death for many people. A dying child is a sad event in most cultures and times; in the contemporary United States, the event may often be seen as a cruel absurdity, challenging our most fundamental images of life.

Dying children are unique in their understanding of death, compared with healthy children. Until fairly recently, dying children under ten years of age were thought not to experience anxiety about dying. This was because they were believed to be incapable of knowing what death meant. Now, researchers are finding that the dying child is aware of his or her condition but is often so socially isolated in a closed context as to be unable to discuss his or her condition with anyone. Children who are terminally ill rapidly develop an understanding of their condition, which points to the importance of personal experience in developing an awareness of death. As Stillion and Wass state, dying children often "know more than they feel safe in saying."[52]

Eugenia Waechter studied sixty-four children in four categories; those who were terminally ill, those with chronic illnesses, hospitalized children with nonthreatening conditions, and healthy children.[53] The terminally ill children scored twice as high as other hospitalized children on a test of their level of anxiety. They frequently depicted death and dying in their stories, often attributing their own symptoms to the dying child in their stories. How do children arrive at such knowledge? Part of our difficulty in understanding this is that, as adults, we learn many things through the assimilation of data. We memorize, study, and learn. Children, on the other hand, may gain knowledge in nonverbal ways as well. So it is with dying children.

Myra Bluebond-Langner became interested in the world of the dying child.[54] Working in a hospital, she befriended dying children, and they opened up to her. She was amazed at the degree to which the children were able to discuss their illnesses, their prognosis, the purposes of the drugs they were taking, and the treatments and procedures that they were undergoing. The children were also aware that the cycle ended in death.[55] The most poignant part of Bluebond-Langner's work was the fact that the children, for the most part, were working hard to protect their parents. The mutual pretense context was predominant among the terminally ill children, the hospital staff and doctors, and the children's families. The children had quickly learned that if they asked for information, their parents and hospital personnel would give evasive answers and then leave the room. The result was that the children soon realized that to try to deal openly with their condition was to court isolation.[56] It was safer to go along with the pretense, for "by reinforcing the adults' hopes, the children thereby guaranteed their continual presence."[57]

When a mutual pretense context became difficult to maintain, Bluebond-Langner observed that the children would often use distancing techniques such as lashing out, withdrawal, or feigning sleep, in order to control the amount of interaction.[58] For instance, she asked one boy why he yelled at his mother so much. The youngster said that he did it so that his mother could then leave, and she needed to leave the room because she couldn't stand watching him die any longer. When he sensed that his mother needed a break, he would begin to yell at her. She would respond that if he kept it up, she would leave the room. He would continue. She would leave, go have a cup of coffee, and return later. He confided in the researcher that he acted as he did to give her permission to get away for a few minutes. Of course, the dysfunctional aspect of this process is its negative effect upon the relationship.

Bluebond-Langner points out other "advantages" to a mutual pretense context: It allows the doctors to continue to act as healers; to carry on in their usual ways.[59] For the parents, defending the child against the awful truth is, in a way, the only thing they have left that they can do for their child.[60] Bluebond-Langner reports that she never saw the mutual pretense context give way to open awareness. Also, the awful truth about the child's dying was too much for the parents to deal with openly. Staff or family members would have to withdraw from openly dealing with the child about his or her death, because the emotional cost to them was too high. As a result, in order to keep some semblance of social interaction alive, a mutual pretense context was necessary. "Interaction could take place as long as everyone acted as if they still had their social roles," states Bluebond-Langner.[61] The saddest part of all this was the loneliness of the children, who were unable to discuss their fears and preparatory grief with those who meant the most to them: the doctors and nurses who cared for them, and the parents they loved and trusted.

Bluebond-Langner describes the process whereby a child becomes aware of his or her condition. Following the initial diagnosis, there are five stages in the child's growing awareness: First, the child realizes that he or she is seriously ill. This becomes modified in the second stage when the child realizes that he or she is seriously ill, but is convinced that he or she will get better. In the third stage, the child becomes aware that he or she is continually ill, but still believes that he or she will get better. The fourth stage is characterized by an awareness that he or she is always ill, and will never get better. Finally, in the fifth stage, the child realizes that he or she is dying.[62]

The child learns of his or her condition by assimilating information from other ill children, from the behaviors of the doctors, nurses, and family members. For example, children observe parents either openly crying or in a state of emotional upheaval and grandparents who travel great distances to visit, or they see the fate of other children with the same disease. All this is assimilated quickly by the child. Easson describes the process:

> He discovers that extra visiting privileges mean that death is fast approaching. He discovers that patients as they approach death somehow tend to be moved nearer the door. He notices that the treating staff seem to pass more hurriedly by the patients who are failing physically. The doctor even has a special face and manner of greeting when the case is doing badly. Though the child of grade school age quickly learns the fears and the anxieties of his hospital unit, he also becomes part of the total group denial process that exists on such a unit. With the support of those around him, he will find that he does not really notice when the bed pattern changes. He will be taught not to become outwardly disturbed when a member of the patient group disappears and never returns.[63]

Occasionally, where the resources are present to help the parents, staff, and children to deal openly with the fact that the child is dying, open awareness can be maintained. Feelings can be talked out, and issues such as some children's decision that their illness or painful treatments are a punishment (perhaps for thinking bad thoughts) can be resolved.[64] A closeness and a resolution can be achieved, and a more satisfying closure to the child's life experienced.

The Dying Aged

At the other end of the spectrum from dying children are the dying aged. Benoliel points out that the number of frail elderly, those over eighty as a general category, is increasing more rapidly than those over sixty-five.[65] Our growing medical technology is producing a group of people who are dependent upon care services, as their advanced years make them unable to fend for themselves. The quality of life of the frail elderly is often quite poor. As Benoliel puts it, dying is what is being prolonged, not living. This is a negative aspect of our advancing technology; the additional time won by medical intervention is spent in institutions fighting the chronic conditions and illnesses associated with aging.[66]

While technology may fend off biological death, it has little effect upon social death. The extended institutionalization and dying of the elderly often result in a withdrawal of family and friends. The result of this process is that social death may occur long before physical death.[67] Marshall points out that the elderly are aware of this process and will, as a result, consider themselves as dead. Most elderly do not fear being dead as much as they fear the process of dying.[68] The elderly have little control over their dying, as they are most usually institutionalized and their "well-being" is the assumed responsibility of the bureaucratic institution within which they live. With the loss of almost all social significance to family and friends—those who matter to the person—combined with a loss of personal autonomy due to institutionalization, the elderly may lose all reason to live, to exist in a society that does not affirm them as persons. Our theoretical perspective holds that the individual strives to bring meaning to his or her existence, to form and maintain meaningful images of the world. Our elderly are all too often denied a meaningful existence by the same society which refuses to let that existence end. The result is a prolonged meaningless existence in a debilitated and sometimes physically painful limbo—a kind of technological purgatory.

Roles Surrounding the Dying

Roles can be thought of as the ways in which society tells us to behave. The values and attitudes of a society can be seen in the various behaviors which are associated with different roles. For example, the teacher is seen as influencing young people, and thus is expected to behave in socially acceptable ways. Each status in our society—that is, a socially defined position in the social world—has certain role expectations. For example, society expects doctors to act in certain ways, and there are sanctions for proper or improper behavior when one does not act in ways appropriate to a particular role. I have heard of hospital patients refusing to speak with a doctor simply because he was not wearing a white coat. In the patients' minds, the role of the doctor required a certain way of dressing.

In this section, we will examine the major roles that surround the dying person: the doctor, the nurse, the social worker, and the hospital chaplain. By understanding the various role behaviors, we can better grasp the underlying attitudes and values that determine many of the role behaviors of those who work with the dying.

The Doctor

> He should be objective and scientific. He should be warm and personal. He must exert himself with equal vigor to save all lives. He is free to be selective, favor the "more valuable" lives over the "less valuable." He is responsible only to himself and his professional code of ethics. He is responsible to the community. He is responsible to the patient. He is a sage and all-around authority on life. He is a technician, a repairman.[69]

Thus do two researchers characterize the physician. In their description, we can see many of the dilemmas that surround the physician. He or she works within the confines of the medical model, which describes illness as a failure of the physical system. Death is a pathological state, one that arises when the physician is unable to reestablish the physical system to a state of wholeness (health). As such, death represents a failure on the part of the doctor.[70]

Kasper, in his description of the role of the physician, points out that as science and reason came to dominate modern thinking, sin became less important as death became more manageable.[71] The doctor, who had held a somewhat questionable status in society prior to the rise of modern medical science, found himself gaining in power and prestige as the clergy diminished in public favor. The centuries-old edict that at the time of illness or accident one should summon the clergy first and the doctor second, was reversed in modern times as the physician began to acquire knowledge and technologies that were effective against disease.[72]

In examining the role of the contemporary physician, Eliot Friedson points out that the physician gains his position in society by subjecting himself to an educational program "perhaps unparalled by any other conventional professional training in its duration, its detail, and its rigidity."[73] As a result of the successful completion of this training, the physician is licensed by the state, which permits him to perform medical procedures and administer drugs as well as to hospitalize patients.[74] The physician's attitude toward death and dying will influence the decisions that are made about the kinds of care a patient receives. Most obviously, for our interests, the physician is directly involved in decisions which affect the patient not only in terms of survival, but also in terms of the quality of his or her living and dying.

For most people in America today, dying is a medical problem. A simple statement, but one with implications for almost every chapter in this book. As Ivan Illich points out, natural death became, with the advent of modern medicine, clinical death. To avoid death, contemporary people have become medical consumers. As a patient, one is cared for and "managed" (a common term in medical literature) by the physician who serves as our expert defender against death:

> Just as at the turn of the century all men were defined as pupils, born into original stupidity and standing in need of eight years of schooling before they could enter productive life, today they are stamped from birth as patients who need all kinds of treatment if they want to lead life the right way.[75]

If the physician is our protection against death, then it is vitally important that we understand the image of death that the physician holds. After all, the physician stands between us and eternity. We assume that he or she is skilled in combating disease. But is he or she genuinely ready to confront death, to deal with humanity's ultimate helplessness? This question may seem melodramatic, but it points to the very nature of the doctor-patient relationship, and our expectations of those who claim to be physicians.

In medical school, the students' first confrontation with death is in the dissection laboratory. The student quickly learns to desensitize him- or herself to the cadaver, and thus to objectify death. Like the funeral director, the doctor learns to accept as routine the symbols of death that would disturb the lay person.[76] Success in medical school is based upon the student's ability to demonstrate a knowledge gained from the classroom, the laboratory, and the medical literature. This exemplifies the importance of the medical model. The patient is not considered as a whole person, but as a collection of symptoms representing a pathological state.[77] Since medical knowledge is expanding at an exponential rate, the student is often confronted with more information than he or she can possible assimilate. The solution to this problem, as described by one doctor, is to socialize medical students "to simulate more knowledge than they possess and greater mastery of the situation than they could actually achieve." This encourages a kind of "counter-phobic bravado" when dealing with situations in which the physician comes face to face with death.[78]

This fragile bravery in dealing with threatening situations, arising out of the need to desensitize oneself to death while also learning to present a professional (i.e., capable, controlled) image to society, also serves to help repress the doctor's own fears of death. Studies have shown that doctors as a group have greater fears of death than others, including seriously and terminally ill patients as well as a healthy control group.[79] This has led to much conjecture as to why people with a high fear of death would choose to go into medicine.[80] Usually the explanantion is similar to that of a young doctor who said, "I think it is the innate fear of one's own death that draws a person into medicine because he feels that it is as close as he can come to conquering it."[81] In the words of another physician, the doctor "takes his own fears, puts them as intellectual questions, and tries to answer them for other people."[82]

If we reflect upon this for a moment, we can see that the dying patient represents to the doctor not only failure as an expert, but also a failure to help the doctor deal with his or her own fears by getting better. However, the physician is provided an escape from a direct confrontation with death. This escape is provided by the medical model. Simply put, the dying person is medically no longer interesting. Typically the doctor withdraws from his or her personal involvement with the patient, often avoiding acknowledging the patient's true condition (and the doctor's helplessness to do anything about it). The patient's David, whose small stones have failed to stop the giant, appears to have decided to retire from the field of battle, leaving the patient alone to face death.[83] As one doctor stated,

I must admit that when the anxiety, the fear provoked within me as the physician becomes too great, it's very very comfortable to deal with the dying process on a technical level. Because then there is no real involvement. There have been times when I haven't been able to cope with an individual patient in a terminal situation, and in a cowardly way, I have run to the stereotyped role of myself as a scientist and technical expert, who doesn't concern himself with people's feelings. Certainly, depending upon the individual physician, some may find the anxiety so great that they always deal with it in this way.[83]

We can infer from the reports of the doctor's tendency to withdraw from the dying patient that the dying provoke a kind of existential grief within the doctor, threatening the physician's emotional equilibrium. The medical school's desensitization no longer prevails, and so the physician must withdraw or confront his or her own ultimate helplessness in combating death.[85] Doctors may recommend that a psychiatrist be brought in to deal with the dying patient and his needs.[86] This strategy may have very different results than one might anticipate: Feifel's study of doctors showed that psychiatrists are the medical specialty with the highest fear of death.[87] In an excellent study on this point, Churchill argues that psychiatrist Elizabeth Kubler-Ross's stage theory, discussed earlier, attempts to impose a "quasi-medical model of dying" upon the patient, thus depersonalizing the death process into "rationally-ordered scientific data."[88] Disallowing the personal, idiosyncratic meaning of death, the stage theory allows the physician and/or psychiatrist to remain emotionally protected from the real, human aspect of the person's dying. Pattison calls this approach by physicians "exaggerated detachment," in which death becomes objectified into a therapeutic process.[89]

Another strategy open to the physician threatened by death is to deny that the patient is dying. Vigorous protocols may be undertaken by the doctor, in spite of the fact that the patient is dying and the treatments will do little good.[90] This may be especially true when the patient is young, and the chances are greater that the child might survive the medical onslaught. The result can be, in some cases, that while the cause of death is listed as a disease such as cancer, the patient actually dies from the body's inability to cope with the toxic chemicals used to fight (but not defeat) the disease.

Hales describes a study in which patients were found to be

receiving a less than adequate supply of pain-killing narcotics. The concern among the attending physicians was that their patients might become addicts. The doctors involved were apparently assuming that their patients were going to be cured of their illnesses and return to a normal social life. Again, as in the case above of continuing useless treatments, one has to ask who was served by the withholding of drugs: the patients or the doctors?[91]

It has been shown that, especially in teaching hospitals, dying patients no longer hold the interest of the physician. Further, Herman's questioning of doctors in a large teaching hospital revealed that 36 percent admitted to being unable to establish a "good emotional rapport" with their dying patients.[92] Interestingly, 89 percent of those doctors queried did not care to become emotionally involved to any greater degree with their patients.

Clearly, this approach can place the dying patient at best in an isolated position, and at worst can make him or her the victim of unwarranted treatment. In their reluctance to face their ultimate defeat by death, doctors are reluctant to see their patients as dying. Thus hospices find that many doctors are unwilling to refer their patients to an organization that might make their dying a more meaningful and comfortable process. Ivan Illich takes an even harsher position: "The doctor's refusal to recognize the point at which he has ceased to be useful as a healer and to withdraw when death shows on his patient's face has made him into an agent of evasion or outright dissimulation."[93]

One solution to this problem that has been suggested is to offer a course in death and dying as part of the medical school curriculum.[94] In 1975, Dickinson found that of the 107 medical schools responding to his survey, only 7, or 6 percent, had a course dealing exclusively with relating to dying patients and their families. By 1980, he found this number had increased to 13 percent of the responding schools.[95] It is unfortunate that the number is so small, in light of Dickinson's finding that the effects of a death education class are to produce more positive interactions with patients by those who do attend such a course.

One of the major issues involved in doctor-patient communications has been whether or not the patient should be told his or her true condition. The attitude among most doctors prior to 1970 tended to be one of refusing to confront the patient directly about his or her disease and its prognosis.[96] Doctors usually said that they would avoid telling their patients, although they would want to be told themselves, if they were the dying patient. While one could accuse the medical profession of applying a double standard to this issue, it may, on the other hand, point out the doctors' lack of awareness about what it is like to be a patient. Recent studies have shown a shift in attitudes in favor of truth telling, especially among younger doctors. Blumenfield's 1980 study revealed that the majority (over 80 percent) of medical students, interns, and residents felt that patients have a right to be told of their condition.[97] It should be noted that there was no significant difference between the attitudes of those who had taken a course in thanatology and those who had not, suggesting that attitudes favoring truth telling are developed prior to entering medical school.

Increasingly, it is being argued that what is needed is a reconstruction of the medical model, which is the basic image governing many of the behaviors of the medical community.[98] All too often, the physician attempts to reduce human behavior to a problem solvable through the informed application of chemistry and physics. Engel argues that the medical model has now reached the status of dogma, in that it dominates all thinking about human ailments, with its unquestioned assumption that there is a somatic basis for all complaints.[99] When prescribed medications fail, the doctor retreats from the scene, rather than question the universal applicability of the model.

What is needed is to modify the medical model to include the social and psychological aspects of illness. As Churchill says, "there is, roughly speaking, a discernible medical model for disease, but there are innumerable patient models for illness."[100] The effect of a given illness or its treatment upon the individual's self-image, and upon society's image of the patient, is a necessary consideration of humanistic care. Without such consideration, the patient becomes a dehumanized collection of symptoms, to be managed while confined to the hospital. It appears that as the population becomes more knowledgeable and less prone to accede automatically to the medical profession's desires, doctors are becoming more sensitive to the patient as a person. Unfortunately, the older medical model approach to the sick is still a powerful attitude among physicians. Unaware or unwilling to acknowledge his or her feelings toward the dying patient and death itself, the following instructions from a doctor to a nurse are typical:

There is nothing we can do; that thing has attacked everything—lungs, spleen, everything. Go and help them [the family and patient], go talk to them. You're her nurse today, you go talk to them. You should be able to help them; I've done all I can.[101]

The Nurse

The role of the registered nurse has been, in a sense, victimized by the organizational context in which it most typically exists—the hospital. The low pay of the institution encourages nurses to seek promotion; and this is available only to those who are willing to supervise or administrate.[102] Both roles are further from patient contact, from the daily interaction with those who need care. The hospital organization does not set out to undermine the caring aspect of nursing, but in a need to maximize efficiency, the hospital seeks the most economical use of its staff. This means using nurses in manager and supervisor roles, and leaving patient care to less skilled (and less expensive) licensed practical nurses and aides.[103]

In the Middle Ages, religious orders of nuns established institutions for the care of the sick and dying.[104] As medicine progressed, the primary care role of the nurse was usurped by the cure role of the doctor. Florence Nightingale, the nineteenth-century nurse who defined modern nursing, saw the nurse as carrying out the doctors' orders; no initiative, no thinking.[105] Carol Germain describes the traditional stereotype of the nurse in this manner:

> The traditionally enculturated nurse is passive, compliant, non-questioning, a doer rather than a thinker, practical, intuitive, and socially insecure. Her practice emphasizes physical aspects and expressive, giving care. She relies upon symbolic objects, such as the uniform, cap, and pin, as important media to communicate her identity as a professional. Her manner is dignified, self-controlled, and passive.

While there may be many nurses who would still fit this characterization, many more have responded to the increasing specialization and technology of the hospital organization by becoming better educated, socially assertive, and by taking on more responsible and complex duties. The result has been a lessening of emphasis upon patient care, and a greater concern with medical issues. In reviewing the current nursing journals, one finds articles dealing with such topics as malpractice, patient illness assessment, and third party reimbursement. Universities, in developing registered nurse programs that are longer and have more depth than the hospital nursing programs (which are diminishing in number), tend to emphasize skills needed in supervisory and management positions as a part of their added years of nurse training.[107]

Nurses hold a unique position in hospitals, which employ two-thirds of the nursing population. The nurse is clearly subservient to the doctor, as well as to the hospital administration which employs her. At the same time that he or she is responsible to those two lines of authority, the nurse is also the only person who is constantly interacting with the patient. This adds to the strain of the role of nurse, as each line of responsibility requires its own kinds of responses.

At the same time that the organizational context of nursing is changing, one cannot overlook the importance of the women's movement in raising the consciousness of those who were seemingly locked into subservient roles. One author comments on this by pointing out that "the definition of the nursing role, built into law, guarantees their ultimate subservience to the physician."[108]

The nursing profession is, in many cases, acting on this new social awareness by redefining the nurse-doctor relationship, and is reexamining the nurse's relationship to the dying patient. A leading nursing journal, *RN*, reported the results of a survey of 12,500 nurses, showing that "unquestioning support" for the doctor is giving away to a position that emphasizes patient advocacy.[109] Germain, whose traditional definition was quoted earlier, sees the contemporary nurse as much different from the traditional model:

> In contrast, nurses of the new culture are concerned with sharing power and decision-making with physicians and hospital administrators, being independent in practice, meeting their own needs and goals, and using collective bargaining rights to negotiate both economic security and practice issues. They resist authoritarian norms, place less emphasis on doing and more on thinking, and fuse expressive (nurturant) and instrumental (technical) role behaviors. They are also described as less concerned with symbolic crutches, more self-expressive, candid, open to their limitations, and socially very secure.[110]

The literature on nursing would contend that, for the most part, the expressive content of nursing is being replaced by a more instrumental approach to work. The change in the role of the nurse may leave a gap in the caring aspect of the patients' needs, as the nurse seeks to improve his or her position by moving away from the patient and into the hospital hierarchy.

However, some qualification is necessary here: We are viewing an entire profession, and when we speak of "the nurse," we are considering a generalized work role. There are many nurses who are dedicated to the more traditional nursing values, and who surely will bristle at the derogatory characterization of the traditional role that Germain puts forth.[111] One of the issues in nursing centers on reconciling this "mother surrogate versus the healer" controversy in the profession.[112] Some studies report a move to return to the caring role, but in a position that is greatly enhanced through the recognition of the nurses' special skills and responsibilities.[113]

Studies of nurses' attitudes toward death and dying do not give a clear picture, with results tending to vary by study.[114] There appears to be some indication that younger nurses have a more difficult time accepting the deaths of their patients, but the import of this is tempered by the finding that younger nurses deal more frequently with the dying than do older nurses.[115] Concerning truth telling, the closed awareness context, whereby the patient is denied information concerning the terminal nature of his or her illness, appears to be reinforced by nurses more out of obedience to hospital policies than because of their own fears of death.[116]

It appears that the nurse is caught in what we might call an evolving organizational context. This context calls upon the nurse to succeed in the organization by moving away from the patient and toward an administrative or supervisory role. At the same time, due to hospital efficiencies and nurse shortages, those who eschew the success model are finding greater and greater demands placed upon them, forcing them to set their priorities in such a way that patient contact and care take up less and less of their time. Ronald Preston, who studied nurses as a participant observer, describes the results of these conflicting demands upon the nurse (and the pitfalls of participant observation as well):

> If one followed a dedicated and competent nurse through the course of a busy shift, one would likely be impressed by how she meets the multiple demands of her work. The leg work alone seems ample inducement for varicose veins. Among the treatments, the charts, the basic physical patient care, the strains of staff relations, this nurse manages a kind word and an attentive ear for her patients, and a bit of jauntiness to cheer them up. On some days, that she manages this at all seems miraculous. If one gets a feeling for her work, one is not likely to question the focus of her effort. Ready explanation jumps to mind for

any action that seems less than humanitarian. She seems to be hemmed in by imperatives. She is hardly to be blamed that she often does not hear what patients tell her or that she does not ponder their fates.

However, if one remains dispassionate and watches the nurse without attempting to rationalize her acts, one sees a somewhat different picture. The nurse seems engaged in an elaborate act, the production of which consumes much of her attention. Her behavior denotes more concern for her duties than for her patients. She seems to care for them, and she also finds them tiring and aggravating. She keeps her distance.[117]

Many nurses *are* committed to the caring role, and are deeply concerned about the dying and their treatment in hospitals. These nurses believe it is possible to maintain a contemporary sense of personal integrity and professionalism, while advocating better patient care. Unfortunately, the dominant trend in nursing seems to be in other directions, as institutions continue to offer rewards to those who are willing to move away from direct patient care.

The Social Worker

Of the over 100,000 professional social workers in the United States, a third of them are in health services work. As a group, medical social workers have not been studied to the same extent as have doctors and nurses. Those studies that have been completed show an occupation that suffers from a lack of definition both internally and among other professions.[118] While social workers hold to a creed espousing patient rights, consumer protection, federal government control of health policy, and consumer participation in decision-making, their daily activities often are involved in mundane activities as they make arrangements for continued care for discharged patients. The position of the social worker has been institutionalized within the bureaucratic hospital in such a way as to minimalize the "casework" (clinical counseling) aspect of the occupation, and to encourage a lesser range of duties.

Olsen and Olsen point out that the social work department is a "secondary, ancillary service within a hospital."[119] This description implies a relationship to the medical model of care. However, the social worker is not involved in curing the patient's illness. The social worker is seen as an assistant by the doctor; one who organizes patient care outside of the hospital.[120] Doctors and social workers differ in their perceptions of the social worker's role; doctors attribute many less professional duties to social workers than do social workers themselves.[121] Since the overwhelming majority of referrals to the social services department come from doctors and nurses, this perception of the social worker's role is very important. For example, as a result of the perception of social workers by physicians and nurses, most of the patients who are referred to the social work department are over sixty-five, and about ready to leave the hospital.[122] In order to do casework (counseling), the social worker must often reassign a referral from external manipulation of the environment (finding a nursing home, arranging transportation, etc.), to casework. In a medically dominated environment, the social workers' skills are usually underutilized. Even if the social services department of the hospital received more referrals, they would be unable to take care of them, because the departments are most often small in size, again reflecting the values of the larger organization.

Friedson characterizes social work as a specialty without roots.[123] Organizational constraints, misperceptions by the powerful, and a lack of a clear definition of their role by social workers themselves have all contributed to keeping the medical social worker in a marginal position within the hospital. Medical social workers, adequately trained, could meet many needs of the dying. Their clinical skills, along with their knowledge of family processes and community resources, could meet many needs that have been articulated by the dying and their families. Instead, they are relegated to other tasks, subject to rivalries with nurses who still favor the caring values of nursing, and are not considered as professional people by the doctors. Perhaps the position of the social worker, with its emphasis upon patient advocacy and well-being, demonstrates the power of the medical ethos within the hospital bureaucracy. Unfortunately, it is the patient who suffers the most from the hospital organization's underutilization of a valuable resource.[124]

The Chaplain

The most marginal role of all those surrounding the dying patient is that of the hospital chaplain. The role of the chaplain can be described as falling into two categories: the humanist or the traditionalist.[125] The latter is concerned with the patient's spirituality, and presents a paternal, pastoral image. The humanist is more psychological in his or her approach, usually adhering to the perspective of Elizabeth Kubler-Ross. While most patients feel that a visit from the chaplain should be a part of their hospital stay, his or her role should be that of a friendly visitor.[126] As a friendly visitor, the chaplain tends to float through the organization, spending time with those who indicate a desire to do so. This is somewhat analogous to the chaplain in the "M*A*S*H" television series, who had a minor role in the organization and was held in sympathetic respect by the powerful. Like the chaplain in the "M*A*S*H" series, the hospital chaplain often relies on his or her own personality to influence matters in the hospital, and not upon the power of the position itself. While others in the hospital organization are supportive of the role, the doctors tend to give the chaplain the least amount of support.[127] The chaplain's role is generally thought to be one of helping to reduce patient anxieties (although not as a patient advocate), and of consoling the bereaved.

As we saw in our analysis of the social worker, the chaplain is caught up in a reality not of his own making, where the dominant values run counter to his or her understanding of the world. For example, while the doctor may see suffering as something to be treated with pain relievers, the chaplain may see it as an intransigent part of the human condition. Suffering may be humanity's enemy, but it may also be a way in which life can be given meaning, and through which such words as nobility, courage, and understanding can take on their true meanings.

As a result of the secular, bureaucratic ethos within which he or she must work, the chaplain most often plays a minor role in the hospital. The sacred symbols of old are not as powerful as they used to be, and the importance of the human spirit appears to have a far lower priority than EKGs, medications, and treatment protocols in the modern hospital environment.

Notes

1. Philippe Aries, *Western Attitudes toward Death* (Baltimore: The Johns Hopkins University Press, 1974), pp. 1–25.
2. The male pronoun is used advisedly; Aries tends to rely heavily upon examples of males dying.

3. Aries, pp. 3 and 55.

4. Ibid., p. 27.

5. E. Mansell Pattison, *The Experience of Dying* (Englewood Cliffs, N.J.: Prentice-Hall, 1977), p. 55.

6. Ibid., p. 44.

7. Ibid., pp. 44–59.

8. Ronald Philip Preston, *The Dilemmas of Care* (New York: Elsvier, 1979), pp. 35–39.

9. Ibid., pp. 4–5.

10. Richard A. Kalish, "Social Distance and the Dying," *Community Mental Health Journal* 11 (1966): 152–155.

11. Sister Rita Jean DuBrey and Laurel Amy Terrill, "The Loneliness of the Dying Person: An Exploratory Study," *Omega* 6, no. 4 (1975):357–371.

12. Diana Crane, "Dying and Its Dilemmas as a Field of Research," in Orville G. Brim, Jr., et al., *The Dying Patient* (New York: The Russell Sage Foundation, 1970), pp. 303–325.

13. Louis Lasagna, "The Doctor and the Dying Patient," *Journal of Chronic Diseases* 22 (1969):65–68.

14. Russell Noyes, Jr. and John Clancy, "The Dying Role: Its Relevance to Improved Patient Care," *Psychiatry* 4 (1977):41–47.

15. Richard A. Kalish, "The Onset of the Dying Process," *Omega* 1, no. 1 (1970):57–69. Also, Kathy Charmaz, *The Social Reality of Death* (Reading, Mass.: Addison-Wesley, 1980), pp. 159–162. For further discussions of the sick role, see Talcott Parsons, *The Social System* (New York: The Free Press, 1951), and Alexander Segall, "The Sick Role Concept," *Journal of Health and Social Behavior* 17 (1976):163–170.

16. Benita C. Martocchio, *Living while Dying* (Bowie, Md.: Robert J. Brady, 1982), pp. 68–71.

17. Ibid., p. 70.

18. Ibid.

19. Kenneth A. Chandler, "Three Processes of Dying and Their Behavioral Effects," *Journal of Consulting Psychology* 29, no. 4 (1965):297.

20. Loma Feigenberg, *Terminal Care* (New York: Brunner-Mazel, 1980), pp. 13–14. Also Jeanne Quint Benoliel, "Dying in an Institution," in Hannelore Wass, ed., *Dying: Facing the Facts* (Washington, D.C.: Hemisphere, 1979), p. 146.

21. Leo Tolstoy, *The Death of Ivan Ilych* New York: Health Sciences, 1973).

22. Elizabeth Kubler-Ross, *On Death and Dying* (New York: Macmillan, 1969).

23. Ibid., pp. 2–4.

24. Ibid., p. 4.

25. Ibid., p. 138.

26. Ibid., p. 47.

27. Ibid., pp. 56–79.

28. Ibid., pp. 79–80.

29. Ibid., pp. 81–84.

30. Ibid., p. 86.

31. Ibid., p. 112.

32. Ibid., p. 138.

33. Ibid., p. 176.

34. Ken Kesey, *One Flew over the Cuckoo's Nest* (New York: Viking Press, 1962).

35. Robert Jay Lifton, "Thought Reform: Psychological Steps in Death and Rebirth," in Alfred R. Lindesmith, et al., eds., *Readings in Social Psychology* (Hinsdale, Ill: The Dryden Press, 1975), pp. 274–289.

36. Charmaz, p. 155.

37. Richard Schulz and David Aderman, "Clinical Research and the Stages of Dying," *Omega* 15, no. 2 (1974):137–143.

38. Daniel Cappon, "The Dying," *Psychiatric Quarterly* 133, no. 3 (July 1959):466–489.

39. Feigenberg, p. 138.

40. Edwin Shneidman, *Deaths of Man* (New York: Quadrangle, 1973).

41. Kubler-Ross, p. 138.

42. Susan Groenwald and Phyllis Bermansolo, "Are We Death and Dying Our Patients to Death?" in Ellen Zinner and Stephen Steele, eds., *Selected Proceedings of the First National Conference of the Forum for Death Education and Counseling* (Lexington, Mass.: Ginn, 1979), pp. 251–259.

43. Avery Weisman, *On Dying and Denying: A Psychiatric Study of Terminality* (New York: Behavioral Publications, 1972).

44. Pattison, p. 56.

45. Shneidman, p. 10.

46. Albert Camus, *The Plague* (New York: Random House, 1948), pp. 194–197.

47. Samuel S. Epstein, *The Politics of Cancer* (San Francisco: The Sierra Club, 1978), pp. 14–15.

48. Richard Hughes, *The Tranquilizing of America* (New York: Harcourt Brace Jovanovich, 1979), p. 8.

49. Viktor F. Frankel, *The Doctor and the Soul* (New York: Alfred A. Knopf, 1972), p. 107.

50. Harold S. Kushner, *When Bad Things Happen to Good People* (New York: Schocken Books, 1981).

51. Nathan Kollar, *Songs of Suffering* (Minneapolis: Winston Press, 1982).

52. Judith Stillion and Hannelore Wass, "Children and Death," in H. Wass, ed., *Dying: Facing the Facts* (Washington: Hemisphere, 1979), p. 218.

53. Eugenia H. Waechter, "Children's Awareness of Fatal Illness," reprinted in Sandra G. Wilcox and Marilyn Sutton, eds., *Understanding Death and Dying* (2nd ed.) (Sherman Oaks, CA: Alfred, 1981), pp. 281–288.

54. Myra Blubond-Langner, *The Private Worlds of Dying Children* (Princeton, N.J.: Princeton University Press, 1978).

55. Ibid., p. 161.

56. Ibid., p. 202.

57. Ibid., p. 229.

58. Ibid., p. 207.

59. Ibid., p. 219.

60. Ibid., p. 217.

61. Ibid., p. 232.

62. Ibid., p. 169.

63. William M. Easson, *The Management of the Child or Adolescent Who is Dying* (Springfield, Ill.: Charles C Thomas, 1970), p. 47.

64. Ibid., p. 26.

65. Jeanne Quint Benoliel, "Dying in an Institution," in Hannelore Wass, ed., *Dying: Facing the Facts*, p. 144.

66. Ibid., p. 145.

67. Hannelore Wass, "Death and the Elderly," in Hannelore Wass, ed., *Dying: Facing the Facts*, p. 198.

68. Victor W. Marshall, *Last Chapters* (Monterrey: Brooks/Cole, 1980), p. 155.

69. Robert Kastenbaum and Ruth Aisenberg, *The Psychology of Death*, concise ed. (New York: Springer: 1976).

70. Ralph A. Redding, "Physiology of Dying," in Hannelore Wass, ed., *Dying: Facing the Facts*, p. 80.

71. August M. Kasper, "The Doctor and Death," in Herman Feifel, ed., *The Meaning of Death* (New York: McGraw-Hill, 1965), pp. 259–270. Also, William F. May, *The Physician's Covenant: Images of the Healer in Medical Ethics* (Philadelphia: Westminster Press, 1983).

72. Charles W. Bodemer, "Physicians and the Dying: A Historical Sketch," *The Journal of Family Practice*, 9, no. 3 (1979):827–832.

73. Eliot Freidson, *Professional Dominance: The Social Structure of Medical Care* (New York: Atherton, 1970).

74. Ibid., p. 83.

75. Ivan Illich, *Medical Nemesis* (New York: Random House, 1976), p. 198.

76. See Kasper; also Michael Simpson, "Social and Psychological Aspects of Dying," in Hannelore Wass, ed., *Dying: Facing the Facts*, p. 117.

77. Simpson.

78. Ibid.

79. Herman Feifel, et al., "Physicians Consider Death," *Proceedings of the 75th Annual Convention of the American Psychological Association* 3 (1968): 545–546.

80. Ibid; see also Kasper, and Simpson.

81. Joan Arehart-Treichel, "Teaching Doctors How to Care for the Dying," *Science News* 107 (15 March 1975):176–177.

82. Kasper, p. 263.

83. Anonymous, "Death of a Colleague," *Man and Medicine* 3, no. 4 (1978):230–283.

84. Louis R. Zako, quoted in David Hendin, *Death as a Fact of Life* (New York: Warner, 1973), p. 116.

85. Kastenbaum and Aisenberg, pp. 215–216.

86. Robert E. Hales, "Dying Patients: A Challenge to Their Doctors and Consultation Psychiatry," *Military Medicine* (October 1980): 674–680.

87. "Fear of Death Linked to Career Decision."

88. Larry R. Churchill, "Interpretations of Dying: Ethical Implications for Patient Care," *Ethics in Science and Medicine* 6, no. 4 (1979):217.

89. Pattison, p. 14.

90. Terri A. Herman, "Terminally Ill Patients," *New York State Journal of Medicine* (February 1980):202.

91. Hales, p. 676.

92. Herman, p. 200.

93. Illich, p. 103.

94. David Barton, et al., "Death and Dying: A Course for Medical Students," *Journal of Internal Medicine* 47 (December 1972):945–951; Sidney Bloch, "A Clinical Course on Death and Dying for Medical Students," *Journal of Medical Education* 50 (June 1975):630–632.

95. George E. Dickinson, "Death Education in U.S. Medical Schools: 1975–1980," *Journal of Medical Education* 56 (February 1981): 11–114. Cf. Marc Smith, et al., "Characteristics of Death Education Curricula in American Medical Schools," *Journal of Medical Education* 55 (October 1980):844–850.

96. P. Ley, "Psychological Studies of Doctor-Patient Communication,"

in S. Rachman, ed., *Contributions to Medical Psychology*, Vol. 1 (Oxford: Pergamon Press, 1977), p. 10.

97. Richael Blumenfield, et al., "Current Attitudes of Medical Students and House Staff Toward Terminal Illness," *General Hospital Psychiatry* 1, no. 4 (1979):306–310.

98. George L. Engel, "The Need for a New Medical Model: A Challenge to Biomedicine," *Science* 196, no. 4286 (1977):129–136. Also, Churchill; Illich.

99. Engel, p. 130.

100. Churchill, p. 213.

101. Martocchio, p. 138.

102. Philip A. Kalisch and Beatrice J. Kalisch, "The Nurse Shortage, The President, and Congress," *Nursing Forum* 19, no. 3 (1980):138–164.

103. Sam Schulman, "Mother Surrogate—After a Decade," in E. Gartly Jaco, ed., *Patients, Physicians, and Illness* (New York: The Free Press, 1979), p. 272.

104. Elliott A. Krause, *Power and Illness* (New York: Elsevier, 1977), pp. 48–50.

105. Ibid., p. 49.

106. Carol Germain, *The Cancer Unit: An Ethnography* (Wakefield, Mass: Nursing Resources, 1979), p. 7.

107. Schulman, p. 274.

108. Krause, p. 54.

109. "Probe Report on Death and Dying," *Nursing 75*, August 1975, pp. 16–24.

110. Germain, p. 8.

111. Lisa H. Newton, "In Defense of the Traditional Nurse," *Nursing Outlook* 29, no. 6 (June 1981):348–354.

112. Schulman; see also Gerald R. Winslow, "From Loyalty to Advocacy," *The Hastings Center Report* 14, no. 3 (1984):32–40.

113. Leon S. Robertson and Margaret C. Heagarty, *Medical Sociology: A General Systems Approach* (Chicago: Nelson-Hall, 1975), p. 115. Also Jeanne C. Quint, *The Nurse and the Dying Patient* (New York: Macmillan, 1967).

114. Lisa R. Shusterman and Lee Sechrest, "Attitudes of Registered Nurses Toward Death in a General Hospital," *Psychiatry in Medicine* 4, no. 4 (1973):411–426; Christina M. Gow and J. Ivan Williams, "Nurses' Attitudes Toward Death and Dying: A Causal Interpretation," *Social Science and Medicine* 11 (1977):191–198.

115. Schulman.

116. Barney G. Glaser and Anselm L. Strauss, *Awareness of Dying* (Chicago: Aldine, 1965), p. 136. Also, *RN*.

117. Ronald Preston, *Dilemmas of Care*, p. 103.

118. Neil F. Bracht, "Social Work Practice in Hospitals: Changing Directions and New Opportunities," in Neil F. Bracht, ed., *Social Work in Health Care* (New York: Haworth Press, 1978), pp. 165–183.

119. Katherine M. Olsen and Marvin E. Olsen, "Role Expectations and Perceptions for Social Workers in Medical Settings," *Social Work* 12, no. 3 (July 1967):70–78.

120. Mary S. Watt, "Therapeutic Facilitator" (D.S.W. dissertation, University of California at Los Angeles, December, 1977).

121. Olsen and Olsen.

122. Alice Ullman and Gene G. Kassebaum, "Referrals and Services in a Medical Social Work Department," *Social Service Review* 35, no. 3 (September 1961):258–267; Barbara Berkman and Helen Rehr, "The 'Sick-Role' Cycle and the Timing of Social Work Intervention," *Social Service Review* 46, no. 4 (December 1972):567–580.

123. Eliot Freidson, "Specialties Without Roots: The Utilization of New Services," in W. Richard Schott and Edmund H. Volkart, eds., *Medical Care* (New York: John Wiley, 1966), pp. 445–450.

124. For an indication of the strengthening of the status of the social worker in the hospital, see Elfriede G. Schlesinger and Isobel Wolock, "Hospital Social Workers and Decision Making," *Social Work in Health Care* 8, no. 1 (1982):59–70.

125. Sr. Cashel Weiler, "Patients Evaluate Pastoral Care," *Hospital Progress,* (April 1975):34–38.

126. Eleanor LeBourdais, "Pastoral Services Rated Important," *Dimensions in Health Service* (May 1976):18–19.

127. Juanita Wood, "The Structure of Concern," *Urban Life* 4, no. 3 (October 1975):369–384.

CHAPTER FIVE

Grief and Mourning

GRIEF CAN BE DESCRIBED as an overwhelming and acute sense of loss and despair. The entire personality is helplessly engulfed in strong, sometimes frightening, feelings. The individual can feel out of control as monstrous waves of emotions sweep over him or her. Tossed about on this emotional sea, the familiar and secure landmarks of life are no longer in their usual places; the old meanings do not apply, and the individual may see him- or herself as the victim of forces outside of his or her control.

This description of grief underscores the powerful feelings involved as the individual becomes aware of a significant loss. *Grief is that state of mental and physical pain which is experienced when the loss of a significant object, person, or part of the self is realized.* The realization of the loss is important in that the individual who does not decide that a particular loss is of personal significance will not grieve over that loss. There is, then, a psychological process whereby the individual acknowledges or "owns" the loss. This is a realization not just that the death has occurred, but that it is of personal significance to the individual. For example, reading a headline in the paper stating that three women have died in a car accident will not necessarily produce a grief reaction. However, grief will ensue when it is learned that a person significant to the reader had been among the three killed.

To a certain degree, who or what we consider to be personally significant is culturally defined. For example, in the contemporary

United States, the individual is generally expected to grieve over the loss of a biological offspring. The further the individual is from the nuclear family, the less amount of grief displayed. Volkart and Michael describe primitive tribes wherein the care of the newborn is shared among many people.[1] As a result, rather than having a few people experiencing intense loss, the grief is felt less intensely by many. Grief is a function of the intensity of the relationship, and the nature of relationships is strongly influenced by the culture within which they exist.

From the sociologists's point of view, the individual's reality is socially defined: we grieve over those losses which are socially appropriate to grieve over. Psychologists, on the other hand, tend to argue that grief is an intensely personal process, and that without considering the internal psychological dynamics of the individual we cannot arrive at an understanding of grief. The question of the relative importance of psychological and sociological factors in the grief reaction is not one that we can settle here. For our purposes, we shall examine what the psychological and sociological perspectives each have to offer us in developing our understanding of the grief process. While grieving is an intensely personal emotional experience, it takes place within a social reality that defines appropriate grieving behavior as well as the significance of the loss itself. We will first consider grief as a psychological process. Later in this chapter, taking a sociological perspective, we will consider the process of mourning which is the behavior in a social context that manifests an acknowledgment of loss.

The Psychological Dynamics of Grief

In the earlier definition of grief, two aspects were stressed; the mental and physical pain experienced, and the loss of something or someone of significance to the individual. First we will discuss the types of losses that the individual may experience, and then we will examine the emotional processes of experiencing and resolving grief.

Loss of a Significant Person

The death of someone who is deemed significant by the griever—a member of the immediate family, close friend, lover, or mentor—

is one of the most common losses evoking grief. An infant will grieve over the loss of its nurturing biological mother because the infant is aware that many emotional and physical needs are met by the mother. However, the severity of grief does not necessarily depend on some form of social interaction between the two persons. An individual may grieve over the loss of someone with whom he or she had only a brief, cursory relationship. One may grieve deeply over the loss of someone with whom one has not actually interacted, but with whom one has a strong sense of identification. The determining factor is not necessarily the proximity of the individuals or the social significance of the relationship, but rather the importance which the griever assigns to the lost person.

Another example of the grieving over the loss of a nonintimate other is the death of a famous personality or leader. In these cases, people who have never interacted with a celebrity, but who strongly identify with that person, will grieve over the death. The assassinations of President Kennedy and John Lennon produced grief among many with whom there had never been personal contact. The grievers identified with these famous men and their deaths were seen as personal losses to a great many people—perhaps not so much as individuals, but as symbols of values held dear to the grievers.

These examples underscore the importance of individual decisions as to the significance of another person in someone's life. While it may be difficult to think of a child as "deciding" that his mother is important, there is an inner process of discrimination that takes place. As the child grows in awareness, he or she becomes aware of the importance of his or her mother. The process of assigning a value to something, even something as obvious as a child's nurturing mother, requires the child to decide to assign importance to the mother. Likewise, the young teen-ager decides to idolize a popular singer, assigning importance to that other person even though the two people have never known one another. Often in the minds of teen-agers, the idol is fantasized as the only person capable of truly understanding them, or able to meet their emotional needs. In both cases, the loss of the significant other person will elicit a grief reaction in the individual.

Separation from a significant person can produce reactions similar to those experienced at times of loss through death. Bowlby's extensive studies of attachment and loss have contributed significant insights about the process of integrating the experience of loss into our lives.[2] Working first with young children and then validating his findings through clinical work with children and adults, Bowlby shows how separation can lead to intensive grief reactions in individuals. A temporary estrangement of infatuated lovers can also be so devastating as to produce a grieving reaction.

To summarize, our first category of loss involves the loss of a significant person. This loss is determined to be significant by the griever. Even temporary loss, where the attachment is seen as vital, may precipitate grieving.

The Loss of a Love Object

The second category of loss is the loss of an object in which the griever has placed special significance; anything that a person decides is important to his or her life. A toy (be it a teddy bear or a yacht), material goods that signify success, pets, and symbolically linked objects such as national flags are important objects to different people. As much as a person may grieve over the loss of an individual, so can he or she grieve over the loss of an object. A miser will feel the loss of his money as deeply as a lover the loss of his sweetheart.

Most generally people do not involve themselves as deeply with objects as they do with other people. However, the loss and concomitant grief process may occur and should be appreciated in the context of what the lost object means to the grieving individual.

The Loss of a Part of the Self

The third category of loss involves losing something which is central to the individual's being, such as a part of the body, the ability to do tasks, physical or mental capabilities, or roles that the individual has performed. Activities or accomplishments external to the self may become ego-extensions of the individual, and as a result the person may grieve when a loss of part of the self takes place. For example, an elderly person may feel sorrowful in having to accept the loss of an ability that was a significant part of his or her life. To give up driving, for example, may mean the loss of the individual's autonomy, and symbolize the encroaching debilitation of old age.

The loss of a limb or an organ, such as the eyes, may be seen as a significant loss, perhaps jeopardizing the major means of self-expression that the individual has developed. The loss of attractiveness, perhaps through disfigurement or aging, can produce grief reactions. In American society where personal attractiveness is considered very important, the loss of beauty may be seen as a tragic event by the victim.

The loss of one's role is another form of loss of self which may foster a grieving reaction. The loss of the role of mother, for example, may produce a grieving in some women as part of the "empty nest syndrome," the time when children are no longer dependent upon the mother. The woman's sense of self can be intimately involved with her role as a mother, and the loss of that role may provoke a grief reaction. Geoffrey Gorer, writing about his research among the grieving in England, states that he found the greatest amount of grief among parents whose children were grown and who had placed a great deal of meaning upon their roles as parents.[3] The greater the importance of the parenting role, the greater the grief that was felt. It may also be that because parents of adult children are most likely to be beyond their child-bearing years, the possibility of them reestablishing themselves in the parent role would be remote. Thus some adult parents not only lose their loved ones, but are thus forced to give up meaningful activities as well.

I have delineated these three types of losses in order to demonstrate that grief need not be solely a product of a significant death. More research is needed in the field of loss and loss management. For example, we need to know how the little losses that we have all had in our lives which entail a "giving up" prepare us for dealing with the larger losses of significant persons in our lives. In considering grief in the context of this book, we will limit ourselves to the larger losses which are experienced through the death of a significant person.

A Typology of Grief

Appropriate and Inappropriate Loss

An important aspect of the degree of significance assigned to the loss lies in the extent to which the death is viewed as an appropriate death. The term "appropriate death" has been used extensively by Avery Weisman.[4] His concern is more with a sense of the appropriateness of the death for the dying person, while ours focuses upon the appropriateness of the death for the griever. Both uses of the term are similar, in that the meaning of the event (death) is judged in terms of its purposefulness, meaningfulness, and acceptability. Weisman warns that one person's acceptable death may be unacceptable to another; this holds for the griever as well as the dying. Typically, the death of one's ninety-year-old grandfather is seen as more appropriate than the death of one's thirty-year-old spouse. As people age, the appropriateness of their deaths becomes more accepted, because everyone must die. Inappropriate death, on the other hand, is an unexpected or unjustifiable occurrence. The injustice, along with the shock of the loss, will precipitate stronger grief reactions than are found in appropriate deaths, as the survivor must struggle with the inappropriateness of the loss as well as the loss itself.

Fulton refers to these two types of grief as "high grief" and "low grief" situations.[5] Unfortunately, he tends to pursue a social definition of high grief (death of a child) and low grief (death of an elderly relative) as indicating the amount of grief to be expected. However, the appropriateness of the death must be considered from the perspective of the griever. For example, while the rest of the family may see the death of an elderly member as appropriate in the scheme of things, the surviving spouse may feel a great deal of rage because he or she might always have expected to die first. The death of the spouse will then be seen as unfair and therefore inappropriate. Only by understanding the meaning of the death to the griever can we come to understand the meaning of the grief.

During the grieving process, to be discussed later in this chapter, the individual may be faced with two distinctly different problems. Both these problems involve the meanings that the griever places upon the death. The death may represent the loss of a loved one upon whom the individual placed a great deal of importance. The death may also represent a dramatic reminder of the reality of death in the griever's own life. A well-known researcher in this field disclosed during an interview with me that at the death of his parents he found his grief involving not only the loss of people, but also the realization that he was, chronologically, next in line in his family to die. This internal turmoil, which we shall call *existential grief,* may absorb the individual as much as the grieving over the loss of the loved person, which we shall refer to as *reactive grief.*

Existential Grief

At the onslaught of grief, the individual usually feels a great sense of disorganization. The way in which the survivor meaningfully interacted with the world in the past no longer makes sense, often calling into doubt the meaning of all of life. The individual is thrown back on his or her own inner convictions as to the meaning of existence. For some, their image of the world may be frightening or inadequately developed. Relationships with others may superficially meet these personal inadequacies. Some persons may seek to escape from their internal fears by establishing a relationship with someone else who, in a sense, makes life worth living. In other words, the meaning of life is found in another person. When the relationship is terminated, the person must again face his or her own internal doubts and fears.

For the person who finds meaning in life exclusively through another, the loss of the relationship may force the person to confront his or her own internal doubts and fears. The lost relationship may have served as the individual's defense against death. To one who has repressed his or her fears of death, or who has not satisfactorily resolved or defended against the issues surrounding existential mortality, the experience of a significant death may reawaken dormant death anxieties. Infatuated romantic lovers may experience a transcendence of worldly reality which seems to diminish death by its very intensity. The loss of such a loved one may cast the survivor into the depths of his own despair, not only over the lost love, but also involving the grim reappearance of death as a fact of life. The fear of death, which is rooted in the primary images described by Lifton, now returns to haunt the person.[6]

The roots of the issues in existential grief can usually be found in childhood. Early in life the infant must confront the reality of the world external to the self. There is a need to be able to interact successfully with the environment. Erikson describes this early interaction as providing the basis for a sense of trust or mistrust of the world within the child.[7] Lifton adds that the individual has a need to develop a sense of connection with the external world.

This is "a fundamental issue in human life."[8] Most typically, this initial connection is made with the mother. The infant develops a sense of trust for rewarding connections with the environment. The child learns of his own separation (individuality) from the environment, and develops a sense of being connected with the environment by interacting with objects in the environment in rewarding ways. In forming these early relationships with the external world, the infant invests emotional energy in those objects and experiences which give him physical and emotional substance. Internally, the infant builds images that represent his external experiences.

Robert Jay Lifton sees the issue of developing a sense of integrity—a sense of personal wholeness—as a part of the early psychological development of the child. Pointing to Melanie Klein's studies, Lifton argues that the polar opposite of integration, which is disintegration, is rooted in the infant's fear of annihilation. Lifton states that

> there is from the beginning some sense of the organism's being threatened with dissolution, disintegration. The terms of this negative image or fear are at first entirely physiological, having to do with physical intactness or deterioration; but over the course of time, integrity, without losing its physiological reference, comes to assume primarily ethical-psychological dimensions.[10]

So from early in our existence we have known images of life and death, and one form of our aliveness lies in organizing ourselves in order to deal satisfactorily with those things external to ourselves.

The relationship of Lifton's argument to our discussion of grieving lies in the vital importance of our own sense of organization, our purpose, confidence, and wholeness. When this is lacking or incomplete, the individual will seek out ways of defending against the reality of death. When a death occurs which is so close as to threaten the person's defenses, or when death takes away the individual who was the person's meaning in life (a defense against meaninglessness), then the person experiences existential grieving which is rooted in primary issues involving the reality of death itself.

As Lifton has shown, early in life the individual must grapple with the reality of death, which he or she experiences in rudimentary images of separation, disintegration, and stasis (inactivity).[11] These images also have polar extremes which are a part of the infant's consciousness as well. These are images of connection, integrity, and movement. The struggle to master the polar realities of life and death engage us all, probably on a repressed unconscious level, all of our lives. An encounter with an actual death, especially the loss of a loved one, may force us again to encounter our own death, "the terror we carry around in our secret heart."[12] In existential grieving the person's words and feelings connote an inward, rather than outward, orientation (which characterizes reactive grief): "Why was I born, if only to suffer so?" is an expression of existential grief, while, "My life is so empty without my lover," is an example of reactive grieving.

Almost all grievings involve elements of both reactive and existential grief. While the individual grieves over the loss, he or she generally realizes that what is being experienced is a part of life, and that all life, even one's own, ultimately involves death. The underlying motive behind the immature vow to "never love again" is an attempt to avoid one's humanness. Humanness can be hurt; and in its vulnerability, it reminds us of our mortality. But if one never loves, one never feels pain (that is, experiences his or her own mortality). Of course, the fallacy in this kind of thinking is that one forfeits humanness in the process of rejecting love, and death still exists, even if love is denied.

Reactive Grief

While existential grief focuses upon the mortality of the griever, reactive grief is concerned with the loss that the death represents to the person. This type of grieving is most evident in those who lose someone who is their significant other. For example, elderly widows and widowers who have lost spouses with whom they have spent the majority of their lives often experience a great deal of reactive grief. The loss of an elderly spouse in a world of few intense relationships may deliver a blow from which one may never recover. The advancing years, with their accompanying loss of energy, may find the survivor ill-equipped to complete the reorganization of his or her life so necessary to a satisfactory resolution of the loss. Bereft of the primary other person in the world, the older widow and widower may never resolve the extensive grief in their lives.[13]

Past unresolved griefs may also be triggered off by the recent loss. This may be especially powerful where there has been some lack of resolution over the previous loss. The severity and the extent of reactive grief that the person experiences will depend upon several factors: The degree to which the person was dependent upon the former relationship will affect the intensity of the existential grief. The individual's perceived ability to establish new relationships which could meet the needs now unfulfilled will also be a factor in grieving. Finally, the social reality of the world of the griever will influence the person's grieving by establishing acceptable modes of conduct concerning grieving and reestablishing relationships in order to meet the needs once satisfied by the deceased.

In order to fully understand the grieving person, we must become aware of the degree to which the grief is reactive or existential. Both types of grief require distinct and separate ways of resolving the emotional crisis brought about by the experience of the death of a significant person. This is often referred to as grief work and may involve the establishment of new meanings in life, the resolution or repression of issues surrounding one's own mortality, or the development of new relationships to meet one's needs. In the following section we will explore this process in more detail.

The Grieving Process

In discussing the grieving process it is impossible to account for the entire range of possible idiosyncratic manifestations of grief. While we can speak of three general phases in the process, it is difficult to account for individual responses to grief. As Bowlby states, "Grief, I believe, is *a peculiar amalgam* of anxiety, anger and despair following the experience of what is feared to be irretrievable loss" (italics added).[14] In this definition Bowlby argues, for the inclusion of those factors which combine in unique ways within each individual, and thus make grief a very personal process. The following descriptions of the phases of the grief process should be seen as presenting general stages through which the individual passes in his or her own unique working out of the bereavement. The phases are not delineated by particular entry or exit criteria, but should be seen as representative of that point in the grieving process when the characteristics described are most prevalent.

While we may speak of a general process of doing grief work, it is important to be aware that the process can also be seen as a series of repeated experiences of grief. Rosenblatt points out that often the bereaved will put aside grief work for a while, only to be reminded of it by reencountering the reality of the loss. "If it is granted that there are fresh reminders, that losses cannot be worked all of a piece, it becomes possible that normal grieving involves repeated surges of grief."[15] A person may manifest a denial of the loss in one aspect of his life while appearing to have resolved the issues of grief in another. An example of this would be a woman who assumes many of the duties previously performed by her late husband (an acceptance of the loss), but still keeps all of his clothes hanging in the closet as they were they day he died (denial). The following phases, then, are general categories wherein the predominant characteristics are those described under each phase. As C. S. Lewis wrote:

> Grief is like a long valley, a winding valley where any bend may reveal a totally new landscape. As I've already noted, not every bend does. Sometimes a surprise is the opposite one; you are presented with exactly the same sort of country you thought you had left behind miles ago. This is when you wonder whether the valley isn't a circular trench. But it isn't. There are partial recurrences, but the sequence doesn't repeat.[16]

Phase One: Reaction

> The intellect is stunned by the shock and but gropingly gathers the meaning of the words. The power to realize their full import is mercifully wanting. The mind has a dim sense of vast loss— that is all. It will take mind and memory months and possibly years to gather the details and thus learn and know the whole extent of the loss.
>
> Samuel Clemens, *Autobiography*

The initial phase of grief is generally described as a shocking blow, and the person is stunned to the very essence of his being by the loss. Numbness sets in. One doesn't feel, one just "does." A grieving parent told me, "It is as if I'm in a daze, and I can only manage to dumbly put one foot in front of the other." People in the early part of this stage have been known to do what needs to be done; making funeral arrangements, notifying others, and

handling these tasks in matter-of-fact tones. They are continuing
to function on an intellectual level, but often with strongly repressed feeling.

> I just don't want to go on. There are times when I'm suspended
> . . . I think that the normal reaction after six months is that
> so many little things come up. There is such a gap between
> just knowing and really feeling all this.[17]

This numbing of feelings may be a life-preserving way of
adapting to some emergency situations which might, as in a disaster
or accident, allow the individual to survive immediate danger. Instead of dissolving into incapacitating grief, the person becomes
emotionally numb, as if in a state of shock, and this allows the
person to focus on the tasks necessary to save his or her life. Such
was the case of a young boy involved in a private plane crash
which took the life of his father. He was able to save himself by
remembering what his father had taught him about survival. By
suppressing his grief he could concentrate on saving himself. In
a less dramatic example, occasionally a family member who plays
the role of a nurturing parent for the others may put aside his or
her own grieving in order to minister to the needs of others. In
both these examples, if this numbing becomes a permanent state,
it will inhibit the resolution of grief.

The early part of the first phase of grief is usually characterized
by a state of bewilderment. The individual tries to assign some
meaning to what has occurred. The more inappropriate and unexpected the loss, the greater the challenge for the individual to make
sense out of this event. This attempt to understand the news of
an inappropriate death may have two motives: one is to understand
the news itself. The other motive is involved with the existential
issues provoked by the loss. In the first case, the survivor's bewilderment lies in realizing that the loss has occurred. A person struggling with this issue might typically say, "I can't believe she's
dead. I talked with her just yesterday." In the second case, the
bewilderment centers on existential grief, and the person might
communicate this by asking, "What kind of a world is it that
allows innocent babies to die?"

> My wife had immediate acceptance. But me! I said to God,
> why such a hurt? Why such a pain? Why did you call?[18]

As the reality of the loss begins to be accepted into the person's
understanding, there is a great urge to recover the lost object. This
may be an involuntary or unconscious action, but nevertheless it

is a very common theme in this initial stage of grief. The person cries out in sorrow. Bowlby argues that there is a biological basis for such behavior.[19] When animal infants lose their mothers, their crying sounds will often bring about the mother's return. However, in case of loss through death, the infant's crying will not bring about the return of the lost loved object. Human beings, Bowlby maintains, are moved by the same urge to cry out in order to regain the lost object.

We are all aware of the building tension, perhaps the attempt to suppress the welling up of feelings, and the final resignation and giving in to a torrent of tears. There is a release of internal tension as the body is racked with anguished sobs. The power of crying to aid in recovering the lost object is not merely a lower animal adaptive function. In the case of loss through death, the cries may produce solace from others (a positive function in itself), but they cannot regain the loss by bringing the deceased back to life. Averill, in a lengthy discussion of this issue, points out that a psychobiological basis for the grief reaction exists. While the grief process is influenced by both the social environment and one's peculiar life experiences, research has shown that there is "a stereotype set of psychological and physiological reactions of biological origin"—most notable in the mother-offspring dyad—that we know as "grieving."[20] The strong feelings of wanting to do something to restore things to the way they were before, and the need to cry out in sorrow are basic to the grief process.

Anger also can be seen during this first stage. Often in the more common forms of loss, a "small or large dash of aggression will be fruitful in bringing about a satisfactory solution to separation."[21] As with the crying behavior described earlier, we can see how this urge to action might be functional in common threats of loss, but these efforts are to no avail in bringing back the dead. In death loss, obviously, this anger will not produce the desired result of restoring the lost relationship, but it may occur anyway.

> Tumor . . . an unknown virus . . . fibrosis . . . I wanted to hammer that tumor out.[22]

Bereaved persons may, to their own bewilderment and perhaps guilt, find themselves reproaching the dead for having deserted them (the dead are the perpetrators of this evil deed). Anger and disrespect for the dead are generally not approved of in our society, but are acceptable behaviors in others, where the dead are openly

reproached for having died. This is an effort to undo the wrong
that has occurred, to reestablish the former relationship.[23] Sometimes God is seen as the cause of the pain that is felt, and the
individual later feels anxious and guilty for having cursed God.
A hospital chaplain described this process to me, saying that he
would not reprove the griever for this initial outburst, because
he understood the deeper need to find a cause for the loss. He
reconciled this with his reverence for God by stating that, "God
is big enough to handle and understand this anger."

> Then they told me the little one was gone . . . God hates
> me!
> After I lost my son, sometimes I would get up and walk
> out of the church. I think it was resentment of God, really.[24]

The anger a bereaved person feels may take other forms as
he or she attempts to regain control of his or her life. Often an
attempt will be made to assign blame to anyone or anything. The
assignation of blame may serve many purposes. It may provide a
protection against guilt by assigning the cause of death to someone
or something else. By finding fault or assigning blame, the griever
may be able to relieve himself of any fears of responsibility for
the death.[25] This is often a difficult problem for parents who lose
a child. Since in our culture parents accept a great deal of the
responsibility for their children, a child's death often evokes a
great deal of guilt on the part of the parents.

Blaming may provide a target for revenge. A sense of restitu-
tion can be achieved as a wrong is corrected. The bereaved seeks
to restore things to the way they were, to recapture the old relationship and at the same time give vent to the anger which is a part
of his or her grief. This explanation of the root motivations behind
angry activity provides an irrational yet understandable context
for the urge to strike out, to do something in response to the felt
loss.

In this initial stage of the grieving process, after the first shock
wave has passed, the most common activities involve crying and
aggressive, angry efforts that are motivated by a desire to restore
the lost loved person to the bereaved. Even though the deceased
person is gone, the needs persist on the part of the bereaved. The
griever cries out for the lost loved one, feels a desire to "do something" about the loss to somehow correct this terrible event. But
these efforts are in vain.

Another form of anger may be the hostility that is shown toward those who would comfort the bereaved. The hostility has its roots in the aggressive urge to reestablish contact with the lost person. The comforter is attempting to help the bereaved to accept the loss, which is exactly what the bereaved does not want to do at this point. Accepting the grief by working it through means accepting the loss as well. For example, one grieving parent stated, "I keep a photograph of the (stillborn) baby on the mantle. I don't plan on ever getting over it."[26] Many a well-intentioned friend has been shocked by the anger with which an offer of support was met. The consoler is unaware that the grieving individual may feel a need to regain the loss (however unrealistic that might appear to the observer), and may not want to accept the death of the lost person. In effect, the bereaved person is saying, "Do not ask me to give up my grief—it is all that I have left."

The Reaction Phase of Grief: "The Raven." Literature can often serve to describe the emotions and motivations of people better than case histories. Illustrative of the initial phase of grief, Edgar Allan Poe, in his poem, "The Raven," lyrically describes his efforts to accept the loss of his loved one.[27] So strong is his urge to regain her that, upon answering what he thinks to be a knock at his door and finding no one there, and "Doubting, dreaming dreams no mortal ever dared to dream before," he calls out to his dead love. His irrational hope is that somehow, in some inexplicable way (and one that is terrifying in its implications), Lenore has returned to him. But there is nothing there, save an echo of his own words, "Merely this and nothing more."

As Poe encounters Death in the form of the raven, he initially tries to deny its impact by stating that death too will pass quickly through his life. The raven encompasses the reality of death into one word and replies, "Nevermore." Poe then decides to confront the visitor in an intellectual manner, by reasoning about what this "grim, ungainly, ghastly, gaunt, and ominous" bird could mean by his curious uttering of "nevermore." But even this fails, for he suddenly realizes that he is resting his head upon a pillow which reminds him of Lenore and his loss. Suddenly overwhelmed with grief, he begs for release from sorrow. Again the bird replies, "Nevermore." The urge to recover the lost object wells up in him once more, and Poe asks Death if he will at least be reunited in heaven with his lost love. The bird replies, "Nevermore."

Now shrieking in anger, the poet orders Death to leave him

and to "take thy beak from out of my heart." Again, relentlessly, the reply is, "Nevermore." Finally, realizing his efforts are in vain, Poe resigns himself to what he perceives as an eternity of sorrows. For Death, in the form of the raven, "never flitting, still is sitting, *still* is sitting," perched in the narrator's personal world, and the shadow of death, which is sorrow, covers his soul. In resignation to his fate, the poet admits that the shadow of his sorrow shall never be lifted from his soul.

In the poem, Poe describes the strong and quick mood shifts which can be a part of early grief. One moment rational, the next angry, suddenly despairing, as the narrator attempts to come to grips with his loss. But every effort to control or mitigate the pain of loss is fruitless. Poe, with the use of almost maddening and repetitious understatement, sums up in one word the stoic and uncompromising reality of death. The efforts to resolve the pain fail, and the narrator resigns himself to what he sees as never-ending sorrow. The second phase of grief now begins.

Phase Two: Disorganization and Reorganization

As the attempts to recover what has been lost fail, the disappointment mounts. Deep, sometimes incapacitating despair set in. No longer does the individual focus his efforts to find the lost person. The realization that the person has died leaves the griever with no place to focus his thoughts. Lindemann describes this as "a painful lack of capacity to initiate and maintain organized patterns of activity."[28] This characterization implies that the grief process itself somehow imposes upon the person this lack of organization. We should be aware, on the contrary, that the griever still has the mental ability to organize his activities, but the old patterns of organization *just don't make sense anymore.* So, rather than the ability to organize life being somehow taken away by grief, we would argue that the grieving person ceases activity because the usual forms of activity have lost their meaning. In view of the circumstances, this cessation of activity may be a logical decision. With the loss of a loved person, a great many of the bereaved's former activities are no longer rewarding in the same way. The individual must stop old habitual behaviors; actions and the motives for them must be rethought. A process of internal reorganization must go on. Deciding to stop many activities certainly makes sense in view of the situational context. To continue in former patterns of activity would be, in a sense, reality-denying behavior.

> I supported that child. I took that child to school the first day. I took that child to the doctor. Now what the hell do I do?[29]

Lindemann points out that if some pre-loss activities persist out of habit, or if the person finds him- or herself ceasing what were formerly important activities, he or she may begin to realize how many of those activities had meaning, at least in part, in the lost relationship.[30] This new lack of meaning in one's life may lead to a strong, if temporary, dependency on others who, in their willingness to help the bereaved, in effect, say, "I will make sense out of your world for you."

During the second phase of grief the individual may appear to be in a state of disorganization. As Bowlby points out, before the person can rebuild his life, he must dismantle the old mental constructs.[31] While externally the person may appear unable to focus his own activities, important internal adjustments to loss may be taking place. The former frame of reference which had guided the individual's behavior no longer applies. Before the griever can reorient him- or herself to the changed external world the old image of the world must be dismantled and a new one constructed. This is the primary work going on during the second phase. Marris describes the reorganization process as "painful, because it begins in such helplessness and uncertainty."[32] The person experiencing grief may feel a loss of a sense of personal integrity or personal wholeness. The one who supplied so much meaning to life and around whom so many of the person's activities were focused, now has been lost to death.

> I had been so used to buying four items, and for awhile I would actually forget, you know, and get four things, and I would just keep the other for myself.[33]

C. S. Lewis, writing about the loss of his wife, says, "Did you ever know, dear, how much you took away with you when you left? You have stripped me even of my past, even of the things we never shared."[34] That vital sense of internal integrity, perhaps never consciously realized before, is now useless.

In their study of the first year of bereavement, Glick, Weiss, and Parkes found that some widows described their loss as a loss of an actual part of themselves, so deep was their grief.[35] In a sense, this description is apt. They have lost a great deal of the symbolic organization they had developed; a symbolic organization that gave meaning to their world. Since so much meaning was based upon the spouse, his dying destroyed their inner world. Often this grieving takes the form of obsessional reliving of the past. This reviewing of the old patterns of symbolic organization is a way of taking apart the old image of the world and preparing a new one which applies to a world without the lost person. The death event forces the individual to reorganize his or her life around a new reality. The denial of this reality only lengthens the grieving process, or may lead to forms of inappropriate behavior.

The desolation and despair that the individual feels are deeply rooted in primary images of disorganization and disintegration. A person who reports a fear of being destroyed by grief is closer to the truth than we might think at first glance. The inner symbolic organization no longer works because it is no longer an adequate image of the relationship between the person and the world. Because the individual's image of the world can no longer be applied to reality, the bereaved person cannot use it as a basis for action.

Erich Lindemann, in his important study, "Symptomatology and Management of Acute Grief," presents his findings from studying over 100 grieving persons.[36] He describes the bereaved as often avoiding those who would console them, because these meetings would release a flood of feelings of desolation and distress. The person may feel a sense of unreality, and a lack of emotional closeness with others. Sometimes there will be a preoccupation with the deceased, as the formerly accurate internal symbolization of the world, not yet completely dismissed, reasserts itself. There may be also a fear of forgetting the lost person if the grief process is completed. Giving up grief may also be resisted because of feelings of guilt. To grieve is to pay a debt. The loss itself may be seen as a punishment, and to grieve is to accept that punishment, to "serve out the sentence," in a sense.

Sometimes an individual may remain deeply involved in grief, seeming to make no progress because, in fact, he or she finds a certain amount of satisfaction (secondary gain) in grieving. The person suffers well, and to finish grieving would mean giving up the tragic role. And the tragic role, while painful, may be the one at which the person is most adept; and which thereby gives him or her the greatest amount of reinforcement and satisfaction.

During grieving, our disorganization and lack of a sense of

personal integrity are further shattered by our lack of experience with the strong feelings that appear to be overwhelming us. An underlying feeling which many are afraid to share openly is that of fear. C. S. Lewis, describing his bereavement over the loss of his wife, says, "No one ever told me grief felt so much like fear."[37] Often this is a fear that the loss of inner integrity and the onslaught of terrifying emotions means that the person is actually losing his or her mind.

> I've been numb from my toes to my head and I can hardly breathe at night. . . . I have weird reactions, fantasies . . . I'm scared. I have been a person I don't know.[38]

The bereaved person needs to become aware that the thoughts and feelings being experienced during normal grief are to be expected, and that they make sense in the context of loss of a dearly loved person.

Phase Three: Reorientation and Recovery

In the final phase of grief, the loss has taken on different meanings for the griever. The memory of the lost person no longer elicits strong grieving reactions. The griever may sense a resolution of previously felt strong feelings. The lost person may be referred to in reminiscences which may entail feelings of pleasure as well as sadness.

As the griever reorganizes his or her symbolic world, the dead person may be given a new image, and the griever may state that the lost person is now in a particular place, such as "heaven," which is a more concrete description of the new status of the deceased.

The dead person is now characterized much differently than when he was alive. The deceased, at least in the imagery of the griever, enters a timeless state. He or she is no longer associated with our time-bound world, but takes on a new identity in the mind of the griever. This is a necessary step if the griever is to reorganize his or her image of the world so that it is congruent with reality. The new identity assigned to the dead person removes him from the everyday world, thus allowing the griever to adapt to life without the deceased. The ceremonies that surround death are, in part, social affirmations of the changed status of the dead person.

The new symbolic world of the griever may be formed in part on meanings and values attributed to the deceased. I visited the home of a deceased test pilot, whose memory was an active part of the family's shared images. There were many mementos, pictures, and awards won by the late father around the house, and the teen-age children spoke openly and matter-of-factly about their father. They continued in active leadership roles in school and athletics, and the son eventually became an Air Force pilot himself. Even after the father's death, the values he had set down continued to be an influence in his children's development.

As the deceased is put into a new perspective by the survivors, new meanings are taken on regarding the lost person's life. The griever attempts to make sense out of the loss, and incorporates these new meanings as a part of his or her changed image of the world. The child may have a desire to become a doctor in order to find a cure for the disease that killed a loved one. The adult may decide that the deceased person died for a cause that must be carried on. The image of the deceased takes on new meanings as the griever orients himself to a world without the loved one. As Marris observes, "The grief is mastered, not by ceasing to care for the dead, but by abstracting what was fundamentally important in the relationship and rehabilitating it."[39]

> I held her a long time after she died and nobody made me budge. I stayed in that room with her about 40 or 50 minutes after she died and it was really neat. But my little girl did have a message. She has a message for me, she has a message for everybody here: the only thing when the chips are down that really matters is kindness. That's the only thing that really matters. You can spell it any way you want. Some people say love, some say compassion but when you act it out what is it, it's kindness."[40]

In the statement above we see that the parent recognizes that the loss has occurred. Meaning has been given to the loss because there was something that the little girl had left behind. To the parent, the lesson learned was that the only thing that matters is kindness. This message gives meaning to the child's life and death. As the individual begins to interact with his or her surroundings, he or she begins to implement a new perspective on the world. This reorganized image may develop almost immediately following death, or it may take much longer. An older child may begin to take on some aspects of a deceased parent's role soon after the parent's death. (This may or may not be appropriate; nonetheless, it is an attempt to build an image of the world without the dead parent.) Aging widows and widowers may choose never to rebuild their lives, but to spend the rest of their days almost totally immersed in memories.

The successful resolution of grief is accomplished when the individual is able to reintegrate him- or herself in the external world. This new inner symbolization of life will contain elements of the individual's past experiences, and a reorientation toward life without the lost loved one. The person is no longer influenced by overwhelming feelings of despair. Feelings involved in the grieving process are no longer as uncontrollable as they were in the past. The individual regains a sense of personal integration and connection and can now redirect and take charge of his or her life. Life begins to move forward again, and the individual regains the ability to interact openly with others.

Bertha Simos sums up the resolution of the grief process in this manner:

> The task of mourning is completed when a personality reorganization takes place, through which the old self and the new self now without that which has been lost, are integrated. This is different from the attempt at retrieval of the loss that characterizes the first phase of grief. That which has been lost is now retained in memory. A sense of identity, a new stability, a hopeful and positive interest in the present and future mark the end of grief and mourning. The search for new avenues of gratification leads to restitution for the loss through new relationships, new interests, new values, and new goals. With restitution comes a restoration of the sense of self-esteem damaged by the loss. The new self is enriched by the memories of that which has been lost as well as by the growth through suffering and the mastery of grief. Healthy grieving should end with new avenues for creative living.[41]

Factors Affecting Successful Grief Work

Throughout our discussion of grief, we have implied different factors which can be seen as affecting the grief process. The death fears and anxieties of the griever may exacerbate the grieving; existential grief can present more of a problem than the loss itself. The intensity of the lost relationship will be a factor in reactive grieving, as will the availability of other love objects to support the griever and to provide for the needs once met by the deceased.

The degree to which the death may be seen as preventable can become a factor in the grief process.[42] Most obviously this question of preventability may produce feelings of guilt. Anger at a needless death, perhaps one easily avoided by stronger laws or better medical care, may affect the ease with which the person can resolve his or her grief. Also, the basic personality and emotional makeup of the survivor will affect the ability to cope with the crisis. Past losses, and the individual's experiences in resolving them may provide valuable information on how the individual can cope with the current loss. Conversely, a great many recent losses can leave the individual in a weakened emotional state. This has been noted among the elderly, who may lose a number of people close to them within a short period of time. Because grieving also takes a physical toll, the health of the griever may affect his or her ability to cope with the loss and regain his or her former state of emotional composure.

As we mentioned earlier, the degree to which the death is seen as appropriate will greatly affect the individual's grief reaction. Appropriate losses, though painful, may be seen as "right." However, inappropriate death may destroy not only the relationship, but one's sense of the meaning of existence itself.

The Social Process of Mourning

We will now shift our perspective from concern with the internal dynamics of grief to the social world in which one acts out the loss. One sociological perspective, strictly defined, states that the emotions are a product of the social reality in which the person exists. According to this perspective, society tells us what and how to feel. This is a result of socially proscribed patterns of interaction, as well as socially reinforced ways of feeling. The sociological perspective differs from the psychological perspective in that it does not emphasize internal feelings. Emile Durkheim, one of the founders of sociology, believed that "mourning is not a natural movement of private feelings wounded by a cruel loss; it is a duty imposed by the group."[43]

This sociological position immediately raises questions concerning the biological basis for grief. Rather than become involved in a debate, let us assume that the interplay of both the individual's psyche and the social environment will affect feelings and behaviors. The development of personality includes not only the external experiences, but also the individual's ability to internalize the experiences in internal symbolic thinking. Attitudes toward death and feelings involved in acknowledging loss (grief) are a product of both social and psychological processes. Mourning, the social experience of grief, permits the individual to experience external validation for his or her feelings. In examining mourning, we will focus on the effect and importance of mourning for the griever. When we consider social rituals surrounding a death, we will examine the significance of mourning for the larger society.

The social environment provides us with a stage upon which to express our inner selves. Our lives and ways of looking at the world may be enhanced or constrained by our environment. A pessimistic investigator may focus on how we are constrained by the social environment, as did Freud and Marx. Others argue that we tend to limit our vision, and that our potentials are more self-constrained than socially repressed. A good deal of the current wave of popular psychology argues that we tend to limit our own abilities more than they are limited by the social environment. This kind of "bootstrap psychology" focuses upon the individual taking responsibility for his or her life, and thereby bringing about the changes that are desired. While accepting responsibility may be an important part of change, this perspective often implies a naive and potentially dangerous approach to the social environment. In our discussion of the mourning process, we will examine both the positive and negative aspects of the social environment, and its influence upon those who are grieving.

The Repression of Feeling in American Society

It is necessary at this point to examine the social contexts in which grieving takes place in this country, in order to understand the reality within which the individual experiences grief. We do this in order to appreciate the ways in which the social environment can facilitate or discourage the grieving process. Also, the judgment that people make about acceptable and appropriate mourning will influence the ease with which the individual is able to mourn. In the extreme, it can be argued that negative social influences on the mourner may promote exceptional grief reactions.

A useful sociological concept to introduce at this point is that of labeling.[44] In this process, the individual is placed in a category of persons, a status, because of behavior which has been judged by some authority (consensus, the legal or traditionally powerful, etc.) as deviant. Deviation implies a digression from the norms of society. What are the norms of American society concerning emotional behaviors such as mourning?

Thomas Scheff argues that industrial mass society is predominantly involved in a denial of the value of "the unalienated individual, passionately engaged, and in intimate contact with at least one other person."[45] Instead, Scheff describes industrial societies as modeled after Martin Buber's I-it relationship, wherein the person is emotionally isolated from society, others, and even him- or herself. On a societal level, these values are epitomized in the bureaucratic as opposed to a more humanistic communal form of organization.

Living in a bureaucratized and industrialized society, one finds the norms and values influenced by and, in turn, influencing the social organization. Feelings, spontaneously expressed, are not approved of in the bureaucratic society, which values instead predictability, control, and efficiency. Scheff notes that "the ideal person for such servitude is reliably obedient, predictable, and orderly."[45] In socializing children, the control of children's feelings is one of the major centers of conflict. Sadness and anger, the two earliest expressions of emotions by the child, are objects of parental control. These two emotions, so basic to the grief process, are suppressed through socialization. This goes beyond the immediate family, as society reacts negatively to "spoiled brats" and "cry babies." Important also is the fact that the social world in which we live does not take an interest in the child's inner state—the source of emotions—but instead punitively socializes the child into the suppression of feelings and compliance with society's norms. Scheff's description of the results of this process is worth quoting directly:

> The first consequence is usually an adult whose emotions are so severely repressed that he seems to others and even to himself to be virtually emotionless. Although the personality of this adult is well suited for human contact in which hierarchy, order, and predictability are emphasized, he is likely to be quite rigid

in most areas and lacking in spontaneity and creativity. Like the bureaucracy he is apt to serve, he is suited for short-term efficiency in using means to an end, but is unlikely to be innovative, creative, or responsive to changing conditions.

A second consequence of the punitive socialization of emotions is likely to be an individual who's as intolerant of emotions in others as his parents were of his own emotions as a child.[47]

Scheff, describing Tomkin's work on the socialization of crying, points out how the emotions are suppressed and given a negative connotation through socialization.[48] The second consequence described by Scheff results in a society intent on labeling as deviant those who would display their feelings openly.

In sum, American society does not approve of mourning, except within the rigid confines of a funeral. Any other display of emotion, or indication of one's emotional state (such as wearing a black mourning band on the arm), is no longer normatively accepted behavior. The individual is expected to return to the workaday world quickly, and not to burden others with open displays of grieving after that time. The bureaucratic world has little tolerance for feelings.

What are of interest to us at this point are the ramifications of such a social reality upon the individual. The result of this kind of a normative order is to encourage denial and suppression of the griever's feelings. Grief is something to be mastered, rather than experienced. At the funeral for the late President Kennedy, his widow was admired for her stoicism. Triumph over one's feelings, suffering in silence, and refusal to be overcome by emotions are seen as admirable traits in American society. To deviate from the norm is to invite social disapproval, and to be labeled as "weak," a "bleeding heart," or perhaps even "crazy." This final label of "crazy" is worth further comment. I was told by one person of his fear of his own strong emotions at a time of grieving. Since strong emotions are not acceptable in American culture, experiences involving them are often feared. This applies to positive as well as negative feelings. A chief cause of reluctance to enter fully into sexual interactions is often given as a fear of losing control. Likewise, an individual who experiences the overwhelming emotion associated with grief, and who has been socialized to suppress (and hence not experience) the strong emotions of anger and sorrow, may feel that he or she is losing his or her mind. In an unresponsive society preoccupied with control, the fear of unsuppressible feelings may contribute to morbid grief reactions. A lack of familiarity with the possible range of human emotions may place the individual in a precarious position when confronting a significant loss, to say nothing of impoverishing life in general.

It is generally accepted that the initial phase of grief may last as long as several weeks or even months, during which time the individual is often overwhelmed with feelings. When one must return to work before the process is complete, a great deal of effort must be expended by the individual to maintain a facade of nonemotionality. It may be necessary for the person to deny his or her feelings in order to continue to function in the world of work. Something of one's humanness must be sacrificed in order to bring home the paycheck. This imposition of behaviors on the mourner may be a product of the bureaucratic form of organization.[49] In the bureaucracy, death is not known. As Marris points out, there is always a replacement available to step in and fill the vacancy in a bureaucracy. While returning to work may be a sign of reintegration for some, when it is imposed upon the individual prior to his being in a position to cope with the realities of the work world it may do much more harm than good.

Usually our society demands a brief mourning period. The individual, forced to play a part contrary to his emotional concerns, is caught on the horns of a dilemma. If he takes the time to work through the grief, he may have to sacrifice his form of livelihood. If he returns to the public world, it may be at the expense of his emotions. Marris has observed that until the "thread of continuity is reestablished, the individual cannot authentically interact with the world." The process of reconnecting with the world in positive ways is ". . . itself the only deeply meaningful activity in which the bereaved can be engaged."[50]

Other societies, and even our own in the past, have recognized the personal needs of the mourner, and have provided a context in which the mourner could express his grief. Phillippe Aries has described the purposes of the seclusion of the family in mourning during ancient times.[51] First, the person was allowed to do nothing but grieve. This custom, still a part of Orthodox Jewish tradition, does not leave room for denial, which so easily occurs in contemporary grieving patterns. Second, the seclusion of a family for a specific period of time would not allow the family to mourn too quickly and thereby not fully resolve their grief.[52] Taking an historical view of mourning customs, Aries states:

If one were to draw a "mourning curve," there would first be a peak stage of frank violent spontaneity until somewhere around the 13th Century, then a long phase of ritualization until the 18th Century and then in the 19th Century a period of impassion, self-indulgent grief, dramatic demonstration and funeral mythology. . . . In the mid 20th Century the ancient necessity for mourning—more or less spontaneous or enforced depending on the century . . . has been succeeded by its prohibition. During the course of one generation the situation has been reversed: what had always been required by individual conscience or social obligation is now forbidden; what had always been forbidden is now required. It is no longer correct to display one's grief, nor even to feel any.[53]

The rise of individualism and technology have combined to devalue individual processes in favor of the larger organization. Today it would appear that to the extent the individual allows him- or herself to become an extension of the bureaucratic organization, he or she must sacrifice some of his or her unique humanness. While in everyday life this may be a rewarding bargain, in times of overwhelming loss the personal need to mourn is often subjugated to the demands of bureaucratic society. The bureaucracy is not concerned with the individual's feelings, but with his or her ability to do the job assigned. Rational thinking must take priority. While one may be rewarded financially, emotionally the person may become impoverished. As Benoliel points out, "The process [of grief work] cannot be hurried beyond the individual's capacity to assimilate the change into his definition of reality."[54] To rush this process in order to meet social demands may foster more severe reactions at a later date.

Thus far we have seen that the value which the society places on individual death will affect the ways of mourning available to its members. Where loss of the individual is considered important, the society will provide a means of acknowledging the loss, such as a state funeral. In mass societies such as the contemporary United States, where individual death (except of significant leaders) is not usually an important national or community event, a social recognition of loss is almost nonexistent.

In American society there is a lack of ritual in interacting with one who is mourning. "I don't know what to say," is the most common statement one hears during mourning. As an example of this avoidance mechanism, Vernon describes a study in which he asked people how they would respond if they met someone who had lost a loved one through death since their last meeting.[55] Only 25 percent of the respondents said that they would mention the death, while 64 percent stated that they would either wait for the other party to mention the loss or would prefer that no mention be made of the loss at all. Another 10 percent stated that they just didn't feel prepared to answer the question. This preference for avoiding the subject by the majority of people interviewed is an example of the lack of socially acceptable behavior when interacting with one in mourning. From the mourner's point of view, the situation is most likely to be similar to Glaser and Strauss's mutual pretense context, as an inauthentic interaction drama is played out. In this type of interaction, the mourner receives no validation or reinforcement for the grief being felt. In fact, the mourner is being encouraged to deny that he or she is grieving at all.

Vernon went on to ask his respondents how they would like to be treated if they were in mourning themselves. While 38 percent stated that they would prefer to be left alone, another 38 percent stated they would prefer some form of interaction with others concerning their mourning. Interestingly, over 22 percent had no opinion as to how they would prefer to be treated during mourning. One thing that stands out is the desire of a large portion of the sample for some form of social validation for their feelings; another is the large proportion of people who had no idea of how to act or how they think they would like to be treated during mourning.

The lack of customary mourning behavior can leave the mourner with an even greater sense of personal disorganization than was felt previously. This points out the attractiveness of denying one's need to mourn in order to become accepted back into society. Gorer speaks to this point as well, and contrasts the kinds of nonnormative behavior with that of the Orthodox Jewish community.[56] Within that group, mourning is rigidly proscribed. Initially, the individual must do nothing for seven days but grieve. After that period of time, the men must not shave or cut their hair for one month, and twice daily someone must go to the temple and say prayers (Kaddish) for the deceased for the next eleven months. Then a grave marker is erected and the mourning ends. The group, in this case as in many traditional societies, provides a format within which the survivors may mourn. It provides for acceptable mourning behaviors within a social context.

Even though the individual may express extreme behaviors during mourning, as in some primitive tribes, it is taking place within a social context.[57] The people may inflict wounds upon themselves, scream and tear out their hair, and manifest other behaviors which would be considered harmful if not pathological in our society. But they do so within a defined social context, which controls the behaviors and will guide the individual back to the normal patterns of social interaction upon completion of the mourning ritual. When the mourning behavior is ended, the individual reaches a closure around the loss and is ready to reintegrate himself or herself into the mainstream of society. In contemporary American society, oftentimes people do not feel a sense of resolution of the loss because of the lack of recognition of mourning by the social group and disapproval of the open display of strong feelings.

Anger, a basic emotion in grief, is often expressed in a social context. Rosenblatt points out the need a society has either to channel the anger of mourning into socially acceptable or nonthreatening behaviors or to isolate the mourner in order to protect the society's members from harm. In the contemporary United States, there are not the specialists who direct the mourner's anger, as in other societies where designated group members such as priests prescribe ritual behaviors for the mourners. The mourner is left to his own devices. A lack of a socially defined and safe means of releasing anger during mourning may contribute to the violence so prevalent in American society. Much of the violence may be the product of unreleased anger reactions stemming from loss.

Another by-product of the lack of normative patterns of interaction with those in mourning is the social isolation which results from this avoidance. At a point in time when the individual is most in need of social support, he or she often is without support from others.[58] Mourning behavior involves those outside of the immediate family only through the funeral. Many grieving people report a great sense of loneliness after the funeral, when others return to their usual routines.

Exceptional and Anticipatory Grief

The acceptance of loss through the grief process enables a person again to interact with the external world in gratifying ways, and to continue a meaningful existence. In this section we will examine two special cases of grief: exceptional grief, wherein the individual does not successfully complete the grieving process and anticipatory grief, involving knowledge that a loss will take place some time in the future.

Defining Exceptional Grief

Perhaps one of the most difficult issues to grapple with in studying grief involves the question of successful and unsuccessful grieving. Bowlby acknowledges the complexity of this issue, and agrees with Lindemann's view that pathological responses to loss are best seen as "exaggerations and caricatures of the normal process."[59] Siggins argues that where the process of grieving is "abnormally delayed, protracted, or intense," we are witnessing a morbid reaction.[60] De-Vaul and Zisook state that unresolved grief involves the absence or prolongation of the grief process.[61] They cite three clinical symptoms of exceptional grief: (1) painful response when the deceased is mentioned, (2) realization of unresolved grief by the individual, and (3) unaccountable depression or the emergence of medical symptoms on the anniversary of the loss.

Welu has addressed the issue of criteria for pathological grief and offers the following tentative guidelines: (1) self-destructive behavior (suicide attempts, excessive use of alcohol and drugs), (2) suicidal thoughts or feelings, (3) physiological problems, (4) social withdrawal, (5) depressive states with obvious clinical symptoms, (6) hospitalization for psychiatric symptoms, and (7) the taking of psychotherapeutic drugs.[62]

Siggins states that a noticeable exaggeration of any of the reactions typical to the grief process may signal a morbid reaction.[63] More specifically, she speaks of the persistent reactions of an emotion usually associated with grief, the appearance of a lack of progress—indeed, what could almost be termed a determination on the part of the griever not to give up the lost object—in the grieving process, and the distortions of the grieving process described by Lindemann and outlined in some detail later in this chapter.

This brief review of the existing literature points out the imprecise and subjective nature of psychological diagnosis. Anthropological studies describe a great many grieving reactions which are contained in the descriptions of pathological behavior given above, but are considered normal (typical, expected) behaviors in differing cultures.[64] Nevertheless, it is probably safe to assume that a lack of recognition of a significant loss, an extreme reaction far in excess of normative cultural expectations, and a lack of movement through the grief process can be considered to indicate difficulty in resolving the loss, which we label exceptional grief.

The pioneering work in describing distortions of the typical phases of grief resolution was done by Erich Lindemann. In his study, Lindemann describes several manifestations of unsuccessful grief work.[65] Since Lindemann's work was published in 1944 others have contributed to both the symptomatic and theoretical perspectives of unresolved bereavement. The following is a compilation of typical manifestations of unresolved grief.

Denial. Probably one of the most common forms of an exceptional grief reaction is denial. In situations where the individual does not allow him or herself to grieve the feelings and images involving the loss are repressed. The factors that influence the individual's decision to repress his or her grief may be external or internal in origin. Internal processes that inhibit open grieving may be based on the desire to be strong for others who are grieving, or perhaps on earlier resolutions not to express feelings of sorrow due to a traumatic experience.

An example of such a resolution is a young man who told me of a boyhood experience in which he was forced by his father to skin and clean his pet rabbit who had died because, said the father, "we don't waste food in this house." The experience was so traumatic for the young boy that as an adult he often denies his feelings of sadness and grief. Robert Jay Lifton uses the term "psychic numbing" to describe the inability of the individual to meaningfully incorporate the information (death) into his symbolic framework. "Psychic numbing refers to an incapacity to feel or to confront certain kinds of experiences, due to the blocking or absences of inner forms or imagery that can connect with such experience."[66]

Lifton states that the impact of death, when judged to be intolerable in its destructiveness of all meaning in life, is severed from all thinking and feeling:

> To say that emotion is lost while cognition is retained is more or less true, but does not really capture what the mind is experiencing. What is more basic is the self's being severed from its own history; from its grounding in such psychic forms as caring for others, communal involvement, and other ultimate values.[67]

By numbing oneself to what are perceived as shattering events, the individual manages to preserve his or her integrity; a sense of personal organization. But the cost of this numbing is exceedingly high. Denying the emotional impact of the loss of a loved person impairs the individual's vitality. The very things that mean life, such as spontaneity, open and emotionally satisfying relationships, and a sense of wholeness, must be sacrificed in order for the individual to numb himself to the awful reality of death. Thus the person stops feeling in order to survive. Ironically, the flattened emotions that result contribute to the characterization of that person as a member of the living dead. In order to survive, one must kill his or her feelings.

Lifton, in his studies of Hiroshima victims, described their numbness as so powerful that it became a permanent part of their personalities.[68] In that particular situation, the nuclear holocaust had so traumatized the entire community as to make the recovery process difficult to achieve. In the case of the individual griever, he or she may be intellectually aware of not functioning as a complete person, or the social environment may react to his or her denial of emotional involvement in the loss in ways that encourage the individual to seek help with resolving the grief.

Barry presents case material of individuals who had not fully acknowledged their grief.[69] One patient sought treatment for psychosomatic ailments, another because of difficulties in social interactions, and the third because of persistent dysphoria. All of these cases involved individuals who denied the emotional impact of their loss through death of a significant other, and reported having no feelings about the loss. The awareness that they were not functioning in appropriate ways had led them to seek professional help. However, few of them were aware that the locus of their problem lay in a morbid reaction to grief when they presented themselves for therapy. In the following case history, the man who presented himself for therapy complained of dysphoric feelings, although he was a noted success in his chosen profession, was surrounded by luxurious possessions, and would generally be considered a "success" by standards of contemporary American society. Barry describes the interaction that took place during his initial interview:

> His demeanor was one of aloof arrogance and he seemed determined to keep others at a distance. When asked how it was that he grew up in an orphanage, he replied impatiently that it was because his parents had both died when he was six years

old. He resisted answering questions about what happened to his parents, saying that "all that ancient history couldn't have anything to do with the way I feel now." The question was pressed. He finally answered in a matter of fact tone that his father had become psychotic, had shot and killed the mother, and had then committed suicide. I was completely taken aback and asked lamely, "Who told you about this?" He glared at me. "Nobody had to tell me; I was in the room when it happened."

Out of my shock and sympathy I said with deep feeling, "You poor guy." At this he literally catapulted out of his chair on to the floor, sobbing convulsively, and I found myself sitting on the floor beside him, holding him in my arms. In the next half hour he alternately wept uncontrollably and apologized for his childishness. Later he told me that after his parents' death, the surviving relatives had been so shocked and horrified at this terrible scandal that they could not seem to bear to be around him. After numerous shiftings from one home to another he was finally placed in the orphanage. This is where he had chosen to begin his story.

He had never allowed himself to weep, grieve, or even think about his loss before.[70]

The delay of grief reaction may last a lifetime, or only a few moments until the mind can incorporate the information that the loss has taken place. In cases of natural disasters such as floods or tornadoes, this numbing may last only until it is "safe" for the individual to release his feelings. Often there are release mechanisms which serve to trigger the suppressed grief. For example, discovering an object that is strongly linked to the image of the dead person, or emotion-triggering music may bring about the release of pent-up feelings.

Anniversary Reactions. Another source of renewed grief may be the anniversary date of the loss. Bornstein and Clayton, in a study of ninety-two widows and widowers, report that 67 percent described a grieving reaction on the anniversary of the death of their spouse.[71] Anniversary reactions may also serve to release feelings that were denied at the time of loss, such as anger at being deserted. Anniversary reactions may also take place when the griever reaches the age at which the person died. Lindemann, among others, speaks of the survivors' belief that they would live to be no older than the deceased, and reports that they can manifest emotional turmoil during the year that matched the age of the deceased person.[72]

Thinking that they are fated to die at the same age as the deceased, these people may feel a sense of impending doom or manifest somatic complaints at the anniversary of the death of a significant person. Anniversary reactions usually refer to some chronological factor that exacerbates an unresolved grief. It is quite possible that the recurrence of social situations which were an important part of the relationship may also trigger a grief reaction. The return to a memory-laden place, or a social gathering that was important to the dyad may foster the same kinds of grief reactions as those linked to an important date.

Ambivalent Reactions. Being unable to resolve grief may also be due to ambivalent reactions to the death of a loved one. If the individual had both love and hate feelings for the other person when he was alive, then those feelings will often continue after death. The grieving process then becomes confused, as the individual is both sad and glad that the other is dead. Often feelings of hatred for the loved one are unacceptable to the person, and so they must be denied. The feelings of sadness are also mixed with unacceptable feelings of satisfaction ("He finally got what he deserved") or anger ("She left me all alone"). Guilt may now become a part of the grief, and the person may seek some form of self-punishment for the unacceptable feelings. Verwoerdt speaks of this process as hostile identification, which may manifest itself as an unhealthy identification with the deceased in the form of taking on symptoms of the deceased's illness.[73]

Identifying with the Deceased. The griever manifests the symptoms or problems which are the same as those of the deceased prior to death. This may be an attempt to keep the deceased with the survivor. Instead of successfully completing the grieving process, the individual keeps the lost one "alive" by acquiring the symptoms that the deceased person manifested prior to death or by developing a problem which was a significant part of the character of the deceased person. DeVaul and Zisook describe a patient who never drank alcohol but became an alcoholic after the death of her alcoholic husband.[74] The acquisition of symptoms belonging to the last illness of the deceased, as described above in depth, was also noted by Lindemann.[75] Psychsomatically based disease such as asthma, rheumatoid arthritis, and colitis may also be aggravated by suppressed grief.

Lindemann lists several other distortions of behavior that manifest themselves in cases of unresolved grief: an overactivity *without a sense of loss* wherein the person's psychic numbing process is compensated by a hysteric "sense of well-being and zest," may be displayed.[76] *Alterations in relationship to friends and relatives* occur as the individual continues to defend against emotional involvement with the external world. *Furious hostility against specific persons* allows a vent of the pent-up anger which may be a basic part of the grieving process. This, Lindemann points out, may often be directed against hospital staff and doctors. We should also be aware, however, that "furious hostility" may not always be a morbid grief reaction, but may be appropriate anger at incompetent or inconsiderate care of the deceased. As was pointed out in the last chapter, many societies provide through ritualistic behavior a means for the venting of anger in socially acceptable ways. Where there is no way of releasing this anger, it may take the form of extreme anger at someone who can be blamed as a cause of the death.

The state of denial which reaches the point that the individual becomes psychically numbed to the trauma of the loss is described by Lindemann as state of affect *resembling wooden pictures*. The person appears totally without feelings. The individual fears the manifestation of any emotions as a result of the immense repression of strong feelings around the loss, and thus supresses all displays of affect. Also Lindemann notes that a *lasting loss of patterns of social interaction* may occur. The individual is unable to reorganize his symbolic world, and therefore cannot continue to interact meaningfully with those who were a part of his world prior to the loss. In other words, the inability to work through the grief process has left the individual unable to continue previous patterns of interaction. The person is stuck in the second phase of grief, unable to reconnect with the external world. Occasionally, when the guilt and need for self-punishment are unresolved, the person will engage in behaviors that are *detrimental to his or her own social and economic existence*. For example, individuals manifesting this morbid grief reaction may start spending money with reckless abandon. In extreme cases, this takes the form of *agitated depression* which may lead to suicide.

Mummification. Another more morbid grief reaction described by Gorer is one of mummification.[77] In this case the griever preserves a part of the house and the objects contained in it exactly as it was at the time of death, as if expecting the deceased to return at any moment. Rituals may develop around the daily activities involved in keeping things as they were, such as laying out clothes to be worn, displaying fresh flowers, and cleaning and care-taking of the area—activities that can take on a sacred air. Gorer contends that these rituals of unresolved grief develop as maladap-tations in a ritualless society. The lack of grieving rituals, especially those in a religious context, leave people to their own devices. The morbid reactions of mummification may be unhealthy attempts by individuals to create their own forms of mourning ritual.

In the above descriptions we see examples of the grieving process going awry; of people getting stuck at some particular phase of the grief work. There are two factors in this process which have been touched upon but need further clarification: First, the social environment may do much to facilitate the grief process and thereby improve the chances of a successful resolution. Many societies provide for the grief process by imposing behaviors upon mourners, and provide rituals for the acting out of the grief. Con-versely, societies may also act in such ways as to encourage the individual not to successfully complete grief work. Two examples of this in the contemporary United States would be the emphasis upon grief as a private experience and the reinforcement of denial by the current mourning customs which serve to mask the reality of the loss. The second factor to be taken into account is the psycho-logical makeup of the individual. The individual who is just able to cope with daily living may find the experience of grief too much of a burden for his or her fragile psyche. Obviously, the psychologi-cal well-being of the individual at the time of the onslaught of grief is going to be a factor in his or her ability to adequately cope with the grieving process.

Pseudo-Resolution: A Special Case of Exceptional Grief. Albert and Bar-bara Cain present us with some startling case histories involving families who sought to replace a dead child with another.[78] Their study included cases of disturbed children whose parents conceived the child with the specific intention of replacing another tragically lost child. As one might suspect, the parents had had severe grief reactions at the time of the death of their former child. At the greatest intensity of their despair, the idea of having another child to replace the dead one appeared to offer a possible resolution.

The idealized image of the dead child came to dominate the life of the replacement child. The replacement "was born into a world of mourning, of apathetic withdrawn parents; a world fo-cused on the past and literally worshiping the image of the dead."[79] The new child found himself in a world where he was constantly compared to a hyper-idealized image of the dead child—a perfect ghost. While the living child was unable to achieve recognition for his own uniqueness, he also lived in a world of fear for his own well-being. Normal parental concerns over the health and safety of the child were magnified to phobic proportions because the parents feared losing this child as they had an earlier one. The children, presented at a child guidance center for evaluation, all showed signs of fearfulness and vulnerability. All were convinced that they would die as children, and some exhibited physical symptoms similar to those present in the dead child. The children had internalized the parents' derogatory comparisons of themselves with the dead child, and saw themselves as never measuring up to the deceased sibling.

The parents in this situation had on the surface manifested a successful grieving process, but in fact were exhibiting pseudo-resolution. While appearing to move through the third phase of the grieving process by having another child, in fact they were creating a new version of the old world. What appeared to be progress was really an attempt to use the future to hold on to the past. Again we see the importance of the symbolic meanings placed upon behaviors by the individual. The Cains point out that the reinvestment of emotional energies in new objects may have negative consequences if the grief has not been adequately resolved. Bereaved parents who continue to work as volunteers in the wards where their children died may often be tragically trapped in the grieving process.

The pseudo-resolution of grief may be fostered in a society that is uncomfortable with grief, and seeks to resolve the process as soon as possible. It is noteworthy that several of the parents in the Cain study reported that their doctors suggested that they have another child, even though they themselves had decided not to have any more. In these cases, society was offering a way out of the grieving process that in reality turned out to be an unhealthy way of coping with grief.

While this manifestation of pseudo-resolution is not a common one, the hyper-idealization of the deceased is a common theme in grief work. The clinical example of replacing a child is a morbid reaction to the grieving for a lost child. It is useful, however, in pointing out the vulnerability of the griever to derailment in the grief process, and the power of the external world to impose itself upon the disorganized symbolic world of the griever.

Anticipatory Grief

As modern medicine becomes more exact, it is becoming more commonplace for people to know of impending death. Since death can be anticipated, grief ensues before the death has occurred. Anticipatory grief, a term first used by Lindemann, refers to *the emotional reaction which occurs before an expected loss*. While retaining many of the characteristics of the typical grief reaction after a loss, anticipatory grief has some unique characteristics that are worthy of separate discussion.

As was evident in our exploration of the grief process, many factors enter into determining the nature of one's grief reaction. The individual's personality, including his emotional well-being, the nature of the relationship, the appropriate/inappropriate nature of the loss, and the social reality in which the loss takes place are some of the contributing factors. In anticipatory grief all of these factors are present, but the nature of their relationship to anticipatory grief differs from that of a typical grief reaction. In this section, we will examine anticipatory grief in terms of the model of the grieving process developed in the last chapter, and consider the differences and similarities that exist in both typical and anticipatory grief.

Like typical grief, the initial phase of anticipatory grief involves the reaction to the news of the impending loss. When the patient is diagnosed as "terminal," the others involved in relationships with the patient may experience the shock of loss, and yet it may be tempered with hope. This is one of the subtle differences that makes anticipatory grief unique. The patient has not yet died, allowing room for hope. While the descriptions of usual grief spoke of the depths of desolation felt by the grievers, anticipatory grief may resemble more of an emotional roller coaster, depending upon the type of illness involved. Experiences of physical degeneration, a worsening of symptoms, or more heroic medical measures may be interspersed with remissions, good days, and seeming progress toward health.

Doris Lund, in her story of her son's fight against leukemia, describes both the shock and the hope of entering anticipatory grief:

> A tremendous splash split the world. The bolt entered the top of my skull as I got the message. Eric had leukemia. It was

something happening right this minute in his bones. We'd been struck. It was ours.

Our first goal, then, was remission. I didn't know exactly just what a remission was. But I'd read enough to know it was a good period of time, maybe lasting for weeks or months, when the disease was under control and retreated for awhile. In remission you could live your life again.[80]

This roller coaster effect inhibits the grieving process by aiding in what might be considered to be denial. This is an interesting point that bears further scrutiny. One cannot deny what might occur. In other words, the loss is anticipated; but it has not occurred, and there is a chance, however small, that it might not occur. While the individual is integrating the anticipated loss into his or her awareness, he or she is also becoming aware that the loss is not a *fait accompli*. The reality of the situation is that the death is expected, but exactly when it will take place is not known. It is entirely possible that others may die before the person designated as "terminal." For, in fact, we all are terminal. This indefinite nature of the information complicates the grieving process, as it discourages the acceptance of the impending loss.

As a result, the social context within which one is existing has an influence on anticipatory grief. American culture rejects a fatalistic approach to life, and many aspects of life are seen as solvable problems in American society. Does one move the family to a foreign country to try a new cure? Will the family be impoverished while trying exotic new treatments? Should experimental drugs be tried? If death itself is seen as problematic, then the responsible person must bear the guilt for not having tried everything in order to save the patient's life. Guilt may arise out of concern as to whether or not one did everything possible to solve the problem of death.

Most obviously, as with the typical grief reaction, sadness and anger are present in the initial stage of anticipatory grief. The anger may be directed at the patient who is deserting the griever. Also, it may take the form of impatience at the suffering one must endure. Like the pragmatic death-as-a-problem definition in American society, so too suffering has been defined as a waste of time; a needless imposition on one's life. Many anticipatory grief reactions may include a number of ambivalent feelings: sorrow over the possible loss, anger, impatience (a wish that it would end), and even thoughts as to how one will live on after the death.

Some of these thoughts may naturally cause feelings of guilt in the griever.

The second phase of grief, disorganization and reorganization, is the phase the person will most typically stay in during anticipatory grief. Although the old symbolic patterns of organization still must be maintained, they are not going to last. Becker claims that although we delude ourselves into assuming that things will last forever, that death will not touch us, the diagnosis of terminality brings us back face-to-face with the reality of death, a reality that we have sought to deny.[81] Limitless time now becomes limited, and perhaps this is the basis for all anticipatory grief. But unlike the typical griever, the anticipatory griever does not totally abandon the old symbolic constructs and build a new image of the world as long as the dying person lives. Sometimes this ambiguous status is too much for the person to maintain, and so he or she continues to resolve the grief, even though the dying person is still alive. Lindemann describes a pattern of resolved anticipatory grief following World War II. Some returning soldiers found that their wives had never expected them to survive the war, and now, having successfully grieved, no longer loved them.[82]

Glick and his colleagues cautioned against encouraging the grief process among those experiencing anticipatory grief, arguing that this can only be done by withdrawing from the terminal person.[83] This, in turn, may lead to feelings of guilt at a later time. Also, it is entirely appropriate for the individual to remain in a state of non-resolution; for, in fact, the entire matter has not yet resolved itself in death.

The person experiencing anticipatory grief may find that he or she is caught between meeting his or her needs, such as finding new love objects, and remaining faithful to the old. During anticipatory grief one may feel that time spent away from the dying person is somehow "stolen." Since the time left is limited, shouldn't as much time as possible be spent with a terminal patient? How much time can be taken away from other obligations, other roles? Again we find ourselves facing questions to which there are, in our society, no cut and dried answers.

Successful anticipatory grieving does not mean moving ahead to readjustment and recovery. Successful anticipatory grief means being aware of the disorganization that is taking place and living with it. Within the confines of current American social reality, this is a difficult position to be in. Our society favors problem solving, progress, and a mastery over the world. To be involved in anticipatory grief means to acknowledge and live with death; to acknowledge one's inability to master it, and one's ultimate helpless position in the world. Understandably, Americans feel ill-equipped to deal with such a traumatic situation.

Although the prolonged period of anticipatory grief may be a very difficult experience for the individual to go through, there are some beneficial aspects that should be noted. Because the loss has not yet occurred, the anticipatory grief period may provide an opportunity for resolution of past interpersonal issues and a reorientation can be begun with the approval of the dying person.[84] There have been cases of divorce and marriage taking place with the understanding of the first spouse, who was terminally ill with a debilitating disease. A man who was permanently hospitalized could thus see his wife and child taken care of, and presumably he could draw some pleasure from this. While this case may illustrate a particularly heroic form of action, other people may find that preparatory grieving provides the time needed to resolve the questions of existential grief. Both existential and reactive grief may be worked through on a partial basis as the individual uses the time of anticipatory grief to prepare to deal with the expected loss.

Rando interviewed parents whose children had died from cancer, and suggests that there is an optimum length of anticipatory grief (six to eighteen months). A shorter period did not give parents enough time to prepare for the loss, and a longer period had a debilitating effect on them. The longer the illness, the greater, the anger and the number of atypical responses found among the sample in her study.[85]

Just as typical grief can be physically debilitating, so it is with anticipatory grief. One can find that the constant emergencies and the inexorable diminishing of life in a loved one take their toll. A long-term anticipatory grieving period may exacerbate the negative aspects of the relationship. It may also affect other relationships, which may tend to be ignored because of the closeness of the impending loss.

One issue in the existing literature concerns whether or not anticipatory grief allows the individual to adjust better to the actual loss when it does occur. Clayton reports that having experienced anticipatory grief did not lead her respondents to a more satisfactory resolution after the death, but that a possible correlation existed between those experiencing anticipatory grief and post-death depression.[86] However, it should be noted that those experiencing depression symptoms prior to death may have been depressed prior to anticipatory grief, and hence the outcome is not the result of anticipatory grief as much as a personality trait unrelated to the crisis itself. Others have reported that anticipatory grief aids in the resolution of the grief. Glick, Weiss, and Parkes report that anticipation of the husband's death among their sample of widows is "one of the most important determinants of the adequacy of recovery."[87] They agree with Clayton's findings, stating the widows in their sample who were most upset by their husband's illness tended to be the most upset at his death. Still, 94 percent of those who anticipated their husbands' deaths moved toward reorganization, as compared to only 77 percent of those who had not anticipated the death. Glick and his colleagues do not attribute the successful reorganization among those who had anticipated their loss to successful anticipatory grieving or to an ability to free themselves from the old relationships, but see the process of recovery from anticipated and unanticipated loss as being different from each other:

> In the anticipated death, there has been a period preceding the death during which the wife and husband together gradually have given up hope as they were progressively failed by therapies and regimes. The death, when it came, was traumatic, but its cause was understood. But when the death happened unexpectedly there might be no such sense of the death having resulted from what had become a familiar, if hated, process. Now the widow might not know what to feel.[88]

Our theoretical perspective would predict that those experiencing anticipatory grief would be better able to reorganize their lives following the loss. The partial grieving could allow a preparation for the inevitable collapse of the old symbolic organization. While the intensity of the grief may not be determined by having anticipated the loss, the eventual reorganization and resolution should benefit if the anticipatory grief has been used to begin tentatively to reorganize the individual's symbolic construct. Clinical researchers speak of the guilt and ambivalence present during anticipatory grief. These studies, although focusing on the pathological, indicate that during anticipatory grief the individual is beginning the process of integrating the expected loss into his or her symbolic organization. This would indicate that anticipatory grief may serve to prepare the individual for the loss in some ways. This is not meant to ameliorate or lessen the burden of anticipatory grief. The stress, both physical and emotional, of a long grieving over an expected loss may take a terrible toll on the individual. However, it is important to realize that vital processes may be at work during that time, which may be beneficial in the final resolution and acceptance of the loss.

One of the emotions present at the end of anticipatory grief, the time of death, is a feeling of relief. In a sense, the anticipated loss can be anticlimactic. Something inevitable yet so long battled, perhaps denied to some degree, and most often experienced through sadness and despair, has finally occurred. One victim of such a struggle against inexorable death experienced a tremendous surge of energy after the loss finally took place, which lasted for more than a day. This was followed by an extended period of grieving. This tremendous release of energy, so bound up in months of anticipatory grief, describes the very nature of the anticipatory grief process, as it binds the individual through sorrow to an event that has yet to occur.

Although exceptional and anticipatory grief are two very different aspects of grief, they involve similar factors. They both involve the person who has not completed the grieving process. In exceptional reactions, we see that the individual becomes fixated at some point in the grieving process, which inhibits the successful resolution of the loss. In anticipatory grief, the individual is in a state of emotional limbo, unable to resolve the loss because it has not yet occurred, and unable to avoid the authoritative diagnosis that the death will occur. Where therapeutic intervention may be used to aid the exceptional griever to continue to move through the grieving process, this would not be beneficial to the person in anticipatory grief, as it might lead to a premature withdrawal from the dying person.

The Mid-Life Crisis: A Form of Anticipatory Grief. Recent literature has focused on the concept of a mid-life crisis, that point at which the individual must come to grips with the finiteness of his or her life.[89] Elliott Jacques, writing some years prior to the recent studies, describes the role of death in the mid-life crisis. Jacques contends that this crisis arises out of the knowledge that one has reached a point where growing up ceases, and growing old begins. The individual becomes aware that life is no longer an infinitude of opportunities. Rather, the realization is that one has made his or her bed, and now must sleep in it.

Death lies ahead. No longer is it easily avoided, no longer is it so far off in the future as to be unseen. Now, as family and friends die, the realization that one cannot go on forever, that the individual is what he or she is, are issues to be reckoned with. The reality of distinct and unavoidable death demands to be acknowledged. And in acknowledging death, perhaps for the first time, the reality of death means accepting the reality of one's life. No longer is life infinite, no longer can one start all over; the reality of what one has made out of life must be accepted and lived with. This may mean dealing with some truths about oneself which have been denied in the past.

As a clinical example of the mid-life crisis, I treated a couple in therapy whose marriage of many years (the children were grown and married) was suddenly in crisis due to the husband's announcement of his deep marital unhappiness. When pressed, he admitted he had almost always been unhappy in the relationship. His recent awareness of his loss of youth and the inevitability of old age made the situation now seem desperate. What had been a familiar misery had been answered by telling himself that "some day things will get better." Now time was running out, and he was realizing that his time was not infinite, that in fact he soon would be growing old.

I have known of other cases that have involved the sudden rejection of a lifestyle of many years in an attempt to recapture youth through more youthful clothes, cars, and lovers. In the contemporary United States, this is much more acceptable behavior on the part of the male than the female. At the base of the behavior is a reaction to death. Sometimes, as above, it is an effort to avoid aging and death by trying to become young again. Other times it takes the form of a depression which clinically may be seen as a reaction to loss; a loss of youth, of opportunities, of endless life.

The working through of this particular form of anticipatory grief can, as most grieving processes, serve as a growing experience. The person can learn to accept the realities of his or her life, and to become more comfortable with himself or herself. This may entail the rejection of some now unrealistic goals. It may mean a reassessment of one's life, as the internal reorganization demands a new perspective. And the realization of the finiteness of life can lead to a new respect for the days that are left, and the placement of higher value on each one of them.

The adaptational value of anticipatory grief has not been researched in great depth. Information concerning the process and possible outcomes of anticipatory grief could aid in better preparing people to work through the experience of expected loss in such ways as to benefit the total grieving process and its final resolution.

The lack of a social structure within which mourning can take place and the grief process successfully worked through can contribute to the sense of helplessness the individual experiences. Overwhelmed by grief, struggling to reorganize his thinking, the mourner finds that his social world offers no direction, no recognition of his plight. There are few expected behaviors that serve to promote grief work. Mourning behavior norms may provide structures within which the grief-stricken can own up to their feelings and acknowledge the loss. A lack of such social structures within contemporary American society forces the individual to cope alone as best he or she can with grief.

Notes

1. Edmund H. Volkart and Stanley T. Michael, "Bereavement and Mental Health," in Alexander H. Leighton, et al., eds., *Explorations in Social Psychiatry* (New York: Basic Books, 1957), pp. 281–307.

2. John Bowlby, *Attachment and Loss*, Vol. I (1969), Vol. II (1973), Vol. III (1980) (New York: Basic Books); also, "The Process of Mourning," *The International Journal of Psycho-Analysis* 42, Parts 4–5 (1961):331.

3. Geoffrey Gorer, *Death, Grief and Mourning* Garden City, N.Y.: Doubleday, 1965, pp. 121–122.

4. Avery D. Weisman, *On Dying and Denying* (New York: Behavioral Publications, 1972).

5. Robert Fulton, "Death, Grief, and Social Recuperation," *Omega*, 1, no. 1 (1970): p. 27.

6. Robert Jay Lifton, "The Sense of Immortality: On Death and the Continuity of Life," in Robert Fulton, ed., *Death and Identity* (Bowie, Md.: The Charles Press, 1976), pp. 19–28, and *The Broken Connection* (New York: Simon & Schuster, 1979), Chapter 15.

7. Erik Erikson, *Childhood and Society* (New York: Norton, 1950), and *Identity: Youth and Crisis* (New York: Norton, 1968).

8. Lifton, *The Broken Connection*, p. 54.

9. Ibid., p. 57.

10. Lifton, "The Sense of Immortality," p. 27.

11. Ibid.

12. Ernest Becker, *The Denial of Death* (New York: The Free Press, 1973).

13. Gorer.

14. Bowlby, "The Process of Mourning," p. 331.

15. Paul C. Rosenblatt, *Bitter, Bitter Tears* (Minneapolis: University of Minnesota Press, 1983), p. 155.

16. C. S. Lewis, *A Grief Observed* (New York: Bantam, 1976), p. 69.

17. J. Fischoff and N. O'Brien, "After the Child Dies," *The Journal of Pediatrics* 88, no. 1 (1976):142.

18. Ibid., p. 142.

19. Bowlby, p. 328–331.

20. James R. Averill, "Grief: Its Nature and Significance," *Psychological Bulletin,* Vol. 70, 1968, pp. 721–748.

21. Bowlby, p. 333.

22. Fischoff and O'Brien, p. 141.

23. Bowlby, p. 333.

24. Fischoff and O'Brien, pp. 141, 142.

25. Erich Lindemann, "Symptomatology and Management of Acute Grief," in Robert Fulton, ed., *Death and Identity,* p. 212.

26. Jane Rowe, et al., "Follow-up of Families Who Experience a Perinatal Death," *Pediatrics,* Vol. 62(2), August 1978, p. 167.

27. Edgar Allan Poe, "The Raven," in *The Complete Works of Edgar Allan Poe* (New York: Crowell, 1902), pp. 94–100.

28. Lindemann, p. 212.

29. Fischoff and O'Brien, p. 142.

30. Lindemann, p. 212.

31. Bowlby, p. 336.

32. Peter Marris, *Widows and Their Families* (London: Routledge and Kegan Paul, 1958), p. 88.

33. Fischoff and O'Brien, pp. 141–142.

34. Lewis, pp. 70–71.

35. Ira O. Glick, Robert S. Weiss, and C. Murray Parkes, *The First Year of Bereavement* (New York: Wiley, 1974).

36. Lindemann, pp. 210–221.

37. Lewis, p. 1.

38. Fischoff and O'Brien, p. 141.

39. Marris, p. 34.

40. Fischoff and O'Brien, p. 146.

41. Bertha Simos, *A Time to Grieve* (New York: Family Services, 1979), p. 45.

42. Margaret S. Miles and Alice S. Demi, "Toward the Development of a Theory of Bereavement Guilt," *Omega* 14, no. 4 (1983–84):299–314.

43. Emile Durkheim, *The Elementary Forms of the Religious Life* (New York: Collier, 1961), p. 443.

44. Howard Becker, *The Outsiders* (New York: The Free Press, 1963).

45. Thomas J. Scheff, "Labeling, Emotion, and Individual Change," in Thomas J. Scheff, ed., *Labeling Madness* (Englewood Cliffs, N.J.: Prentice-Hall, 1975), p. 80.

46. Ibid.

47. Ibid., p. 83.

48. Ibid., pp. 82–84.

49. Lois Pratt, "Business Temporal Norms and Bereavement Behavior," *American Sociological Review* 46, no. 3 (1981):317–333.

50. Marris, p. 92.

51. Phillippe Aries, "The Reversal of Death," *American Quarterly* 26 (1974):536–560.

52. Ibid.

53. Ibid., p. 548.

54. Jeanne Quint Benoliel, "Assessments of Loss and Grief," *Journal of Thanatology* 1 (1971):189.

55. Glenn M. Vernon, *The Sociology of Death* (New York: The Ronald Press, 1970), pp. 166–167.

56. Gorer, pp. 76–80. See also Maurice Lamm, *The Jewish Way in Death and Mourning* (New York: Jonathan David, 1969).

57. Paul N. Rosenblatt, et al., *Grief and Mourning in Cross-Cultural Perspective* (New Haven: Human Relations Area Files Press, 1976).

58. Beverly Raphael, *The Anatomy of Bereavement* (New York: Basic Books, 1983), p. 47.

59. Bowlby, p. 332.

60. Lorraine D. Siggins, "Mourning: A Critical Survey of the Literature," *International Journal of PsychoAnalysis* 47, Parts 14–25 (1966):268.

61. Richard A. DeVaul and Sidney Zisook, "Unresolved Grief," *Postgraduate Medicine* 59, no. 5 (1976):267.

62. Thomas C. Welu, "Presenting Pathological Bereavement," in Bernard Schoenberg, et al., eds., *Bereavement: Its Psychosocial Aspects* (New York: Columbia University Press, 1975), pp. 147–148.

63. Siggins.

64. Durkheim, pp. 442–449; Rosenblatt.

65. Lindemann, pp. 215–221.

66. Lifton, "The Sense of Immortality," p. 21.

67. Lifton, *The Broken Connection*, p. 175.

68. Ibid.
69. Maurice J. Barry, "The Prolonged Grief Reaction," Mayo Clinic *Proceedings* 48 (1973):329–335.
70. Ibid., p. 335.
71. Philipp E. Bornstein and Paula Clayton, "The Anniversary Reaction," *Diseases of the Nervous System* 33 (1972):470–472.
72. Lindemann, pp. 215–219.
73. Adrian Verwoerdt, *Clinical Geropsychiatry* (Baltimore: Williams and Wilkins, 1976), p. 75.
74. DeVaul and Zisook.
75. Lindemann, p. 216.
76. Ibid.
77. Gorer. pp. 85–87.
78. Albert Cain and Barbara Cain, "On Replacing a Dead Child," *Journal of the American Academy of Child Psychiatry* 3 (1964):443–456.
79. Ibid., p. 445.
80. Doris Lund, *Eric* (New York: Dell, 1974), pp. 11–12.
81. Becker. pp. 47–66.
82. Lindemann, pp. 220–221.
83. Glick et al., p. 294.
84. Kathy Charmaz, *The Social Reality of Death* (Reading, Mass.: Addison-Wesley, 1980), p. 286.
85. Therese A. Rando, "An Investigation of Grief and Adaptation in Parents Whose Children Have Died from Cancer," *Journal of Pediatric Psychology*, 8, no. 1 (1983):3–20.
86. Paula J. Clayton et al., "Anticipatory Grief and Widowhood," *British Journal of Psychiatry* 122 (1973):47–51.
87. Glick, et al., p. 256.
88. Ibid.
89. Elliott Jaques, "Death and the Mid-Life Crisis," *International Journal of Psychoanalysis* 46 (1965):502–514.

CHAPTER SIX

Survivors of Death

T HROUGH OUR EXAMINATION of the grief process, we have been able to develop an understanding of the psychological ramifications of death. In discussing mourning, we examined contemporary American society's response to loss, including its normative expectations of the bereaved. In this chapter we will examine yet another dimension of bereavement—its social and psychological effects upon categories of people: children, the widowed, the family, and people whose loved ones commit suicide.

Children as Survivors

As we have already seen, children conceive of death very differently than do adults. The image of death that a child holds is a product of his or her experiences with death, the information available about death, and his or her level of cognitive development. When a death occurs, the child may have to reconcile his or her understanding of death as an abstraction with the reality of a loss of a loved person. For example, a child may conceive of death as a state that is similar to sleeping. When the child realizes that the dead do not wake up, then death must be redefined by the child as a permanent state. When someone who was a source of need fulfillment for the child dies, not only does the child have to change his or her understanding of what death is, he or she also has to cope with the loss of a love object. "Only in childhood can death deprive an individual of so much opportunity to love and face him with so difficult a task of adaptation."[1] The child is often handicapped by an immature reasoning ability as well as little experience in loss management. Thus, in terms of the ability to cope with the situation, the experience of the death of a significant person is generally expected to be more difficult for children than for adults.

While the child's vulnerability to trauma as a result of the death of a loved person is obvious, this does not mean that every child who experiences the loss of a family member is somehow damaged for life. There are many intervening variables which can influence the outcome of bereavement. Furman lists three factors that affect the child's ability to cope with loss: (1) the child's mental ability to deal with loss, (2) the role that the dead person played in the child's life, and (3) the circumstances surrounding the loss and the grieving process which follows.[2]

Let us examine each of Furman's factors in more detail: The child's mental abilities include both cognitive and emotional development. On a cognitive level, it is difficult for a child who has not yet fully developed the ability to understand abstract concepts such as death to integrate the full meaning of death. Generally, the younger the child, the more difficult the process of grieving. The young child is vulnerable to the loss of loved ones, especially his or her mother. The process of childhood development can be thought of as a differentiating of self from parents. When death interrupts this process, bringing it to an early end, the child must go through the grief process in order to resolve successfully the trauma of loss. The importance of the loss cannot be underestimated, especially in the younger child. The older child is beginning to have his or her emotional needs met from diverse sources, such as peers, teachers, and extended family members. He or she is also developing a sense of mastery, or control, over the environment. But the younger child is still dependent upon parents (or parent figures) for all of his needs, both physical and emotional. Further, the younger child lacks the ability to manipulate his environment in order to find new sources of love and nurturance. For these reasons, the younger the child, the greater the potential for damage by the loss of a parent to death.

Without the ability to comprehend death fully, the child may acknowledge the parent's death, and yet still imply living attributes to the deceased. Freud described this in the grieving of a ten-year-old boy, who said, "I know Father's dead, but what I can't understand is why he doesn't come home for dinner."[3] From a psychological perspective, the child may have been defending against the strong emotions connected with the loss. Lopez and Kliman describe a four-year-old, presented for psychological treatment because of her exceptional grief reactions following her mother's suicide, as saying, "I know about my Mommy. Don't talk about her. I get scared."[4] Therapist Jill Miller points out that in children the grieving process has a different aim than it does in adults. While adults seek to reorganize their lives without the dead person, the child often seeks "to avoid the acceptance of the reality and emotional meaning of the death and maintain in a more internal form the relationship that has been ended in external reality."[5] In Miller's description of the psychodynamics of children's resistance to grief work, we can see that for the child to work through the loss means to give up the internalized image of the dead person, which is, in a sense, all that the child has left.

Magical thinking, whereby the child believes his or her thoughts can influence the external world, may play an important part in the child's adaptation to loss. For example, a woman who as an infant wished that her abusive father would go away suffered from guilt into adulthood because she felt that she had somehow caused his desertion of her and her mother.[6] Finally, and perhaps most obviously, the child who somehow either lacks enough resiliency or who has been subjected to other traumas prior to the death may have a more difficult time resolving the loss of a significant person, because past traumas have left the child with depleted emotional resources for coping with stressful events.

The role that the dead person played in the life of the child, Furman's second factor, recalls our earlier discussion of the grieving process, where it was argued that grief needs to be understood in terms of what the loss means to the survivor. A child living an existence isolated from others, with the exception of his or her nurturing mother, will most likely react more intensely to her death than will a child surrounded by many sources of love and support. Or the child may have ambivalent feelings toward the dead person, as in the case of the child and her abusive father described above. Being glad that her father was out of her life, she also felt sad for having lost him. As we saw in examining exceptional bereavement, ambivalent feelings can make the resolution of grief a more difficult process.

Finally, Furman speaks of the circumstances that surround the death as affecting the child's resolution of the loss. As we shall see when we examine the long-term effects of childhood bereavement, many factors external to the grieving child can effect the resolution of loss. Sula Wolff, in her study, *Children under Stress,* states that "the harmful effects of bereavement are more often due to its long-term social consequences and to the emotional reactions of the surviving parent than to the impact of the death itself upon the child."[7] Where the grief of the surviving parent "dominates the household," the children tend to have more difficulty in accepting the loss themselves.[8] A surviving parent's smothering and clinging to the children may make it difficult for them to reorient themselves to a world without their dead parent. Also, if the surviving parent refuses to fully accept the loss, the children may find that this hinders their own grief work. What appears to be more common is the withdrawal of the surviving parent into his or her own grief. As a result, the children feel doubly abandoned—first by the death of one parent, and then by the withdrawal of the surviving parent.

The circumstances surrounding the death itself may be an important factor in the child's coping with the loss. Accidents, which might have implicated the surviving child in some way, may be interpreted by the child as his or her fault. Younger children, with their belief in magical thinking, are particularly vulnerable to this kind of guilt. Cain, Fast, and Erickson report that often, in families where the surviving siblings were involved in the accident, there was a prohibition against discussing the accident.[9] Whenever the surviving children attempted to talk about their involvement in the accident, the parents would interrupt with reassurances and stop the child from discussing the death any more. The authors point out that the parents either believed or had been told by professionals that to let the children discuss the event would only make it linger in their minds all the more, and the best thing to do was to discourage the children from talking about it. Also, the parents were already under great emotional stress, and might have feared that the rage at their surviving children that they were suppressing might be released by further discussion of the event. Finally, Cain, Fast, and Erickson point out that the parents sought to avoid a discussion that might implicate the surviving children in the death. The last thing that they needed at this time was to acknowledge that their terrible sorrow was caused by another whom they loved dearly.

Another facet of the circumstances surrounding the loss which may affect the child's grieving process is the economic impact of the death. Many times the death of the breadwinner can plunge the family into hard times, so that the child is forced to deal with the trauma of poverty as well as grief. The family may have to move from their home. The economic situation may force the surviving parent to leave the home in order to support the family. As a result, the child may feel an additional sense of abandonment and loss with the absence of the remaining parent.

The role of the extended family and the larger community can have an impact upon the child. Having been abandoned by one parent, there is always the possibility that the other will die as well. Knowing that there are other people who will take care of the children can be reassuring. With older children who are developing social lives of their own, the support of peers and others within the community can be positive influences as the child seeks to work his or her way through the crises.

The survivor's ability to grieve successfully over the loss of a sibling is influenced by many of the factors described earlier. The nature of the sibling relationship may lead to unique kinds of problems when the child becomes enmeshed in the process of exceptional bereavement. Guilt, often embodied in sibling rivalry and jealousy, may be a factor in the survivor's reaction to death and may block resolution of the grief.[10] In some situations where younger children survive the death of a sibling, the parents may rebuke them for not seeming to be saddened by the loss, which may be interpreted by the children as an indication of their guilt in somehow causing the death.

Lacking the capacity to fully integrate adult images of death, the child may react to the news of the death of a significant person in his or her life with almost total nonchalance. It may take months or even years before the full impact of the loss is felt by the child. A research assistant of mine related her experiences with a neighbor's young child who matter-of-factly announced that her grandmother had recently died. She added that her mother and father had cried, but she hadn't. When asked about this, she simply replied, "My tears aren't ready yet." Unfortunately, this kind of behavior is often interpreted as a lack of caring, rather than being understood as a result of the child's lack of ability to fully understand what death is. To expect an adult response to death from a child is to demand more than the child is often capable of doing.

To dismiss his or her later incessant questioning or desire to discuss death with an adult is to deprive the child of an opportunity to work through the loss that has occurred.

Another effect of sibling death may be what Krell and Rabkin call "family protective maneuvers."[11] The vulnerability to death felt by the family is translated into overprotection of the surviving children. This may precipitate defensive gestures on the part of the surviving children, which may range from passive acceptance to rebellion against the overprotective actions of the parents.

An extreme reaction to the loss of a child may be a total suppression of any talk about the death. This silence, similar to what we saw in discussing accidental deaths, leaves the surviving child "haunted by something mysterious and uncertain, knowing and yet not knowing, and afraid to ask for clarification."[12] The young child may surmise that even though the death was not accidental, somehow he or she is responsible for this event which is so terrible and mysterious that no one will discuss it. There is no opportunity to share his or her own fears, doubts, and grief.

Adolescence—that intense time of biological, psychological, and social change—appears to be a time when death is not a part of the person's everyday imagery. Kastenbaum points out that the adolescent lives in the present; the past (childhood), and the future (adulthood, aging, and death) are not powerful images in the mind of the adolescent.[13] What is important is *now*. Entering a period of maximum biological energy, freed from the bonds of childhood, life is intense and the new freedoms and energies are all-powerful. Death becomes a romantic, distant image.

Wass, surveying 144 high school seniors, found that 39 percent reported that death was never talked about in their families, while 25 percent reported that the subject was brought up only when it was necessary, and then only for a short period.[14] This would indicate that the adolescent is influenced not only by his or her psychobiological constitution, but also by a social environment that denies the importance of death in life.

Where the denial of death becomes great enough to prohibit open mourning, the adolescent may choose to act out his or her grief in acts against society. Shoor and Speed report studies of adolescents involved in delinquent behavior, all of whom had recently undergone the loss of a loved person. Unable to express their grief in socially acceptable ways, the young people "acted out their tears" through delinquent behaviors.[15] Rosenblatt also raises the question as to how much of deviant behavior in our society is the product of repressed grief and mourning.[16] Perhaps, as Rosenblatt suggests, a great deal of antisocial behavior results from the aggressive, angry feelings of repressed grief.

Adult Reactions to Antecedent Childhood Bereavement

In this section, we will review the literature on childhood bereavement as it affects later life. Since the 1930s, a good number of studies have sought to establish a link between the childhood trauma of parent loss and later psychological pathology. Psychiatric illness, juvenile delinquency, schizophrenia, depression, and the inability to be intimate with one's spouse are a few of the products of childhood bereavement that have been investigated, and often the researchers claimed that childhood bereavement was directly linked to later adult pathology.[17]

More recently, however, several critical reviews of the literature have appeared which challenge the earlier studies on methodological grounds, point out the weaknesses of the studies, and as a result question their conclusions. Joseph Palumbo, reviewing such studies in the psychoanalytic literature, points out that it is fallacious to consider all experiences of parent loss as similar.[18] He goes on to point out several variables that may affect the child's experience of parental death: the cause of death (accident? lingering disease?); which parent dies (mother? stepfather?); the child's age, sex, and developmental level; the quality of the relationship that existed between the deceased and the child; prior psychological maladaptations on the part of the child; the child's understanding of the death; and the child's support system at the time of the loss.[19] Palumbo argues that what might have been an nontraumatic experience for the child may be interpreted differently by the clinical research:

> As observers, we tend to structure and select from the observed data those phenomena that have meaning to us or those with which we feel empathic. We make inferences based on our past experiences. We, unwittingly, permit our subjective responses to structure our observations so that they can fit into our preconceptions. In matters as emotion-laden as death, our feelings can interfere powerfully with our scientific stance. Our humanity is engaged by the suffering of another being, and we lose our objectivity.[20]

Other reviewers of the many empirical studies which have appeared have found that most studies are so methodologically flawed as to render the conclusions questionable at best. Crook and Eliot, reviewing more than twenty studies of adult depression and childhood bereavement, found that many investigators failed to control for such factors as parental age and social class, thus allowing their studies to be biased by such factors.[21] The authors point to several studies which controlled for such variables as age, sex, social class, and marital status, and which find no link between childhood bereavement and later depression. This is not to say that Crook and Eliot wish to dismiss childhood bereavement as a traumatic event that may possibly influence adult functioning. Rather, like Palumbo, they question the conclusion of many that childhood bereavement is so traumatic as to almost inevitably lead to adult pathologies.

Markusen and Fulton also challenge the retrospective studies of childhood bereavement, questioning the ways in which control groups were established in various studies.[22] The use of nonpsychiatric medical patients as a control group, a common practice in many studies, overlooks the known fact that many "normal" patients have illnesses that are psychosomatic in origin. The use of actuarial data, often used for comparison purposes, is biased because of the lack of information on the poor, who don't as often buy life insurance as the middle class. Further, the use of psychiatric diagnostic categories to determine who was experiencing mental illness has long been questioned as a research tool. In addition, Markusen and Fulton point out that these studies have relied heavily upon the memories of the respondents—a notoriously unreliable source of information. For example, parental desertion may be difficult to accept for both personal and social reasons. Thus, over time, it may have become easier for the respondent to speak of a parent's death, rather than admit to having been abandoned by a parent. Over a lifetime, this may be repeated so often that it becomes a "fact" in the mind of the respondent. On the basis of their evaluation of the research methodologies used in past studies, Markusen and Fulton argue that "retrospective studies have not provided a reliable answer to the question of whether early childhood bereavement is predictive of later behavior disorders."[23]

In an effort to circumvent the methodological issues raised by past studies, Bendiksen and Fulton gathered data on the behaviors of 256 subjects who had been participants in a statewide (Minnesota) study conducted when the respondents were in the ninth

grade.[24] The original data, gathered in 1954, indicated which subjects had experienced childhood loss of a parent. A control group
of 324 subjects from intact families, 264 bereaved subjects (as of
1954), and 221 subjects from families that had experienced parental
divorce or separation were initially contacted. Sixty-four percent
returned a completed questionnaire. The response rate was much
higher (70 percent) among those who were from intact homes, as
opposed to a lower (58 percent) response from those who were
either bereaved, or from a divorced or separated home. This indicates a major problem for this kind of a study: self-reported data—
especially when it concerns reporting on one's behaviors that are
not socially desirable, such as mental illness or lawbreaking—is
of low reliability. For example, the difference in response rates
of the total population may indicate a reluctance by people who
have unpleasant memories of the past to report their personal histories. The authors are aware that "various methodologic problems
plague this study," but their pioneering efforts should not be totally
dismissed.[25]

Bendiksen and Fulton argue that those who experienced childhood bereavement were more likely to have suffered from major
illnesses and emotional problems than the control group from intact
homes. The responses were similar for the respondents from divorced homes, who reported more major illnesses and emotional
problems than did the intact home control group. The data reported
for criminal behavior were not statistically significant, indicating
no differences among the three groups. One indication noted by
Bendiksen and Fulton was that children of divorce tend to fare
worse than those experiencing the death of a parent; a fact that
we shall see borne out in other subsequent investigations.

Michael Rutter, an English psychiatrist, has studied maternal
deprivation extensively.[26] His conclusions concerning the later effects of maternal parental loss are similar to the others we have
reviewed. He argues that psychopathology is not necessarily linked
to the disruption of the parent-child bond, but rather to the lack
of bonding initially. Where "discord and disharmony" surround
separation, one will find later antisocial behavior among the
children.[27] For example, Rutter points to studies which show that
children adjusted much better to parent loss when they were kept
in a homelike atmosphere, rather than being put into a cold, impersonal institution where the ever-changing staff precluded the establishment of any new bonds.[28]

Rutter's work, while restricted to maternal deprivation, reinforces the argument that parent death alone is not a determinant of later psychological or social pathology. While it may indeed bring emotional distress and vulnerability to the child, parent loss must be linked with other negative stressors in order to lead to later problems for the child. Rutter argues that what is needed is a better understanding of what is involved in successful as well as unsuccessful coping with the death of a parent. We will now examine one such study, which looks at children who have managed to cope well with life, in spite of suffering major losses.

Resiliency: Effective Coping with Childhood Bereavement

While there is a body of literature available on childhood bereavement, the vast majority focuses upon those children who are experiencing exceptional bereavement. There seems to be little material available which relates to effective coping with death on the part of children.[29] Werner and Smith, in a longitudinal study of children through their adolescence and young adulthood, examined resiliency—the ability to surmount trauma and to do so with little damage.[30] The study took place on Kauai, Hawaii, and dealt with impoverished children. While the study did not limit itself exclusively to parental or sibling death, it was one of the stressors taken into consideration. The authors asked what, if any, were the differences between the resilient children who coped well in spite of traumatic events in their lives (such as death, illness, and physical defects), and those who evidenced maladjustments?

The results of their study tend to dovetail with the findings of those cited earlier which investigated childhood bereavement. The composition of the family can aid children in learning to cope with the loss they have suffered. For example, other caregivers can relieve the primary caregiver, thus lowering the chances of rejection taking place. Primary caretakers who have no relief from their roles are more likely to reject their children.[31] For example, mothers alone all day with their children are more likely to reject them than those who have other adults present to assist with the children, and to provide some relief from the pressures of child rearing.

Another interesting finding in the Werner and Smith study was that maternal employment does not seem to be a negative factor, but may have been a positive influence on resilient girls who tend to be more independent and assertive.[32] However, while the working mother may provide a resilient model for the children, if the absence of the mother with no caregiver present leads to an unstable family environment, negative results may occur.[33] There must be a stable caregiver present in the home in order for the mother's working to become a positive factor. The absence of a father, the authors contend, has more negative consequences for the male than the female children.

Summing up their study, the authors state:

> Among key factors in the caregiving environment that appeared to contribute to the resiliency and stress resistance of these high-risk children were: the age of the opposite-sex parent (younger mothers for resilient males, older fathers for resilient females); the number of children in the family (four or fewer); the spacing between the index child and the next-born sibling (more than two years); the number and type of alternate caretakers available to the mother within the household (father, grandparents, older siblings); the workload of the mother (including steady employment outside the household); the amount of attention given to the child by the primary caretaker(s) in infancy; the availability of a sibling as a caretaker or confidant in childhood; structure and rules in the household in adolescence; the cohesiveness of the family; the presence of an informal multigenerational network of kin and friends in adolescence; and the cumulative number of chronic stressful life events experienced in childhood and adolescence.[34]

It appears from this study that if children are provided with a stable and nurturing environment, they are often capable of overcoming the negative effects of emotional and physical trauma. We should note that Werner and Smith's resilient children lived in poverty; stability and nurturing should not be considered in solely material terms.

Because people often believe that the trauma of childhood bereavement is never to be overcome, the labeling of these children as somehow marred for life may be damaging. The impressionable younger child may feel himself somehow "cursed" when significant others label him as permanently scarred by death. Joyce Phipps describes her son's rejection of this process of labeling when his father died suddenly: "Once, after an especially heavy and gushy experience, Keith exclaimed, 'I wish you'd tell that lady to stop patting me on the head and saying "poor little boy." I'm not poor!

And I'm not little.' "[35] On the other hand, if the child is labeled as competent, and supported in his grieving process and public mourning, there is every indication that childhood bereavement can be surmounted.

Survivors: Widows and Widowers

They are women in a male-dominated society. They are old in a society that venerates youth. Many are grieving and lonely in a country that would deny and ignore such unhappy emotions. They are without mates in a social network of couples. Many are members of ethnic or racial minority groups and already face prejudice on that basis. (For example, about one and a half million of our female elderly are foreign-born.) They are poor in a wealthy land, and they tend to be ignorant and uneducated in a society that increasingly demands knowledge and skills.[36]

Thus does Helena Lopata, a sociologist who specializes in the study of widowhood, characterize the female survivors of the death of a spouse. The widowed in American society are predominantly female, consisting of 13 percent of the total female population, while widowers make up only 2.7 percent of the total male population.[37] Males are more likely to die or remarry, while women are more likely to outlive their husbands. As a result, three out of four women in America today can expect to become widows.[38] Between 1970 and 1979, the number of widowed women under sixty-five decreased slightly, but the number of widows among sixty-five and older females increased.

Since society expects the male to marry a younger woman, and younger women are seen as more highly valued, the widow will most likely not remarry. Men are more likely to remarry, and tend to do so sooner than their female counterparts. Balkwell reports that of widows and widowers over sixty-five, 1.7 percent of the men remarried, but only 0.3 percent of the women. The 1979 census reports that widowers accounted for 24 percent of all males over seventy-five, 9.3 percent of all males between sixty-five and seventy-four, and 3.4 percent of all males between fifty-five and sixty-four years of age. This is in sharp contrast with the percentage of widows among the female population: 69.7 percent of all women over seventy-five, 41.7 percent of all women between sixty-five and seventy-four, and 18.8 percent of all women between fifty-five and sixty-four years of age are widows.[39]

While there are many more widows than widowers, the men tend to have much more difficulty adjusting to their new role than do widows. They are less likely to be able to express their grief openly and thereby aid in its resolution. Many find that they lack the ability to take care of themselves, having previously left the domestic duties to their wives. Also, contact with the extended family is usually the duty of the wife; upon her death the husband is often isolated from family members, and may lack the skills for maintaining or reestablishing those ties.[40] In addition, widowers often find themselves shunned by our couple-oriented, death-avoiding society.[41]

Males in American society are not socialized to the value of close same-sex friendships. While widows may join with other women in order to meet their social and emotional needs, widowers tend to be more isolated. These conditions, along with a greater availability of single women, encourage the widower into rapid remarriage. An indication of the severity of widowerhood upon men is the higher risk of mental and physical illness among widowers, most especially during the first six months of bereavement. Landis and Landis report that women widowed before they reach age forty have a greater chance of remarrying than do those who have never married; women who are widowed before they are twenty-five have a 90 percent chance of remarriage. Also, they are more likely to marry widowers than single or divorced men.[42]

The widowed male tends to suffer more severe emotional effects during the first months of bereavement; the widow tends to suffer more long-term, debilitating effects of spousal death. Economically, the widow is often dealt a severe blow; many times she is catapulted into poverty. This means that many must seek employment for which they often are not prepared either educationally or emotionally.

Lopata lists four immediate problems with which the widow must cope: (1) grief, always a challenge, becomes even more difficult where the loss is sudden and unexpected; (2) financial considerations may require that immediate decisions be made; (3) children, if the widow is young, must be cared for in their own sorrow; and (4) life's usual day-to-day problems must be confronted in the new roles of head of household and single parent.[43]

Many studies have reported the high risk of mortality associated with bereavement.[44] Emile Durkheim first noted an association between widowhood and suicide.[45] The major effects of bereavement tend to show up during the first two years after the loss of a spouse. In widowers, the initial six months of bereavement tend to be the most dangerous. In their extensive review of the literature, Jacobs and Ostfeld offer two explanations for the effect of bereavement on the expected mortality rate: assuming that bereavement itself does not cause death (an assumption that would be challenged by studies of the effect of stress upon the individual), Jacobs and Ostfeld suggest that the higher rate of mortality may be due to homogamy of married couples. In other words, the unfit tend to marry the unfit.[46] Their reasoning is that the widowed population is already at risk by their unfitness, and the trauma of being widowed exacerbates an already existing condition. This would also explain the high death rate among widowers, who would be unable to care for themselves and thus would rapidly decline in health. The alternative explanation put forth by Jacobs and Ostfeld is that the couple shared an unhealthy environment which eventually took its toll on one member of the dyad, and the other succumbed a short time later. Both of these explanations need further study so that we may understand more fully the effects these variables might have upon those who have recently lost a mate.

Widows reporting the greatest difficulty adjusting to their new status are those who are under forty-five.[47] These women, who often have small children, report a sense of isolation. Lack of adequate income means an inability to afford child care, which might make possible a social outlet as well as an opportunity to meet eligible men. Often, young widows state that they would like to continue their old relationships, but find that their interests differ from those of their married friends. Also, widows quickly become aware that they are seen as a threat by their married friends.

"I was always welcomed by my friends," one young widow told me, "until I stopped wearing black." This woman found the isolation in her suburban home to be so great that she eventually sold her home and moved into an apartment in an area more highly populated by single people. The literature on widowhood contains frequent anecdotes about jealousy exhibited by married friends; it is also full of accounts of sexual pressure put upon the newly widowed, quite often by married male friends. This is often a traumatic shock for the widow, who in her loneliness and grief may be vulnerable to such attentions.[48]

Loneliness appears to be a common theme in studies of widows of all ages, especially among those who do not wish to become a member of a group comprising widows and other single women. Rural widows seem more prone to the vicissitudes of loneliness, as a result of their physical as well as social isolation.[49] Lopata is of the opinion that the middle-aged widow is the one who experiences the most difficult time in adjusting to her new role. In facing what is probably the most traumatic and wrenching of all role changes in life, two factors tend to play important parts in the widow's adaptation to her new role, according to Lopata. Those two factors are the widow's financial condition and her level of education, which is usually linked to social class.[50] As we saw earlier, the availability of funds allows the widow to become socially active, and thereby to be able to seek out sources of emotional and social support. On the other hand, a lack of income may leave the widow unable to interact socially and isolated in her poverty. The fact that social class and education enter into successful coping with widowhood is an interesting finding. Lopata, who studied this factor in some depth, accounts for the importance of education in this manner:

> Formal schooling, particularly at the high school and over levels, teaches people to analyze a situation in the abstract, to perceive alternate paths and their consequences in reaching goals, to plan action, and to modify it flexibly if the consequences are not as anticipated. People who are successful in the school system also build self-confidence in their actions and learning abilities, and trust in their own judgment. These abilities are necessary for planned engagement in social relations and social roles and in planned rather than reactive life styles. In addition, formal schooling increases the person's ability to integrate other resources into an upward or at least stable middle-class life style, in terms of occupation, income, and association with others.[51]

Lopata sees social class as a predictor of a successful transition to widowhood for both men and women, because lower-class males and females tend to live sex-segregated lives. As a result, it is more difficult for lower-class people to re-enter the social world, especially after many years of marriage. The middle-class life style, on the other hand, is not as rigid, and as a result the individual is not as isolated from the opposite sex as is the lower-class person.[52] Felix Berardo also found these factors important among widowers;

in addition he found that those with the greatest amount of social isolation were older, less educated, rural widowers. Of all marital status categories, Berardo found the widower the least likely to be living with his children or interacting with his family, as well as the least likely to report having friends to socialize with.[53]

While the studies cited above tend to focus upon the social or environmental factors that affect the widowed, Maddison and Raphael report on several studies that have looked at the perceptions of the world held by the widowed.[54] Those widows who successfully resolved the issues of their new role were those who saw their immediate environment in a helpful and positive light. The widowed population, both male and female, needs to be studied in the same manner as were the resilient children discussed earlier. One might extrapolate from those studies of resiliency that along with environmental factors, the personal resiliency of the individual plays an important part in resolving the crises of widowhood.

In sum, then, we can say that the widow is more likely to be poor, socially isolated, and subject to higher rates of physical and emotional problems than other women of her own age. While the widower is less likely to be impoverished by the loss of his spouse, and is more likely to remarry than the widow, he is at greater risk of emotional stress. Education, financial well-being, and a positive image of the world are other factors that correlate with successful coping with the death of a spouse.

The Family as a System of Shared Images

In order for individuals to interact, there must be shared among them a commonmality of images. These shared meanings, or constructs, are necessary in order to understand the actions of others, as well as to be understood oneself.[55] Behavior that can be anticipated leads to the development of an organized pattern of interaction; a system. The family is such a system, relying upon mutually held images to give meaning to the actions of its members. Bowen maintains that the family system is in equilibrium when it is in a state of calm, with "each member functioning at reasonable efficiency."[56] He classifies the family system in terms of the communication patterns which exist within it. A family with an open communication pattern can be described as dynamic, and sensitive to external and internal stimuli. It is synergistic, meaning that the individual parts, working together, increase each others' effectiveness. The family with an open communication pattern (the open family) will have an image of itself which holds each member in healthy respect, is predominantly instrumental in its approach to problem solving, and is nurturing to its members.

The family with a closed communication pattern is, in its extreme form, the polar opposite of the open family. It tends to be rigid and insensitive to external and internal stimuli. Individuals appear crystalized in their roles, with little tolerance for innovation or adaptive change. The image of itself held by the closed family is dogmatic in nature, indicating that it is not open to question, reformulation, or change. Rather than the shared meanings of the family being subject to modification as a result of experience, the shared images of the closed family are held as sacred, powerful, and mysterious; the shared image becomes a taboo which affects daily life but is never discussed.

Obviously, the open and closed family models have many ramifications for coping with stress. When what Bowen characterizes as "an emotional shock wave" hits the family—when death takes one of the members—the open family is more likely to recognize the full meaning of the loss.[57] While this might seem to evoke more severe emotional responses among family members than would a refusal to acknowledge the importance of the loss, it is an indication that the family may be acknowledging the severity of the loss.

The open family identifies the loss as affecting the family, and in a nurturing and responsive manner each member seeks to support each of others in their grief. In other words, the open family reacts not only to the external stimuli of the death of one of its members, it also responds to the internal stimuli of the bereavement of the living members of the family. The closed family, on the other hand, would be more likely to deny the importance of the loss; for to accept the reality of the loss would mean changing the family image. The closed family, in denying the loss, tends to isolate each individual member. It is unable to respond either to the needs of its members or the demands of the environment to adapt to the new situation. To do either would necessitate fully accepting the loss. The old patterns of interaction and communication, based upon the formerly viable image, may become perverted into the victimization or scapegoating of one family member, who is singled out to act out the pain of the loss which is felt by all.[58]

As with individuals, families will often develop a closed communication pattern around the subject of death. Pattison maintains that as a result of the denial of death so prevalent in America, families create myths that serve the same purposes as do defense mechanisms for the individual.[59] In the face of massive threat to itself, the family promotes an image based upon its own beliefs, rather than upon verifiable information. The whole conception of death and its effects upon individuals becomes mystified, and the family members find that they are confused, unwilling to relate emotionally to the loss, and unable to discuss the death and its effects with other family members. The family myth that denies death is an avoidance mechanism used by the family in seeking to maintain equilibrium within the family system.[60]

Other factors which we saw as affecting the individual's grieving process are at work in the family as well. The inappropriateness or appropriateness of the loss will have ramifications for the family unit. Reactive and existential grief may also be an issue for the family, as it may have difficulty accepting the fact that its members may die. The inability to accept the reality of death may spill over into other aspects of family life, such as the growing, changing, and separating from the nuclear family which is the process of child development. Pattison addresses this issue when he asks, "If we cannot admit death is a part of life, may it be that we cannot face the fundamental psychological issues of separation and individuation that contain the kernals of loss?"[61] Pattison maintains that when a family denies death by so mystifying the subject, the family members will develop a confused, fearful attitude toward it. This not only shuts off all communication about death itself, it also mystifies related issues involved in change and adaptation. In the open family, death is accepted as a fact of life; separation exists and individual members are seen as separate, distinct beings capable of self-expression and self-determination. In the closed family, the subject of death is taboo, and the related issues of separation and individuation are fearful, anxiety-laden matters.

From a sociological perspective, we can examine the degree to which the culture influences the images that are held by families. Families incorporate the values of the larger culture, and in the United States this means a lack of acceptance of the reality of death. The contemporary American approach to death, which we earlier labeled avoidance, is reiterated in the family unit as well as the individual. In addition, as we noted earlier, the immediate, nuclear family is defined as the source of all of the emotional needs of its members. As a result, the loss of one of the members means that whatever needs were being met by that individual are now unmet, and will remain so until that person is replaced. The loss of a member means the disruption of need fulfillment on the part of the surviving members. Additionally, there is in the United States a lack of familial and social support for the grieving family, which is left to its own devices in trying to adapt to the loss that has occurred. The problem of dealing with the loss of a family member is thus compounded by a social environment which does little to support the family in time of crisis. Also, society expects the family to be able to meet all the needs of its members, and not to rely upon the larger society for substantial emotional support. The values of our society, which work against the individual by promoting an avoidance of death, also work against the family in its attempts to deal with the trauma of the loss of one of its members.

One of the major organizational tasks for the family seeking to cope with the problem of loss is the reallocation of roles. Part of successful coping may be the sharing of duties once performed by the deceased person. Sometimes there is an effort by the family to foist off on one member of the family the role played by the deceased. For example, a young woman complained to me that after her mother's death, her father and younger brother began to expect her to perform many of the domestic duties that were formerly the mother's. The younger brother also would seek to have some of his need for nurturing met by his older sister. She resisted the imposition of this role, claiming that her father and brother were demanding more than she, at eighteen, felt she could give or should have to give.

Krupp points out that sometimes a family member will take on the role of the deceased voluntarily in order, in a sense, to keep the dead person "alive."[62] While this interpretation implies a deep psychological motive, it may be that by carrying on for the lost person, the individual is giving meaning to the loss. Death becomes less powerful as the family copes with the loss and continues to function as a unit. Bedell points out that in the families evidencing the most successful adaptation to loss, the duties formerly performed by the deceased were shared among the survivors.[63] This strategy provides for the needs of the survivors while still acknowledging that the loss has occurred.

The fact that many families cope effectively with the death

of a family member indicates that such a death is not, in and of itself, pathogenic. When families fail to respond openly to the loss, the resulting defensive maneuvers and emotional numbing may inhibit individual adaptation through effective grieving. The result, as Paul and Grosser point out, may be a continual acting out of the mourning process.[64]

Validation of our observations about the importance of the family system can be found in the literature on divorce as a result of the death of a child. Spinetta and colleagues point to three factors which they associate with effective coping: life meaning, support, and communication with the child.[65] "Life meaning" refers to the family's image of life which "helped the family accept the diagnosis [of terminal illness] and its consequences as a part of an overall life scheme."[66] This closely resembles some of the characteristics of the open family communication pattern, which describes the family as having a realistic relationship with the world. By "support," the authors mean the degree to which the members of the family can rely upon one another for aid during the stress of the ensuing illness and death. The open family is concerned about the emotional needs of each member, and actively works to support its members during a crisis. In considering "communication with the child," the authors of the study asked whether or not the family openly accepted the problem of having a child with a terminal illness, even though that acceptance entailed a great deal of grief. Here again, an open family will respond to the problem and seek to do so in innovative and effective ways, rather than through avoidance or denial. Spinetta's study gives credence to the positive, adaptive functions of an open family system.

I have often heard speakers on parent bereavement comment on the high divorce rate that accompanies the loss of a child. However, I have not been able to find any scientific studies to support this allegation. What few studies have been done tend to indicate that the reverse is true. Lansky and colleagues reviewed the literature, and report on five recent studies that fail to link divorce with the death of a child.[67] Their own study reported findings similar to the Spinetta study cited above; the divorce rate among families suffering the death of a child was lower than would normally be expected. This is not to indicate that the families emerged unscathed; while many reported that the death of the child had the effect of bringing the parents closer together, others reported increased family problems following the loss. Tew and colleagues found that the divorce rate for couples with a living but severely handicapped child (spina bifida) was three times higher than that for families experiencing bereavement over the death of their handicapped child.[68] This study indicates that the stress of living with a doomed child may exact a greater toll on the marriage than the death of a child. There is evidence from other studies, however, that the parents of spina bifida children who divorced or separated were experiencing marital difficulties previously.[69]

In summary, the family can be viewed as an interacting group of individuals organized into a system that seeks to remain in a state of equilibrium, with the various members homeostatically arranged in more or less stable patterns of interaction. The communication patterns within the family fall along a continuum that ranges from open (dyamic, synergistic) to closed (rigid, dogmatic). When a death occurs within the family, the open family follows a pattern analogous to the individual grieving process; it reacts to the loss, goes through a state of disorganization and reorganization, and finally reorients itself to the world in new ways to meet the needs of the individual family members. The closed family uses denial and mystification to defend against the anxiety of death. It numbs itself to the reality of the loss as it strives to maintain its image. The more closed a family's communication, the more likely that the death of one of the members will be met in ways that are maladaptive for the family unit, and as a result will have negative impacts upon the individual members.

Survivors of a Suicide

The survivor-victims of a suicide must cope not only with the burden of a death of someone significant to them, they must also deal with the stigma of being associated with the suicidal act itself. In this section, we will examine the factors that contribute to the sometimes overwhelming and usually very difficult plight of the survivor of a suicide.

We like to hold an image of the individual as the master of his fate. This leads to seeing suicide as a result of what Henslin calls "personal problems."[70] As a result, we tend to implicate the surviving family members in the suicidal act. What kind of parents were they to raise a child who would do this? What kind of a husband or wife was the survivor, to be a part of such a heinous thing as a suicide?

A lack of an explanation for the suicide, coupled with the fear and loathing of an outrageous death, places the survivors in a stigmatized position in American society. It far exceeds the usual pollution of the bereaved described earlier, and there appears to be no ritual act or penance by which the survivor of a suicide can cleanse and thus rid him- or herself of the stigma. Lindemann and Greer point out that while we no longer punish the survivors of a suicide as was the custom in earlier times, we have also eradicated a means of discharging the anger felt by the survivors.[71] In past times, one might be publicly punished for the misdeed of suicide of another. This functioned, in part, as a way for society to vent its anger at this unacceptable act, and as a way for the survivors to do penance. Today, the suicide survivor must permanently carry the disgrace of having a suicide in the family.

Not only do suicide survivors experience rejection by the larger society, their initial encounters with death are also caught up in the legal system. Many survivors speak with anguish about the insensitive and unfeeling approaches of the authorities when interacting with the suicide's family. (Legal agencies are required to investigate the death, to determine if it was, in fact, a suicide.[72]

Well-meaning friends may, out of their own shock and disbelief, repeatedly ask how and why the suicide occurred. The survivor, still in the early grief state of reaction, is faced with those questions for which there may be no satisfactory answers. Religious organizations may withdraw support for the bereaved by refusing a service or burial for the suicide, thereby denying the survivors the consolation of a religious ceremony.

The social situation prior to the suicide may often be such that the survivor is extremely vulnerable to the trauma of the act itself. Cain reports that pathological behavior, alcoholism, marital conflict or separation all may be contributing factors not only to the suicide itself, but also to the survivors' emotional state in attempting to deal with the loss. A telling example of this is the fact that many survivors report early feelings of relief upon learning of the suicide.[73] The suicide has often attempted the act in the past, or has acted out in so many ways as to become an emotional burden on those around him or her.

As we noted earlier, the bereaved are often seen by the larger society to be death tainted (polluted), and thus are to be avoided. Those suffering a loss due to suicide are even more rejected by society. In order to rebuild their shattered social world, suicide

survivors often must take drastic steps. For example, it is not unusual for the family of a suicide to move to another town, thereby
hiding or diminishing the stigma of the suicide. This may not be
solely an act of those suffering shame or guilt; I have known of
younger siblings of a teenage suicide who were openly teased by
their peers about the death. Typically, our society does not respond
in open and compassionate ways to those who survive a suicide.[74]
The family which chooses to move to a new community is hoping
to be able to hide or at least dimish the social impact of the death
of their child by suicide.

Psychological studies of the bereaved survivors of a suicide
have tended to focus upon those survivors who have sought clinical
aid in resolving their grief. Resnik, in a study of seven families
with an adolescent suicide, found that the parents chose to deny
that the death was a suicide, instead insisting that it was an
accident.[75] This resulted in anger toward those authorities who
classified the death as a suicide. Resnik maintains that, on a deeper
level, the parents felt a strong sense of guilt concerning the suicide
of their child. The anger at authorities served to project the guilt
outward, thus allowing them to avoid the acknowledgment of their
own responsibility for what had taken place. Resnik notes that
so powerful was the defensiveness of these parents concerning
what they termed an accidental death, and at the same time so
transparent was their effort to deny the facts of the suicide, that
he and his co-worker decided not to pursue the issue with the
families. They felt that confronting these families again with the
facts of the suicide would be too destructive of their defense against
this reality.[76]

The survivors have a need to make sense out of an act which
not only results in a loss through death, but also implies an ultimate
rejection of family and loved ones. In American society, the parents
are considered responsible for their children's behavior, often for
the rest of their lives. Thus, the grief and rejection felt by parents
over the suicide of a child may be coupled with a sense of responsibility for the death. By defending the death as accidental, Resnik's
families were trying to avoid the guilt of responsibility for the
suicide, as well as the pain of their rejection by one they loved.[77]

Albert Cain, a noted researcher of suicide survivors, has noted
several reactions to suicide common to survivors.[78] The reality distortion and search for meaning that Cain describes can be seen
in Resnik's study, where blatant facts were denied by the family

in order to construct a guilt-free version of what had occurred. Whitis provides us with a case history that also demonstrates several of the reactions categorized by Cain.[79] After the suicide of a thirteen-year-old son, the mother began to "adopt" other children into the family; usually taking in children from broken or troubled homes. This activity served to provide a replacement for the dead child, and also helped to relieve some of the guilt felt by the mother. The taking in of other children showed what a good person she was, and how adequate she was in caring for children, thus strengthening her self-concept. Her husband's resentment of the extra children served as a lightning rod for her anger, providing a justification for her rage. This case delineates the efforts of the survivor to deal with the many negative results of a suicide.

Cain's survivor reactions of identification with the suicide, depression, and self-destructiveness can be seen in the following studies of children's reactions to the suicide of a parent. Often, as we noted earlier, the family context was disturbed in its emotional make-up prior to the act, a fact that would tend to increase the vulnerability of the children to the trauma of a suicide in the family. In some extreme cases, the child may actually have witnessed the suicidal act itself.[80]

Identification with the parent, a normal part of child development, may take on a pathological, self-destructive quality when a parent commits suicide. The rate of suicides and suicide attempts among children of parent suicides—sometimes years after the parent's death—indicates the powerful, pathological legacy that the suicide may leave behind.[81] We noted earlier that parents often deny the suicide of a child. The effect of this cover-up on the surviving children, especially younger children, is to present them with contradictory evidence concerning the suicide. For example, the children may be told not to discuss the death, to deny what they know or experienced, and to accept a new version of reality. In order to maintain a place in the family system, the child must accept the myth, the distortion of reality. This may lead to later disturbed reactions on the part of the child.[82]

As we noted at the onset of this discussion, a great deal of the literature on survivors of suicide is based upon clinical material. There is little information on successful coping strategies in a family victimized by a suicide. Rudestam's study of thirty-nine families showed that while the negative effects upon the survivors are powerful, both in depth and duration, some families are able to derive strength from the members' common plight. Rudestam points out that his study was conducted six months after the suicide, and that the perceived family cohesion may have been a temporary crisis-reaction, masking deeper difficulties.[83]

Clearly, the legacy of a suicidal act is one that contains destructive and unhealthy elements. The image of suicide in American society is such that the survivors are stigmatized with shame and guilt. The grief over loss of a loved one is compounded by feelings of rejection and disillusionment. To the child, the consequences of a suicide within the family can be pervasive and pathological.

Notes

1. Erna Furman, *A Child's Parent Dies* (New Haven: Yale University Press, 1974), p. 12.

2. Ibid., p. 119.

3. Sigmund Freud, *The Interpretation of Dreams,* Vol. 9 of *Standard Ed. of the Complete Psychological Works of S. Freud* (London: Hogarth, 1953), footnote, p. 254.

4. Thomas Lopez and Gilbert W. Kliman, "Memory, Reconstruction, and Mourning in the Analysis of a Four-Year-Old Child," in *The Psychoanalytic Study of the Child,* 34 (New Haven: Yale University Press, 1979), p. 239.

5. Jill Miller, "Children's Resistance to Parent Death," *Journal of the American Psychoanalytic Association* 19 (1971):701.

6. Author's files.

7. Sula Wolff, *Children Under Stress* (London: Penguin, 1969), p. 75.

8. Ibid., p. 82.

9. Albert C. Cain, Irene Fast, and Mary Erickson, "Children's Disturbed Reactions to the Death of a Sibling," *American Journal of Orthopsychiatry* 34 (1964):743–752.

10. Ibid., p. 743.

11. Robert Krell and Leslie Rabkin, "The Effects of Sibling Death on the Surving Child: A Family Perspective," *Family Process* 18 (1979):473.

12. Ibid.

13. Robert Kastenbaum, "Death and Development through the Lifespan," in Herman Feifel, ed., *New Meanings of Death* (New York: McGraw-Hill, 1977), pp. 30–33.

14. Judith Stillion and Hannelore Wass, "Children and Death," in Hannelore Wass, ed., *Dying: Facing the Facts* (Washington, D.C.: Hemisphere, 1979), p. 210.

15. Mervyn Shoor and Mary H. Speed, "Death, Delinquency, and the Mourning Process," in Robert Fulton, ed., *Death and Identity* (Bowie, Md.: The Charles Press, 1976), pp. 258–262.

16. Paul C. Rosenblatt, Douglas A. Jackson, and Rose P. Walsh, "Coping with Anger and Aggression in Mourning," *Omega* 3, no. 4 (1972):271–284.

17. Herbert Barry, "Significance of Maternal Bereavement Before Age of Eight in Psychiatric Patients," *Archives of Neurological Psychiatry,* 62, no. 5 (1949):630–637. Also, J. Birchtnell, "Early Death and Psychiatric Diagnosis," *Social Psychiatry,* 7 (1972):202–210.

18. Joseph Palumbo, "Parent Loss and Childhood Bereavement: Some Theoretical Considerations," *Clinical Social Work* 9, no. 1 (1981):17.

19. Ibid., p. 18.

20. Ibid., p. 19.

21. Thomas Crook and John Eliot, "Parental Death During Childhood and Adult Depression: A Critical Review of the Literature," *Psychological Bulletin* 87, no. 2 (1980):252–259.

22. Eric Markusen and Robert Fulton, "Childhood Bereavement and Behavior Disorders: A Critical Review," *Omega* 2 (1971): 107–117.

23. Ibid., p. 111.

24. Robert Bendiksen and Robert Fulton, "Death and the Child: An Anterospective Test of the Childhood Bereavement and Later Behavior Disorder Hypothesis," in Robert Fulton, ed., *Death and Identity,* pp. 274–287.

25. Bendiksen, p. 285.

26. Michael Rutter, *Maternal Deprivation Reassessed,* 2nd ed. (New York: Penguin, 1981).

27. Ibid., p. 131.

28. Ibid., p. 133.

29. Bryan E. Robinson and Nell H. Fields, "Casework with Invulnerable Children," *Social Work,* 28 (1983):63–65.

30. Emmy S. Werner and Ruth S. Smith, *Vulnerable but Invincible* (New York: McGraw-Hill, 1982).

31. Ibid., p. 77.

32. Ibid., p. 79.

33. Ibid., p. 80.

34. Ibid., p. 155.

35. Joyce Phipps, *Death's Single Privacy* (New York: Seabury, 1974), p. 55.

36. Helena Z. Lopata, "Living Through Widowhood," *Psychology Today*, (July 1973): 87–92.

37. U.S. Dept. of Commerce, Bureau of the Census, *Statistical Abstracts of the United States: 1980* (Washington, D.C.: U.S. Government Printing Office, 1980), p. 43.

38. Carolyn Balkwell, "Transition to Widowhood: A Review of the Literature," *Family Relations* 30 (1981):117–127.

39. U.S. Dept. of Commerce.

40. Balkwell, p. 120.

41. Helena Lopata, "The Widowed Family Member," in Nancy Datan and Nancy Lohmann, eds., *Transitions in Aging* (New York: Academic Press, 1980), p. 100.

42. Judson T. Landis and Mary G. Landis, *Building a Successful Marriage* (Englewood Cliffs, N.J.: Prentice-Hall, 1977), p. 392.

43. Ibid., p. 98.

44. Colin Murray Parkes, et al., "Broken Heart: A Statistical Study of Increased Mortality among Widowers," *British Medical Journal* 1 (1969):740–743; W. D. Rees and S. Lutkins, "Mortality of Bereavement," *British Medical Journal* 4 (1967):13–16; James J. Lynch, *The Broken Heart* (New York: Basic Books, 1977), Chapter 2.

45. Emile Durkheim, *Suicide* (New York: The Free Press of Glencoe, 1951).

46. Selby Jacobs and A. Ostfeld, "An Epidemiological Review of the Mortality of Bereavement," *Psychosomatic Medicine* 39, no. 5 (1974):354.

47. Lopata, "Living Through Widowhood."

48. See Phipps; also Lynn Cain, *Widow* (New York: William Morrow, 1974).

49. Balkwell, p. 122.

50. Lopata, "Living Through Widowhood," p. 240.

51. Lopata, "The Widowed Family Member," p. 101.

52. Ibid., p. 102.

53. Felix M. Berardo, "Survivorship and Social Isolation: The Case of the Aged Widower," *The Family Coordinator* 19 (1970):14.

54. David Maddison and Beverly Raphael, "Conjugal Bereavement and the Social Network," in B. Schoenberg, et al., eds., *Bereavement: Its Psychosocial Aspects* (New York: Columbia University Press, 1975), pp. 26–40.

55. David Reiss and Mary Ellen Oliveri, "Family Paradigm and Family Coping," *Family Relations* 29 (1980):431–444.

56. Murray Bowen, *Family Therapy in Clinical Practice* (New York: Jason Aronson, 1978), p. 324.

57. Ibid., p. 325.

58. Beverly Raphael, *The Anatomy of Bereavement* (New York: Basic Books, 1983), pp. 115–116.

59. E. Mansell Pattison, "The Family Matrix of Dying and Death," in E. Mansell Pattison, ed., *The Experience of Dying* (Englewood Cliffs, N.J.: Prentice-Hall, 1977), p. 38.

60. Paul C. Rosenblatt, *Bitter, Bitter Tears* (Minneapolis: University of Minnesota Press, 1983), pp. 122–151.

61. Ibid., p. 40.

62. George Krupp, "Maladaptive Reactions to the Death of a Family Member," *Social Casework* 53, no. 7 (1972):425–434.

63. John W. Bedell, "Role Reorganization in the One Parent Family," *Sociological Focus* 5 (1971):84–100.

64. Norman Paul and George Grosser, "Operational Mourning and Its Role in Conjoint Family Therapy," *Community Mental Health Journal* 1, no. 4 (1965): 339–345.

65. John J. Spinetta, et al., "Effective Parental Coping Following the Death of a Child from Cancer," *Journal of Pediatric Psychology* 6, no. 3 (1981):251–263.

66. Ibid., p. 256.

67. Shirley B. Lansky, et al., "Childhood Cancer: Parental Discord and Divorce," *Pediatrics* 62, no. 2 (1978):184–188.

68. B.J. Tew et al., "Marital Stability Following the Birth of a Child with Spina Bifida," *British Journal of Psychiatry*, 131(1977): 79–82.

69. Patricia Martin, "Marital Breakdown in Families of Patients with Spina Bifida Cystica," *Developmental Medicine and Child Neurology*, 17 (1975): 757–764.

70. James M. Henslin, "Strategies of Adjustment: An Ethnomethodological Approach to the Study of Guilt and Suicide," in Albert C. Cain, ed., *Survivors of Suicide* (Springfield, Ill: Charles C. Thomas, 1972, pp. 217–222.

71. Erich Lindemann and Ina May Greer, "A Study of Grief: Emotional Responses to Suicide," in Cain, ed., *Survivors of Suicide*, p. 66.

72. Albert C. Cain and Irene Fast, "The Legacy of Suicide," *Psychiatry*, 29, no. 4 (1966): 406–411; and Samuel E. Wallace, *After Suicide* (New York: John Wiley, 1973).

73. Kjell E. Rudestam, "Physical and Psychological Responses to Suicide in the Family," *Journal of Consulting and Clinical Psychology*, 45, no. 2 (1977): 167–170.

74. Albert C. Cain, "Introduction," in Cain, ed., *Survivors of Suicide*, p. 15.

75. H. L. P Resnik, "Psychological Resynthesis: A Clinical Approach to

the Survivors of a Death by Suicide," in Edwin S. Shneidman and Magno J. Ortega, eds., *Aspects of Depression* (Boston: Little, Brown, 1969), pp. 213–224.

76. Ibid., p. 216.

77. Henslin, 217–222.

78. Albert C. Cain, "Introduction," pp. 3–4.

79. Peter R. Whitis, "The Legacy of a Child's Suicide," *Family Process* 7, no. 2 (1968):159–179.

80. Albert C. Cain, "The Impact of Parent Suicide on Children," in O. Sahler, ed., *The Child and Death* (St. Louis: C.V. Mosby, 1978), pp. 202–209.

81. Ibid.

82. Cain and Fast, 406–411.

83. Rudestam, pp. 167–170.

CHAPTER SEVEN

Ceremonies of Death: The Funeral

W HEN A DEATH OCCURS within a social group, there is usually a public ceremony which provides for a sharing of feelings and an expression of the values held by group members. Across cultures, funerals take many forms; they may be brief or last for many days, they may be public or private. Some funerals involve the group in extreme emotional outbursts and bodily mortification, others involve calm acceptance. The death of a socially important individual may require national recognition by millions of people, while the deaths of the less important may be dealt with without any kind of funeral at all.

When a person dies, the society is faced with two basic tasks: to remove the physical remains which serve as a health threat to the group, and to present to the group an understanding of death that will reintegrate the social group and assist in allaying the terrors awakened by the presence of death. For the individual, the funeral can serve as a means of channeling grief into socially acceptable behaviors.

A death reminds each of us of our own ultimate helplessness and vulnerability. It may remind us that death is not necessarily fair, logical, or a joyful release from this vale of tears. Death may be any number of things in our understanding, because it has no meaning in and of itself. We assign meaning to death, be it the ironic twists of fate described by Sartre, the tragic fate of a Greek drama, or the whimpering demise of the world predicted by

T. S. Eliot. All of these are attempts to bring meaning to the reality of death.

The funeral ceremony seeks to restate the image of death held by the society's members, to define death in such a way as to comfort the living. Death may be seen as challenging the image of life that the members of society hold. It can wreak havoc not just upon the family, but, as was the case when the black plague swept across Europe, it can threaten the very meaning and existence of an entire culture. When the death occurs, society must respond to the question, "Why?" Often this is done by performing a ceremony that restates and reaffirms the values of society which deal with forces outside of human control. Meaning in life is reestablished. All are reminded of why death exists, and of their responsibilities as group members.

On one level, then, the funeral serves to restate the collective image of death. For example, this may take the form of a reminder that the wages of sin is death, or it may be joyous celebration of a transition to Heaven. Through this ceremony, the image that the group holds of death is restated and reaffirmed. Sense is made out of death. By examining the values symbolized in funeral activity, we can come to understand many facets of the collective image concerning the meaning of existence. This also implies that the absence of any ceremony may be indicative of the group's attitude toward death as well, a point we shall return to later.

The funeral ceremony is a structured response to a significant event. In addition, the funeral serves as a method for disposing of the body. The body, once a vital and loved person, has suddenly become a corpse which represents decay and rot—a thing to be abhorred. A funeral ceremony allows society to rid itself of the corpse, while retaining a respectful attitude toward the deceased person. In this chapter we will examine the funeral as it exists in America today, as well as its historical roots. As the United States has changed in its attitudes toward death, the ceremony that surrounds death has likewise changed. We will also examine the role of funeral directors, who are responsible for providing the services needed to carry out the funeral. We will review the current controversies surrounding the funeral industry, and conclude with an examination of some current trends in funeral behavior.

The funeral ceremony is a rite of passage. As such, it is a formal recognition of the changed status of the individual. The deceased is recognized as no longer in the world of the living, but now has a new status as one of the dead. Robert Hertz states that:

> Every change of status in the individual, as he passes from one group to another, implies a deep change in society's mental attitude toward him, a change that is made gradually and requires time. The brute fact of physical death is not enough to consummate death in people's minds: the image of the recently deceased is still part of the system of things in this world, and loses itself from them only gradually by a series of internal partings. We cannot bring ourselves to consider the deceased as dead straight away: he is too much a part of our substance, we have put too much of ourselves into him, and participation in the same social life creates ties which are not to be severed in one day. . . . Thus, if a certain period is necessary to banish the deceased from the land of the living, it is because society, disturbed by the shock, must gradually regain its balance, and because the double mental process of disintegration and of synthesis that the integration of an individual into a new world presupposes, is accomplished in a molecular fashion, as it were, which requires time.[1]

A rite of passage, as first described by van Genepp, has three stages.[2] The first stage is one of separation, wherein the old relationships cease to be valid. In the second stage, limnality, the person is in transition, and is without a status. The third stage, incorporation, reunites the individual with society, but in a new status. The death rites of passage in contemporary America begin with the acknowledgement that the person is dying. This typically involves a physical separation when the individual is placed in a hospital. As Sudnow points out, often the family will stop visiting the dying patient so that by the end of the first stage, the individual is already socially dead.[3] The declaration of physical death by the doctor is usually the peak of the first stage.

During the stage of limnality the individual is without a clearly defined status. The family is notified that the death has occurred. The body is taken to the funeral home or the morgue, where it is kept until directions are given for its disposal. The funeral ceremony typically marks the ending of this transition phase and the beginning of the reintegrating third phase. During the ceremony, consoling sacred literature may be read, to restate and affirm the values of the community. Finally, the person's soul is declared to have attained a new status (such as, "He is with God now"), and the body is committed to the earth or cremated. The individual is now acknowledged to be in a new status in the timeless world of death—the "mythical society of souls which each society constructs in its own image"—never to return.[4]

The funeral may serve to facilitate the grieving process, and to channel it into socially acceptable behaviors. The survivors may find that the funeral is the first time they truly realize that the death has occurred, and can express their feelings of loss. Ideally, the consolation and direction which are a part of the ceremony encourage the grievers to resolve their feelings of loss. The funeral serves to protect against the urge to stay in perpetual grief, and to direct the mourner back into society. At the same time, the funeral may promote community support for the survivors.

Rosenblatt and colleagues, in an anthropological study of funeral behavior, point out that funeral ceremonies and rituals may meet the needs of survivors by giving them something with which to occupy themselves, thus channeling their inchoate grief into acceptable behavior.[5] For example, anger, a basic emotion in the grief process, may be channeled into nonaggressive behavior as the grief-stricken are involved in the process of funeral arrangements. Ritual activity such as praying, singing, or dancing may be the norm of a particular society. These socially required behaviors may serve as a kind of social safety valve, directing anger-inspired energy into nonthreatening behavior. The authors maintain that societies define what are appropriate behaviors during grief. People in various cultures react to loss in many ways which differ from our own. While American widows may be admired for a stoic demeanor at the time of loss, an Indian woman might try to throw herself upon her dead husband's burning funeral pyre. By indicating what is considered to be the proper way of grieving, society rules out those bizarre emotional responses which are dysfunctional or inappropriate. In some societies, because grief is expected to elicit antisocial forms of aggression, the bereaved may be isolated or marked in distinctive ways in order that society may protect itself from their anger.[6]

American funerals, while serving as a rite of passage for the deceased, do not provide identical functions for the bereaved. The important difference lies in the final phase of a rite of passage, integration. While the death is acknowledged and the bereaved are recognized, there is no closure around a new status for the bereaved. They are left in the transition phase with no societal indication as to when that phase should end, or when the individual should reenter into normal social interaction. Gorer recognizes this dilemma among widows, and claims that unstructured grieving causes many to become stuck along the way to successful resolution.[7]

In the United States, where controlling one's feelings is so highly prized, people are admired for suppressing their grief, and returning to work (sometimes referred to as "the best medicine") a few days after the funeral. It is not socially acceptable to wail or to beat one's breast while grieving over a loss, nor are other expressive acts allowed. What is acceptable in our contemporary society is the suppression of feelings as quickly as possible. It may be that, by becoming more and more ritual-less and unemotional, we risk promoting aggressive behaviors in individuals who were not allowed to vent their feelings at the time of loss.[8]

There is another aspect of the contemporary pattern of "open-ended grieving" that has not been studied in depth. Those who come in contact with death are often seen by others as somehow tainted by death, and thus they are to be avoided. People who have experienced the slow dying of a family member often find friends and acquaintences pulling away from them, as if they were stigmatized by their closeness to death. This is a kind of pollution, whereby the individual is seen as unclean; as if tainted by his association with death. Sadly, just at a time when those facing the death of a loved one are most in need of support, the community often seeks to avoid interacting with them.[9] While the common explanation is that we feel inadequate to interact properly with the bereaved, it seems clear that the stigma of death surrounds the bereaved, and we avoid them for that reason. It is as if death were contagious, and we might catch it from the bereaved. Our imagery of death, which is clouded in avoidance, is threatened by the bereaved. As symbols of a reality we wish to avoid, those close to death are to be avoided or unrecognized, lest they somehow confront us with the reality of mortality.

Other societies recognize the pollution of the bereaved, and their funeral ceremonies may include a rite of purification which serves to cleanse the bereaved of death. Today, Americans are left to their own devices in resolving their grief and reintegrating themselves into society.

The larger society as a whole can benefit from the funeral ceremony. The group's values surrounding death may be strengthened. The solidarity of the group is expressed by attending the ceremony. As the group expresses support for those who are suffering, it also promotes a reciprocity in future times of need. In the course of the ceremony, death is acknowledged in a very real way, as in many cases the body is present during the service. At the same time, the people are reminded of their connection with life—through sacred images, restatement of other immortal imagery, and association with other living beings. In this manner, an equilibrium is achieved in the group which has been assaulted by death. The larger social group reorients itself to life as it bears witness to the existence of death. An example of the restatement of social values is found in religions that maintain a belief in a post-death judgment and pray for mercy or compassion during the funeral ceremony. They are also reminding themselves that there is no escape from accountability for one's acts—even in death.[10]

The Funeral in Historical Perspective

The Funeral in the Era of Sacred Death

The eminent French historian, Philippe Aries, described Christian death behavior for the ten centuries preceding the twelfth century as remaining quite constant. "Tamed death," as he called it, was met with a traditional ceremony as the dying person separated himself from the world. What Aries describes is a ceremony that took place during the separation phase of the rite of passage—a simple public ceremony that was organized by the dying person himself, by which he took leave of the world.[11]

The separation phase involving the dying person was followed by a solemn funeral service during the transition phase. In addition, mourning ritual was clearly defined, although its form might differ through the ages. This was still true in Puritan times in America, where the dying individual played an important part in the separation phase. The Puritan funeral, however, was very different from that of other Christian denominations. In reaction to the "Popish ways" of the Church of England, the Puritan funeral was without prayers or religious service.[12] The body was prepared for burial by the family, carried to the graveyard, and deposited there, often in an unmarked grave.[13] A fatalistic acceptance of everyday death is reflected in this simple process. The larger social group would recognize the death at the next Sunday's services, when mention would be made during the sermon. Then the death might serve as the basis for a hellfire-and-damnation sermon, which would seek to restate the group's attitude toward death.

As society became more affluent and life became a bit easier, a civil ceremony was instituted to recognize the death, probably originating with the deaths of well-known leaders. This was acceptable to the Puritans because it was not a religious, but a civil ceremony. Tokens of remembrance to be distributed to funeral attendees such as rings, scarves, books, and gloves became fashionable in seventeenth-century America. These were representations of the death that had occurred, and often included inscriptions of the person's name, age, and date of death. The items varied in quantity and quality according to social status of the deceased. The fashion grew to such an extravagant extent that in 1743 the Massachusetts General Court passed an act restraining the number of gloves, scarves, and rings (as well as the amount of liquor) that could be given away at a funeral.[14]

Funerals came to be seen more and more as major social events, at which one paid one respects and remained for the feasting and drinking that followed. An example of the popularity of the colonial funeral is the death of one prosperous Boston merchant in 1738 which was marked by the distribution of 3000 pairs of gloves; 1100 people took part in the funeral procession. This occurred in a city estimated to have had a population of only 16,000 at the time.[15]

During the eighteenth century, as funerals were becoming more ostentatious, there was a shift from home-centered preparation of the body and coffin to the use of professional labor. The American colonies were growing in wealth, and one way for the newly wealthy to demonstrate their differences from the poorer members of society was through elaborate funerals. The Revolutionary War, which restricted the flow of goods from Europe and diminished the affluence of many colonists, and restrictive legislation curbing ostentatious funerals combined to bring about a decline in elaborate and costly funerals.

During this period of American history, death was considered a sacred event, and there was a sharp distinction between the early religious funeral and the civic event that followed. As time wore on, however, the funeral and civic ceremonies began to coalesce into one. The church funeral would be followed by a procession to the burial site, and a social gathering with much eating and drinking would follow.

The Funeral in a Time of Secular Death

The increasing urbanization of the nineteenth century contributed to changes in the conduct of funeral ceremonies. Urban people were not able to perform many of the tasks that previously had been a part of rural family functioning. Personal service areas of work came into existence, and the increasing specialization and mechanization of production eliminated many former home-centered activities. The preparation of the body for burial was turned over to women who were trained as nurses, and often furniture dealers who sold coffins as a sideline found funeral directing becoming their main occupation.[16]

The secular values of the period were reflected in the funeral ceremony as well. There was an increase in longevity during this period, and death was not as common an occurrence as it once had been. The increase in wealth among the people allowed for a return to public display through elaborate funerals, which again served as a statement of status.

In urban America during the middle and late nineteenth century, family conditions changed in ways that contributed to the development of the funeral home. Smaller living spaces did not provide the room needed for a wake, which had become a part of the ceremonies surrounding death.[17] Originally brought over during Colonial times by immigrants from Scotland and Ireland, the wake, or viewing, was an expected ritual in American funerals by the nineteenth century.[18] The increasing use of embalming made performing these duties in the home more difficult, and the undertakers wished to centralize their operations as well. As a result, funeral homes were established which served as a central location within the city. (The term "funeral parlor" evolved as the funeral home came to replace the parlor in the home, which had been used for wakes and viewings in earlier times.) By the end of the nineteenth century, the funeral director was in charge of the body and most often the funeral ceremony itself.[19]

The funeral ceremonies of this age of secular death were filled with gloom and despair, to the point of being melodramatic. The focus was upon the bereaved, who were expected to remain in mourning for several months—for several years in some cases. For example, it was acceptable for an older woman to wear black to signify her mourning for the rest of her life, in some instances.[20] Black gloves, arm bands, and badges were symbols of grief commonly worn by funeral attenders.[21] In the larger cities there were shops that catered solely to the bereaved, featuring the latest in mourning fashion. Kephart notes that a Philadelphia department store carried a full line of mourning apparel, a vestige of the earlier mourning shops, as recently as 1950.[22]

As we saw in our discussion in Chapter Two, death has had different meanings at various times in history. During the era of secular death, death itself meant a time of joy and hope, for the deceased was surely in Heaven. In other words, the dead themselves were seen in a more positive light. It was grieving that became highly emphasized, as the focus shifted from the dead to the survivors. During the secular period there was a noticeable shift in the values expressed in many religious funeral ceremonies. Farrell cites the Methodist religion as an example of this shift:

> From 1839 to 1916, the Methodists had maintained a delicate balance of fear and hope in their funeral ceremony. In 1868 they had added a few prayers that lengthened the service without altering its tone. In 1884, they added another prayer, confirming the "joy and felicity" of the future life, thanking God for the good example of the dead, and asking for "perfect consummation and bliss, both in body and soul, in thy eternal and everlasting glory." The prayer for the commitment of the body highlighted the positive aspects of death, resurrection, and future life, instead of the fearful aspects. But not until 1916 did the Methodists disturb the balance of the ceremony as a whole in the direction of hope.
>
> In that year, they omitted both quotations from Job, including the reminder that "worms destroy this body." They decided not to mention that "man that is born of woman hath but a short time to live, and is full of misery," and they also omitted the sole reference to the pains of death. . . . At the same time, the new "Order for the Burial of the Dead" included several sections of Scripture designed to console and comfort the bereaved. . . . A passage from Revelations also provided a picture of life in heaven.[23]

By 1920, the Methodist funeral ceremony, typical of trends in other Protestant religions, was centered upon God's mercy and assurances of eternal life in Heaven.

The era of secular death, which lasted until the time of the World War II, was a period of great change in both the popular image of death and the ceremonies that recognized it. The gloom which was symbolically portrayed through extensive use of black fabric and objects began to give way to flowers. This symbolic shift was linked to a growing belief that heaven is assured to those who die by a merciful God. The center of attention shifted away from the dead person and onto the mourners. The consolation of the bereaved became the center of attention.

The funeral, which at the beginning of the nineteenth century had been largely in the hands of family members, had evolved into a commercial activity controlled by funeral directors. America's romance with materialism was in full swing, and the funeral industry responded to public demands and tastes with fashionable products such as ornate hearses and coffins, splendid ceremonies, and mourning fashions—all of which allowed people to display their affluence and genteel tastes.[24]

The Funeral in an Age of Avoided Death

Since World War II, America has intensified its avoidance of death. Death has never been a pleasant subject, but in the past it was impossible to escape its reality. Death was such an evident part of living that some, such as the Puritans, were able to speak about death with something of a sardonic sense of humor. Death was an unavoidable and constant companion to the Puritan. It struck the young and old, rich and poor. Death wiped out entire families as easily as it claimed the solitary. Also, death struck quickly, so that many people were well one day and dead a few days later. There was little that one could do to avoid death, and humor was as good a defense as any during Puritan times.

But during the 150 years since then, during the time that we have called the age of secular death, the rise of science has been changing the very nature of death itself. While death has not been defeated, it is being resisted more and more successfully. For instance, many of the former childhood killers have become rare today. One seldom hears of children dying from whooping cough, diphtheria, or scarlet fever. Our improved sanitation and nutrition, along with improved medical services, have drastically reduced infant and child mortality. The life expectancy of Americans has increased markedly in the past fifty years, and as a result the image of death has changed as well.

Since the ceremonies of death are responses to the event of death, as the meaning of the event changes so does the ceremony responding to it. As we have seen, the reality of death runs counter to many values central to the American image. The result is a feeling of dread and an avoidance of death as well as anything that serves to remind us of its existence. The funeral industry has responded to our increasing secularism and death avoidance by providing more services that defend against the stark finality of death. The funeral home is an intrinsic part of the bureaucratized death system, assuming responsibility for the body from time of release from the hospital until final interment. So much in control is this death system that often hospitals will refuse to release the body to anyone but a licensed funeral director.

After the body has been obtained from the hospital, the funeral director will prepare it for "viewing," which usually takes place in the funeral home. The body is embalmed and dressed, make-up is applied if necessary, and the corpse is placed in the selected casket. ("Coffin" and "undertaker" are terms that the occupation prefers to replace with "casket" and "funeral director," which are seen as more professional and less death-oriented.)[25] The casket is then placed in a room used to view the body, called by some funeral directors a "slumber room," much to the delight of those who oppose current funeral practices.[26] Times during which the family will be present are published, and the public is invited to pay their respects.

Since the turn of the century, more and more funeral homes have been providing chapels where a religious service may be held. While many religions prefer that a sacred service be held in a church or synagogue, the use of facilities provided by the funeral home is often allowed. The service is typically followed by burial, perhaps with a short ceremony committing the body to the earth.

An informal folkway of American society is a group meal of consolation following the funeral. In small towns and in urban neighborhoods where there is a network of acquaintances, this may take place in the home. Friends and neighbors may bring food, and people will socialize informally. In other situations the family may go to a restaurant or have a reception of some sort at the church. This informal ceremony of traditional gathering has been overlooked in examinations of the rites of passage, yet I would maintain that it serves an important function in the reintegration of those who have experienced the loss. It serves as an opportunity for those who have undergone a change in status as well as those who have stopped their normal activities to recognize the existence of death, to start to behave in a normal fashion. The redistribution of rights, duties, and wealth, often a part of the formal ceremonies of primitive peoples, may be carried out on an informal basis during the gathering after a contemporary funeral. At the same time, this social gathering may serve as an opportunity for the group immediately surrounding the bereaved to show their solidarity in the face of death.

One of the best analyses of the meaning and function of American funeral behavior was done by W. Lloyd Warner. In his study of Yankee City, a pseudonym for a city of 17,000 in New England, Warner takes into account not only the ceremonies performed for individual deaths, but also the public rituals for the dead that take place on Memorial Day.[27] This historic ceremony serves to restate the community's common images, as well as to provide for a sense of connection with its history. It appears that the Memorial Day ceremony no longer is as meaningful a collective representation as it was during and immediately following World War II. It may be that it no longer reflects the popular image, and that the sentiments expressed in Memorial Day observations are no longer dominant in the public image. Although the United States has been involved in two wars since that time, the Korean conflict and the Vietnam War were not the triumphs of a righteous America that World Wars I and II were. In fact, they symbolize aspects of the American way that some would prefer not to immortalize in yearly ceremonies. As a result, Memorial Day ceremonies recognizing the war dead tend to be sparsely attended in many communities today.

At the same time that the honoring of those who died in war has become less popular, due to the questionable motives behind our involvement in those wars, America has become more avoidance-prone around the entire subject of death. These two trends have contributed to the demise of the Memorial Day ceremony as a representation of the community's collective image; a demonstration of the community's unity and values. The image of dying for one's country as a worthwhile act has become less popular as Americans have come to question the national priorities that embroiled the country in the Korean and Vietnam wars. In addition, those wars involved fewer Americans than the two World Wars, and there was less of a perceived threat to the nation as a whole.

The American funeral ceremony, from the time of the viewing of the body through to the social gathering following the formal funeral ritual, is an area that has not been thoroughly studied. There is a need to examine the various religious services and how they each define, explain, and respond to death. An historical analysis is needed to examine changes in such activities as Memorial Day services, as well as the changes in religious practices which have occurred over the course of the nation's history. These gaps in our knowledge dramatize the paucity of thanatological data, and the need for continued research in the field.

We have seen that the ceremonies surrounding death have undergone changes as the meaning of death has changed. As with many other facets of our daily lives, death has become institutionalized, and that very process insulates us from the stark reality of it. Improved living conditions have made death the province of older people, those whom we have already shunted away from the mainstream of American life. Death is seen as a failure of medical science, and sacred responses are no longer as paramount to people's needs as they once were. Consolation is no longer found in the Book of Job, but in grief therapy, as the therapist plays the supportive role once filled by family, friends, or religion.

It is an open question whether people's needs are being better met by the contemporary secular approach to death, as compared with the more sacred responses of the past. It is all too easy to look back with a romantic bias, seeing the past as the days when life was good and things were simple. In times of rapid social change such as we are now witnessing, the past is remembered as a time in which life was easier to live. But a caution is necessary: Often social proscriptions lasted longer than the value of ceremony or custom, and people were forced to behave in ways that did little to meet their inner needs. The behaviors of people in an earlier age may have been performed out of a sense of duty, and not because any personal gratification was being gained. The widow who refused to wear black and mourn for a year would feel the censure of her contemporaries.

While we may look back from our position which is relatively free of ceremonial and normative constraints upon an earlier more structured age with a certain amount of envy, a more realistic appraisal is necessary. For example, the worlds of the living and the dead during the nineteenth century were very much intertwined. As a result, the dead were able to influence the living through their presence. This took the form of spiritual messages as well as the very real place that the dead occupied in the public image of the time. One was forced by the collective image of the closeness of the dead to partake in long mourning customs, which might far outweigh the individual's grieving needs. Huge sums were spent on elaborate funerals, graves, and tombstones (as much as one year's salary), because these were socially expected expressions of caring about the deceased. While we might hunger for the emotional support that we see as a part of the old-fashioned funeral, our values are decidedly different. Today there is more of a reluctance to spend lavishly on the deceased if the result is to be a burden upon the living.

Also, I am skeptical about the assumption that the old-fashioned gathering of friends, family, and neighbors would stand by the bereaved through the grief process. S. J. Kleinberg, in one of the few studies of working class death behaviors at the turn of the century, recounts the story of one widow of some years counseling a woman who had just become widowed. She stated that after the ceremony was over, people would quickly forget her. "For a few days everybody is sorry for you; after that you are just another widow."[28] This sounds remarkably similar to the concerns of the contemporary widow.

A society develops the ceremonies and collective images that it needs. Now probably more than ever, it is possible for people to fashion whatever kind of a funeral ceremony they feel meets their needs. There are few laws, except perhaps those of public health, that prohibit or restrict the kind of behavior that the group might wish to engage in. As we shall see later in this chapter, those opposed to current funeral behaviors attempt to label the funeral industry as the perpetrator of vulgar and unhealthy ceremonies. The general public more often demands the services that are provided, however, and these services have remained remarkably similar in their general form over the last 200 years.

As life becomes more bureaucratically routinized and emotions more private, the funeral ceremony appears to have become less popular. There is usually not the need for a community response, as the increasing anonymity of mass society means that society is less and less affected by the loss of a single individual.

While many have discussed this in terms of its effects upon the grief-stricken, few have asked what the effects might be of living in a ritual-less society.[29]

The Ritual-less Society and the Death of Ceremony

As our mourning and funeral behavior become less important in our lives and in the lives of the community, we can ask what purpose they have served and why we have chosen to deemphasize ceremonies which connect us to our history, and are so important in other cultures. This discussion relates not only to the ceremonies of death, but other ceremonies that mark life's changes as well.

The Growth of Secularism. With the increase in secularism and rationalism which has coincided with a decline in sacred values, ceremonies have become suspect. In our growing secularism we have chosen to regard ceremonies as religious activities and, therefore, of little value to contemporary humanity. Also, ceremonies often focus on historically valid symbols, and the future-oriented, rational-scientific outlook is skeptical of the values of the past. Because many values and attitudes of today are radically different from those held by previous generations, symbolic, ceremonial behavior may not be seen as relevant to contemporary life. As a result, many people see no value in ceremonial activities such as funerals or memorial services.

The Bureaucratization of Society. The bureaucratic ethos holds that activity that does not result in some extrinsic end—that is not purposeful—has no value. Ceremonial behavior is a gesture, a representation of some aspect of the collective image. As such, it is performed for its own sake, and not for some quantifiable end result. Since ceremony appeals to our nonrational senses, it can be difficult to justify in terms of such rational standards as cost and efficiency.

Rationalism and Positivism. The rise of science as a predominant value has brought with it a belief in the value of rational thinking and behavior. Ceremony is sentimental—it expresses those parts of our shared image of the world which are neither rationally nor scientifically comprehensible. The same holds true for art. Norman Rockwell, whose art was never considered by critics to be of the highest artistic caliber, still was able to capture a part of the public image that cannot be conveyed rationally. His tremendous popularity was due to his ability to evoke emotional responses from many who shared a collective image of American life. Today, Rockwell's work is often seen as a naive representation of a simpler era. Our current scientific ethos seeks other, less sentimental understandings of life. The trust in science and rationality as ultimate solutions to life's puzzles is a strong part of contemporary American values. That which appeals to the irrational and emotional in us is met with suspicion and distrust. This is the legacy of such as Sigmund Freud. The basis of feelings lies in irrationality. The rational mind must triumph and control the threat of unleashed feeling.

Mass Society and Atomized Man

Ceremonies, as we have said, are representations of the collective image. As society has become more heterogeneous and mobile, the individual has lost many ties to the extended family and large society. Since the time of Emile Durkheim, sociologists and anthropologists have spoken of the need for a collective demonstration of solidarity in the face of death. Today, society is no longer threatened by the death of any one of its members, unless that person happens to be a national leader. Our bureaucratized society has responded to the reality of death by developing a system in which no one is indispensable, and those who stand a greater chance of dying are retired out of important positions in society. As a result, the ceremonies of the past are no longer meaningful in the present. Ceremonial recognition wanes in the face of bureaucratic efficiency and rationality.

But ceremonies continue to exist. There seems to be a resistance to abolishing them completely. As Orrin Klapp points out in *The Collective Search for Identity,* we seem to recognize the need to express ourselves in a collective fashion.[30] Perhaps the problem lies not in the idea of ceremony itself, but in the images that the ceremonies of the past represent. The content may not reflect the shared images of our contemporary society, and as a result they are seen as empty formal rituals to be endured. As Lifton argues, we have become disconnected from history.[31]

This does not mean that we should return to the sentimentalism of Victorian times or mimic a primitive tribe's violent responses to death. But we do need to search for ways of expressing the contemporary images which link the members of our society together. Perhaps, on the other hand, the lack of meaningful ceremonies in our society is symptomatic of a lack of a commonly shared image, though it is doubtful that this is the case. If it were, such a disparity of commonality would evidence itself in other aspects of American life, such as in the political arena.

The lack of public ceremony has taken its toll on our society. We are characterized by some as being the epitome of Simmel's urban man; emotionless, atomized, and calculating in our outlook on life.[32] Our ceremonies of death, in which we also represent our image of life, are unemotional, commercialized, and often materialistic. "Social sentiments" are not reinforced and proclaimed, and as a result our shared images weaken, and our atomization—our individual loneliness in the midst of mass society—is felt even more deeply. Some are turning to immediate body disposal services and eliminating ceremony entirely. Perhaps they are saying, "Better no ceremony at all than one that only a lonely few attend—if anyone attends at all."

Lest we end this discussion on a pessimistic note, let us remember that American society is nothing if not resilient and plastic. Our ability to shape ourselves is great, and we are thus able to experiment with new forms and representations of the feelings and the values that we share. New religious movements, innovative funeral ceremonies, and greater appreciation of individual needs at a time of loss are examples of efforts to develop a new appreciation of death, and to express a new image of our mortality. We can hope to create new collective images of life and death that will speak to the emotional as well as the cognitive needs of society's members.

Images in Stone: The Cemetery

While ceremonies are group representations of collective images, the cemetery serves to represent the meanings of life and death in static form. Warner spoke of the cemetery as the city of the dead, and it is worthy of study because it represents the values and social structure of the living. Warner considered the importance of the cemetery as a representation of the collective image of death when he wrote that "cemeteries are collective representations which reflect and express many of the community's basic beliefs and values about what kind of society it is, what the persons of men are, and where each fits into the secular world of the living and the spiritual society of the dead."[33] As ceremonies changed along with the changes in the meaning in death, so did the cemetery.

The Cemetery of Sacred Death

Early in the history of the United States, the burial place was a site of common burial, usually in the churchyard. Because it was only a temporary resting place until Judgment Day, there was no need to mark the spot. Families in the farmlands usually had a piece of land set aside to use for burial of its members. Also, the Puritans feared that gravestones would serve to focus attention on this world, rather than on the next. When gravestones first came into use, it was forbidden for them to have any kind of decoration, and it wasn't until the middle of the eighteenth century that extensive artwork became part of New England iconography.

As tombstones became more ornate, and their messages spoke of all manner of things from religious verse to humor, the graveyard was still considered an unattractive necessity in the community. The image of sacred death of the Puritans meant that graveyards were places to be avoided except during burials. As a result, by the time the image of death had changed into a more secular and positive condition, the graveyards had fallen into a state of disrepair and neglect.[34]

The Cemetery of Secular Death

As death became something more approachable, concern began to arise about the disreputable condition of the country's grave-yards. Also, by the early 1800s, graveyards that once had been on the fringes of villages were now in the middle of bustling urban areas. In Boston, for instance, a graveyard once on the edge of the common grazing land is today surrounded by office buildings. The growth in population, as well as the longer existence of the graveyards, contributed to their becoming overcrowded and disorganized.[35]

The response to this problem was a civic concern, and as such it marked the beginning of a collective activity which resulted in the development of cemeteries very different from the unkempt and rambling graveyards of the earlier era.

The cemetery consists of concrete representations that express people's images of immortality. These symbols serve as a connection with immortality for the living. The cemetery must also contend with the secular problem of disposing of the rotting corpse and presenting in its stead a more acceptable image of the immortal soul. Naturally, the more pleasant the images, the more the living will be consoled and, therefore, seek out their company. Thus the rural cemetery movement came into existence.

The decaying graveyard of the past, with inscriptions that often warned the reader of his or her own mortality, was not a pleasant place to be. In contrast, the new cemeteries of the beginning of the nineteenth century were to be places of inspiration, beauty, and peace, combined with sentimental statuary—and a good deal of conspicuous consumption.

In the Boston area, for example, Mount Auburn Cemetery was created in order to repudiate the unsightly graveyards of the past. Nature was not supposed to overrun man's efforts. Quite the contrary: man was in charge here, laying out a formal system of roadways and paths, regulating the materials used so that only enduring stone was allowed, and encouraging statuary which would show the living "much of our destiny and duty."[36] The cemetery was to be a chronicle of history, a "perpetual home," representing the highest values of the community.

The rural cemetery movement served as a basis for the development of the art of sculpture in America, although the effort was less than uniform. A visit to one of these rural cemeteries such as Mount Auburn in Cambridge, Forest Hills in New York City, or Magnolia in Charleston, South Carolina, reveals Egyptian tomb architecture and classical Greek revival monuments, sometimes combined with Christian religious symbolism in a rather freewheeling display. Religious symbols were not as common as they had been in the past because of the increasing value placed on science and naturalism.[37]

The graves were removed from the normal traffic of life, and placed in a gardenlike setting supervised by specialists in horticulture and landscaping. Death had now taken another step away from everyday life. At the same time, the area was designated as having cultural value: it was to represent to the living the lessons of life that were to be seen in the uplifting statuary that the cemeteries contained. If this sounds a bit like a statement of social values, it is because the conservatives of the 1820s and 1830s saw in the cemetery an opportunity to instruct the populace about the values which (according to them) had made this country great.[38] The message was conveyed to a large audience, as these cemeteries became popular recreational sites. Families would gather for picnics and outings in the local cemetery. Laurel Hill Cemetery in Philadelphia claimed 30,000 visitors a year during this period, and other cemeteries reported traffic problems due to their popularity.[39]

The statuary in the rural cemetery was very personal, symbolically representing the deceased's accomplishments. A statue might depict some aspect of the individual's work, such as a ship or a fireman's helmet. Other more personal representations were of the dead person's favorite pastimes or hobbies. Graphic descriptions in stone depicted angels opening the coffin to release the spirit of the deceased, or leading the person upward to Heaven. The emphasis upon the grieving so prevalent at this time was not lost in the cemetery. Examples of this are such statues as a man visiting the graves of his wife and daughters, a grieving angel weeping upon a gravestone, and a shroud-wrapped baby lying in his bassinet. One was limited only by the approval of the cemetery officials and one's own finances and resources. As a result ornate mausoleums were built by the wealthy which would command respect from the passers-by. These little buildings in stone often drew their inspiration from famous buildings of the past, and range from replicas of da Vinci's tomb in France to Parthenon-like structures.

Everywhere the values of the time were evident. One man's portrayal of his wife which was immortalized in stone shows her waiting dutifully for his return at the end of the working day. Power is represented by lions guarding a family mausoleum, or achievements depicted by statuary. In Poughkeepsie, New York, there is a gravestone that shows a detailed representation of a fire truck and the simple inscription, "Duty on earth, Reward in Heaven." In these examples we see the Victorian values of woman as homemaker, the importance of private money as social power, and work as the way to salvation (the latter being an updated Puritan theme).[40]

At the same time that the cemetery was becoming a popular place in which to demonstrate society's values (as determined by the wealthy), the changing image of the dead could be seen in the financial and social investment being made to recognize the dead. This follows the same pattern that we saw in examining ceremonial behavior, where elaboration and ostentation became the norm. With death no longer full of hellfire and brimstone, with life expectancy slowly improving, and Heaven depicted as middle-class gracious living at its best, the cemetery came to be a place that represented a resolution of any questions one might have concerning mortality. At the same time, the cemetery became a cultural repository, and a symbolic representation of the collective American image. Of course, *whose* values became immortalized in stone or demonstrated through a mausoleum is another question. It was not the poor, who were dying in the mills and slums, but rather the rich who were able to afford such displays.

Warner found that the location of burial plots within the cemetery could indicate the nature of the social structure of the time.[41] He notes that the collective gravesites for families, often delineated from the rest of society by an iron fence, almost always had the father at the center of the grouping. The image of Warner's Yankee City men as superior to women can be seen in the stonework of the cemetery, where their worldly accomplishments are recorded far more often than women's.[41]

Location of the burial plot within the Yankee City cemeteries reflected one's money and status, with the poor relegated to the most unattractive sections because of their inability to afford anything better. As Warner puts it, "Where the body of a man is placed when he dies tells much about his meaning as an individual, but it may tell even more about his social place and significance to those who survive him."[42] So important was graveyard status, that Warner states that at the time of his study, it was not unusual for newly prominent families to have their poorer deceased relatives disinterred and reburied in more socially desirable locations, which more appropriately reflected the family's new social status.[43] This is an interesting example of post-death social mobility.

The Cemeteries of the Age of Avoided Death

As death has become a subject to be avoided, images in stone in cemeteries have diminished in size. The statuary of the past would most likely be seen as ostentatious, and a sign of bad taste. Cemeteries could be classified as upper, middle, and lower class in earlier times, but today class distinction and racial segregation tend to be breaking down. This is probably the result of an increased standard of living for the population as a whole, combined with the increasing competition for business. However, as recently as 1950, it was still impossible for a black person to be interred in any cemetery within the city limits of Philadelphia.[44]

In the newer sections of cemeteries, gravestones are laid flat on the ground in orderly rows, making it easier to care for the cemetery. The demands of the cost-efficient machine seem to be imposed upon us even in death. The people who wish to erect statues or larger monuments may do so if they wish to spend the extra money. A Southern California mausoleum, containing hundreds of individual crypts, also has vaults available which are topped with replicas of famous religious statuary such as Michellangelo's "Pieta." However, these vaults cost over $15,000, and are not the public's typical choice. The emphasis today is upon a much more simplified grave than in the previous era, again perhaps representing the social isolation of grieving as well as the avoidance of death.

Potter's fields, publicly maintained graveyards for the poor and indigent, still exist in many communities in order to dispose of the bodies of those unable to pay for private burial. Hart Island in New York harbor has served the city as a common burying ground since 1869, and over 600,000 poor people have been buried there. Convicts write the individual's name or "unknown" on the rough pine boxes, and bury the caskets in lots with a simple marker to note each lot.[45]

Warner's thesis that the cemetery reflects society's values is evident in contemporary cemeteries. The desire to avoid death, the economy of machine care, and the deemphasis of emotions are all evident in the popularity of small stones, set uniformly close to the earth, with little in the way of emotion-provoking words or images. The poor are afforded little or no recognition, and are segregated into potter's fields.

The American Funeral Director

Prior to the latter part of the nineteenth century, funeral directing was an unorganized occupation, often performed as a sideline by church sextons, furniture makers, and livery men. Their work as undertakers, as they were then called, grew naturally out of their other occupations as city dwellers of Colonial times became more dependent upon specialists for services.

The actual preparation of the body in the early part of the nation's history was performed by a member of the family or perhaps a neighbor. This was a traditional activity that was passed on to successive generations, much as other abilities necessary to family functioning were passed on.[46] By the beginning of the nineteenth century, cabinetmakers were beginning to advertise as coffin builders as well.

Nurses, who were employed by the family, were the first people paid to prepare bodies in the United States. As nurses became more independent and offered their services to the general public, they included body preparation in describing their activities.[47] Gradually this role was taken over by the businesses supplying the coffin and/or hearse as the industry became consolidated. By 1882, there was enough of a clearly defined occupation with its own specialized interests for the National Funeral Directors' Association to be organized.

As America's image of death was changing, the industry changed its products. In the middle of the nineteenth century, the box-shaped casket was introduced, which was developed to obviate to some degree the disagreeable sensations produced by a coffin with its more human form, the latter now being relegated to horror films.[48]

The promotion of the term "casket" also diverted attention from death, and the caskets themselves took on new meanings as they became more elaborate and concerned with preservation of the body. Embalming, first widely practiced during the Civil War, added to the emphasis upon body preservation. This coincided with the increasingly secular image of death. The body was becoming more important than the soul in funeral activities.[49]

As we have noted, the funeral parlor replaced the family parlor as the location for the funeral director's activity. This was a result of several factors: Living space was changing, and in urban areas a centrally located facility was more convenient.[50] As society became more mobile, the increasing interstate shipping of bodies required some form of receiving facility. At the same time, the development of a central location allowed the funeral director to offer more services, and thereby increase his profit. This shift in location also had another effect: "By banishing the parlor from the home to the funeral parlor, families also banished the associations of death that lingered in the parlor after a funeral."[51] America's aversion to death was increasing, and the availability of facilities to deal with death were quickly accepted by the public.

As the image of death and its concomitant ceremonies has changed, so has the occupation of funeral director. As Farrell describes it:

> Just as naturalists accented the ease of a natural death, and as cemetery superintendents maintained a natural living landscape, so funeral directors aimed for a natural lifelike appearance of the body. As cemetery superintendents improved nature to preserve her charms, so also funeral directors tried to "retain and improve the complexion as one of the conditions of success." Eventually they even applied theatrical cosmetics to attain "the desired natural lifelike color of the face." Funeral directors also began to dress and position the corpse naturally. "Modern custom decrees that the body shall be in all respects as nearly like it was in life as possible," noted one authority. "The custom of dressing it in the kind of clothes worn in life rather than in the sepulcher shroud is a most sensible and natural one."[52]

Today, many funeral homes provide for the entire management of death, to include simple body disposal through cremation as well as elaborate funeral ceremonies, body preservation, and interment in a mausoleum.

The Funeral Director: A Role Analysis

The funeral director functions as what Warner calls a "transition technician."[53] His or her duty is to assist in the rites of passage which transform the person from the world of the living to the world of the dead. The occupation consists of taking the body which is considered by society to be unclean and often is diseased, and changing it into a representation of a person in peaceful sleep. Warner provides the following analysis of the funeral director's activities:

> Basically he is a private enterpriser who will do the ritually unclean and physically distasteful work of disposing of the dead in a manner satisfying to the living, at a price which they can pay. He sells his goods and services for a profit. His salesmen, applying the sound logics of business enterprise, attempt to sell his goods—coffins and other mortuary paraphernalia—at

the highest price possible, and he buys at a price low enough to maximize profit. As a businessman he advertises, enters into civic life, and engages in other activities businessmen use to increase business and compete successfully with their rivals. As an enterpriser he hires employees—drivers and other skilled workers—and by steadily increasing the size of his work force and the effectiveness of his sales organization, enlarges his business, profits, and importance in the community.

One of the important points that Warner makes in this description concerns the unclean and distasteful aspects of funeral work. In many societies, those who perform tasks that are what we might call the dirty work of society are often stigmatized by their occupation. This is called "pollution" by anthropologists, who speak of those who care for the dead as often being polluted by their occupations.[55] (This concept may be extended to other conditions of uncleanliness, such as menstruation.) Often there are rituals that may be performed to cleanse the individual and rid him of his uncleanliness. This kind of stigmatization is not limited to primitive tribes, however. For example, Sudnow describes the role of the morgue attendant in a large hospital as death-tainted. As a result, the man who was trapped in that role worked very hard to dissociate himself from his job in order to mask the stigma of polluted work.[56]

This description applies to the role of funeral director, who is also polluted by his occupation. Pine found that in some cases, urban funeral directors who live at a distance from their work will seek to hide their occupation from their surburban neighbors.[57] This becomes more difficult in smaller communities where such anonymity is not as easily attained.

Pine, in his study of funeral directors, sees striking differences between rural and urban funeral directors. The urban funeral director is characterized as "a bureaucrat" whose work "generally is anonymous and impersonal, often is subject to criticism by the public."[58] This is very different from the picture of the small town funeral director, who Pine characterizes as "concerned with the professional aspects of the work" and who "enjoys high social status, considerable community prestige, political power, and personal respect."[59]

Pine's characterizations seem to typify the rural-urban dichotomy that has been popular in the past, wherein the urbanite is seen as cold, calculating, and mercenary, while the rural dweller is warm, caring and altruistic. Crouch, in attempting a more rigorous study of funeral directors, found that professionalism as measured by adherence to certain values was higher among urban than rural funeral directors.[60] (Pine's findings were based more upon his personal observance of funeral directors in rural and urban settings, while Crouch used questionnaires to gather his data.) The anonymity of role preferred by the urban funeral director may also be preferred by the rural director, but he or she is simply not allowed the luxury of escaping from the occupation. Also, the rural director may be able to counter the stigma of his or her occupation by being active in the community, thereby counteracting some of the negative images associated with the job of funeral directing.

The pollution associated with the funeral director's job may flow from sources other than his handling of the dead body. Because the tasks are so disliked by the public, it is logical for people to assume that only a strange kind of person would possibly want to do them.[61] If this is not the case, then perhaps it is the profit motive that motivates one to become a funeral director. Pine points out that the funeral director cannot gain role distance by joking or denigrating his or her clients, because this would only reinforce the image of the funeral director "as 'more ghoulish' than some people already believe he is."[62] (This technique of denigrating clients is often used by others who work with the less socially desirable, such as the mentally ill or handicapped.) More common ways for the funeral director to deal with the pollution of the occupation are the use of euphemistic jargon to gain distance, such as "making a call" when picking up a body, or attempting to identify the work as a profession and emphasizing the professional aspects of the job.[63]

An important aspect of being labeled as having a polluted occupation is the victimization of the individual or occupation which may occur. As a means of venting society's anxieties, the unclean may be set upon, as if punishing them will punish (or rid the world of) the unwanted, dirty image they represent.[64] One form of this victimization of the funeral director is the low esteem in which the occupation is held by the public; another is the use of the role as a negative or comic relief character in the media.

In a society that seeks to deny the reality of death, the funeral director is a living symbol of this dreaded subject. At the same time, the funeral director may be seen by some as one who profits from another's loss.[65] The anger that is a fundamental part of the grieving process may be projected onto the funeral director, who is a prominent figure in the process of social affirmation that the death has occurred.

In addition to the external strains associated with the occupation of funeral director, there are internal strains as well. Wishing for more funerals, which would spell success, also means wishing for death to strike more often.[66] Most obviously, the funeral director is surrounded by death and grief. Many hours each day are spent dealing with the bereaved, as well as performing tasks that most people would react to with abhorrence. The role of these "dismal traders," and the resulting psychological stress have been neglected areas of research. That work which has been done, however, does not lead to the conclusion that funeral directors are necessarily ghoulish, profit-mad, or unethical characters, as some would like to label them.

In a society that views the corpse with horror, the funeral director reduces those feelings of revulsion by making the body "acceptable" again. In the process, the illusion that is presented again restores a kind of manageability to death. Contemporary people have contended with death by means of science and technology. When these fail, then death reasserts itself as of old; replete with all its primal terror and images. To proceed from a technological battle with death to a direct confrontation with a rotting corpse is too much for us. As a result, we require of the funeral director an intercession to soften the blow. This is not a true denial of death, for if it were so, then the funeral industry would be inventing more and more lifelike presentations of the body. The corpse may look "at rest," but this does not imply "alive." What the public desires is a blunted representation of death, to make its reality easier to confront. When death appears, we avoid it in the abstract, and attempt to mute it in the concrete in order to make it somehow more manageable. This job—making the reality of death more manageable—we delegate to the funeral director.[67] It is a job few of us would take on ourselves.

Occupational Role Strain

Within the role of the funeral director, there also exist competing images that produce a great deal of role strain, as the individual seeks to deal with opposing values.

On the one hand, the funeral director seeks to be treated as a professional, and refers to himself as a professional. On the other hand, he is called upon to be a businessman, to produce a profit, and to run a successful business. The result of this role strain has had ramifications which extend from the highest organizational levels of the occupation to the self-image held by individual funeral directors. The two organizations that represent the vast majority of funeral directors differ on the very issue of professional versus business values. The National Funeral Directors Association espouses professional values, while the smaller National Selected Morticians takes a more business-oriented view of the occupation. The NSM seeks to promote the occupation by emphasizing business practices and concepts to its members. The NFDA, the larger and more powerful of the two organizations, seeks to promote the occupation through community education, mass media, political lobbying, and communicating with association members.[68]

On the individual level, the values espoused by professional organizations are not so evident or easily separated. In a study of over 400 funeral directors, Crouch found that only 18 percent favored professional values, only 17 percent could be classified as favoring business values, and 24 percent were a mixture of the two. The remaining 41 percent could not be classified as holding either set of values.[69] Combining the last two categories, we see that 65 percent of the funeral directors in the study were either conflicted or ambiguous in relation to the two primary values espoused by their leading occupational organizations.

This lack of a clear set of values, when combined with social stigma and the ambivalence in which the occupation is held, produce an occupational group which is extremely sensitive to public criticism, and which works hard to enhance its position in society. Sometimes these efforts have been to its own detriment, as critics have also used trade communications on improving the funeral directors' public image to deride the occupation.[70] Attempts to establish the funeral director as a professional similar to the doctor, lawyer, or minister have generally met with little success, because the funeral director fails to evidence many of the characteristics and values of a professional status. Instead, such efforts often evoke unfavorable comments from those critical of the occupation, who usually prevail in such arguments.[71]

Analysis of the dilemma of the funeral director leads us to argue that, if he or she is truly to espouse professional values, efforts must be made not only to promote a good public image, but in fact to *become professional*. For example, the educational standards for professionals require at least a college education.[72] Altruism and commitment to the profession must take precedence over profit, and practitioners must aggressively seek to eliminate the unethical, untrained, and unscrupulous members from the occupation. Such efforts have met with resistance when attempted in the past, which is indicative of a reluctance of many funeral directors to take on the responsibilities and burdens that are part of the role of the professional. Until the members of the occupation resolve these issues, the role of the funeral director will be subjected to the strains of these conflicting self-images.

Issues in Funeral Directing

The funeral industry has been severely criticized, most notably by Jessica Mitford in her *The American Way of Death*, Ruth Harmer in *The High Cost of Dying*, and Leroy Bowman in *The American Funeral: A Study of Guilt, Extravagance, and Sublimity*.[74] These authors contend that the funeral industry is guilty of several unethical—if not illegal—practices which result in their exploiting the bereaved family in order to amass huge profits. Since Mitford's book has been the most popular of these, we will examine her work more closely.

Mitford has a lucid writing style which she combines with a satirical wit to produce highly readable work. While presenting some valid complaints against the funeral industry, she comingles them with a quasi-British perspective which delights in scathing attacks upon anything that bespeaks the common American. An example of this is Mitford's description of the contemporary American funeral home:

> An appropriate showcase setting for all these treasures assumes a special importance. Gone forever are the simple storefront undertaking establishments of earlier days. They have been replaced by elaborate structures in the style of English country houses, French provincial chateaux, Spanish missions, split-level suburban executive mansions, or Byzantine mosques—frequently, in a freewheeling mixture of all of these. A Gothic chapel may be carpeted with the latest in wall-to-wall two-inch-thick extra-pile Acrilan, and persian rugs laid on top of

this; its bronze-gilt door may open onto an authentically furnished Victorian drawing room in one corner of which is a chrome-and-tile coffee bar. The slumber rooms in the same building may stress the light and airy Swedish modern motif.[75]

For those in need of instruction on gentility and good taste, Mitford provides a chapter on the English funeral. Her description of her visit to a London funeral establishment is enlightening, in view of her description of the typical American funeral home:

> Mr. Aston was a charming host. He led me through his entrance hall, conservatively decorated with neutral wallpaper and wine-red upholstered furniture, up the stairs to his private office where we chatted over a cup of tea.[76]

This is a far cry from her characterization of the American funeral home. While the entertainment value of Mitford's rather waggish approach to her subject matter entertains the general reader, her often valid criticisms tend to get lost in her reachings for the satirical.

Her argument is based upon a belief that the bereaved family is in no condition to make wise decisions about the funeral. She quotes the industry trade publications at length, as they discuss the funeral transaction and how to make it more profitable. Ignorance of the law on the part of the consumer, the lack of price tags on caskets, and the pressure of a polished sales technique combine to separate the grief-stricken from their money, she claims.[77] Mitford also attacks the costs of funerals, claiming that expensive funerals are foisted on those least able to afford it, using up insurance money that could be put to better use. The idea of preservation—a major part of the sales promotions for caskets—is questioned by Mitford, because a sealed container may actually promote a rapid decomposition of the corpse.[78] The allied industries—cemetery management, florists, and casketmakers—are described by Mitford as attempting to promote lucrative funerals, while at the same time discouraging attempts to offer alternative means of body disposal.[79]

Mitford's solution to the high cost of funerals and what she considers their ostentatious bad taste is cremation, which can be much cheaper than a funeral with the body present. What can be distilled from Mitford's work, as well as from other works criticizing the funeral industry, are the following controversies:

Exploiting the Vulnerability of the Bereaved

As we have seen in our examination of the grieving process, the trauma of loss can involve disorientation, emotional imbalance, and extreme dependency upon others. This psychological state, when combined with many people's ignorance and inexperience about funeral practices, may place the consumer in a position which is different from the usual buying transaction. Other factors that may influence decision-making when arranging a funeral are guilt and the pressure of time. It is rare that a person will shop for the best price in making funeral arrangements. The result of these psychological and time-related factors is that the person making the arrangements can be vulnerable to the pressures of the funeral director.

The issue of the mourner's guilt being used as a means of exploitation by the funeral director needs special consideration. This is a charge that is often leveled by critics of the industry, and implies unethical behavior on the part of the funeral director. However, those critiques often overlook the fact that in our materialistic society, one of the ways of demonstrating feelings for others is through giving them material goods. If an individual clearly wants to spend a great deal of money on a funeral for a loved one, and if this purchase serves to relieve the negative feelings of guilt on the part of the bereaved, is it unethical for the funeral director to provide it? This is, of course, different from taking advantage of the emotional or intellectual vulnerability of the bereaved by pressuring them into purchasing something that they do not want or need. While these incidents do occur, they are less frequent than the critics of the industry would lead people to believe, as several researchers have shown.[80]

Critics of the funeral industry generally oppose the materialistic bent of the American ethos, preferring more intellectual and physically simpler styles of living; a value orientation that can lead to its own kind of snobbery. While this approach to life may satisfy a few, the majority of Americans place a great deal of importance upon material possessions. It is a natural extension of this materialism to want to provide a funeral which demonstrates the values held by the family. This may serve to relieve feelings of guilt or sorrow, and, if so, then perhaps it has served its purpose.

It may be that the critics of the funeral industry are misplacing their anger. To accuse the American public of being too involved with material possessions—too wrapped up in worldly pursuits—is a valid criticism. But to attack the funeral director seems to be setting up a straw man. If people did not want what the funeral director offers, they would not purchase it. This is a strong statement to make, in light of our knowledge of the vulnerability of the bereaved. However, two important studies lend credence to this position. Khleif, in an independent study of the industry, found that 94 percent of his respondents reported a high level of satisfaction with the funeral that they had purchased.[81] Another study, done by the State of Minnesota, also confirmed a high satisfaction level among its respondents.[82]

There is no question that some bereaved persons are somewhat vulnerable to sales pressures. But most people (86%) who are making funeral decisions are accompanied by at least one other person, and often there are three or more involved in the decision-making process.[83] This helps to prevent situations where individuals can be talked into purchasing a funeral that they would later regret. Few report feeling a time pressure, or pressure from the funeral director. Also, by and large the funeral industry is aware that a great deal of its business is based upon goodwill and word of mouth, and that a dissatisfied client can do more harm than will be offset by profiteering from a single sale.

It appears that the intense competition within the industry has contributed to a need for a high profit level in each transaction. There are many more funeral homes in the United States than are needed. Of the approximately 22,000 homes in operation, only 2000 could handle all of the needs of the entire country. As a result, the average number of deaths handled by each home is 94 per year, but the actual number of funerals per home differs from this figure. Large firms account for almost half of the funerals in many areas, sharply reducing the number of funerals per home among the smaller homes.[73] The large overhead in each home makes a high gross price necessary.

One of the important aspects of the funeral transaction is ignorance on the part of the purchasers. When making arrangements for a funeral, the typical consumer has less information than when making any other major purchase. The Federal Trade Commission noted this, stating that in our death-avoiding society, "information on death is neither sought or disseminated."[84] In a society where *caveat emptor* is a basic tenet, to enter into a transaction ignorant of its legal and financial aspects may lead the individual to spend

more than he would have had to spend had he been at all knowledgeable. However, few people seem to have the inclination to
become informed about a topic so closely related to death, a subject
most choose to avoid as much as possible.

The Practice of Embalming

Embalming came into widespread use during the Civil War, and
has remained a major part of the traditional funeral. It is also the
focus of a great deal of criticism. The embalming process involves
replacing the body fluids with a preservative chemical. Usually
this is followed by a beautification of the body prior to viewing.
It serves no hygienic purpose, nor does it permanently stop decay.[85]
It serves in the main to make the body presentable for public viewing.

Gorer considers embalming the ultimate denial of death.[86] He
argues that the process of artificially preserving the body impedes
the grief process, thereby hindering its successful resolution. Lifton
is of the opinion that the embalming of the body may confuse
images in the viewer's mind, as the dead body is used to represent
continuity and immortality. This preservation of the body is, of
course, a facade, but Lifton's concern is for those who might not
see through it and attach literal meanings to the symbolic use of
the corpse. Both these perspectives imply an inability to discern
the difference between the dead body and its presentation. There
are no studies to indicate that this confusion is a frequent occurrence, nor am I aware of any studies that imply that seeing the
body in a beautified condition is unhealthy. Opinions as to the
beneficial or deleterious effects of having the embalmed body present at the funeral service or viewing, however, are everywhere.
The only agreement on this issue is that a viewing is appropriate
when there has been a sudden or unexpected death. It is generally
agreed that in such cases viewing the body is often necessary in
order to fully accept the death.[88]

Those who favor having the body present argue that embalming and restoration provide an image that will be acceptable to
those grieving over the loss. It is not an attempt to make the person
look better than they had in life, but to make the body presentable
in such a way as to show the bereaved a final positive image of
the deceased.

May presents an analysis of current funeral practices in which he avoids taking sides in this controversy.[89] Instead, he asks whether or not death is a sacred experience for modern man. Death maintains its sacred power because man is ultimately helpless before it, and has been unable to tame death. We know no more about the state of being dead than did primitive man. The sacred is always powerful, and death is sacred by the very nature of its unfathomability by man. Technological man has engaged death in a battle, attempting to subdue and control it. The result has been a prolonging of life (the quality of which is another issue)—an evasion of "old man death." In a sense, our contemporary image of death is similar to the child's who sees death as a personification which, if one is careful or lucky, can be avoided.

May argues that when death triumphs, as it ultimately does, "we are at a loss as to how to proceed on the far side of this word."[90] Our materialistic, technological defenses abandon us, and we find ourselves bereft of ways of coping with the awesomeness of death. The "ceremonies of acceptance" which the funeral directors provide are congruent with our image of life and death. Technology is used to come to grips with death in all its terrifying power. The corpse is not remade into a perfectly lifelike being. If this were the case, then the best embalming and restoration would be too terrifying to see, as it would blur the line between life and death. Rather it is a sham, a theatrical presentation, but one that can serve a useful purpose. It can help to resolve the fears of those who have sought so long and hard to avoid death, by showing that in defeat before the sacred enemy, peaceful resolution is possible.

In spite of our current preoccupation with death, we have given it a taboo status that implies a great deal of underlying fear and anxiety. Anything that will ease our fears is used to protect us from death. We give millions of dollars to fight disease, we occupy our spare time with staying physically fit, and we blunt death's awful impact with the use of the skills of the funeral director. While critics may consider such activities barbaric or in bad taste, they are certainly in harmony with the basic values of American society.

The Therapeutic Value of a Funeral Service

There are few who would argue that the death of a person should go unacknowledged, that the body be disposed of as quickly and surreptitiously as possible, and that all efforts be focused upon denying the loss and returning to the daily routine of living as if nothing had occurred. As we have seen earlier, the use of ceremony within a society serves both individual and social functions. To deny such a process is to leave people with a greater sense of disruption and loss. But while the need for some sort of recognition of the death seems almost universally accepted, the form and substance of that recognition is subject to debate.

The funeral industry has generally taken the position that having the body present for viewing and holding a funeral ceremony is a way of confronting the reality of the death that has occurred. A complete funeral ceremony allows for the rites of passage which are an important part of the grief process. Sociologically, the funeral ceremony allows for the expression of the collective image, and provides a connection with our history.

The Memorial Society Alternative

For those who wish to avoid the expense of a traditional funeral, memorial (or funeral) societies provide access to simpler and more economical alternatives. The 140 member societies of the Continental Association of Funeral and Memorial Societies contract with local funeral directors for low-cost funerals, using the bargaining power of group purchasing.[91] For a membership fee, usually about $25.00, a member can avail himself of funeral services at prices that are determined in advance of need. The member may choose the method of disposition of his remains, and designate what kind of ceremony he would prefer.

The memorial societies use the membership fees to educate consumers about funerals and to participate in state or local regulatory agencies. In this manner, they have served as watchdogs over the funeral industry, often calling to public attention the excesses or unethical conduct of funeral industry members. While often castigated by the industry, the memorial society movement serves an important consumer function in its scrutiny of an industry which, like most professions, often tends to act more in a defensive and protectionistic manner than in ways that would place stringent ethical demands upon the activities of its members.

Conclusion

The critics of the funeral industry tend to be of a liberal and intellectual persuasion. Their satiric attacks on the industry are often misdirected criticisms of America's materialism and conservative nature. The funeral industry makes an easy target, being sensitive to public ridicule, a taboo subject, and not without its charlatans, hustlers, and confidence men. The critics have served several purposes, among which have been educating the public, making the subject of death more openly acceptable, and exposing some of the fraudulent and unethical activities of the funeral industry.

The industry has responded, for the most part, in a manner that has been detrimental to its own goals. Having developed a nationwide organization (NFDA) which has served to protect the industry through control of state governing boards, political lobbying efforts, and public relations, the industry has been reluctant to set and enforce a high standard of ethical conduct (it does maintain a code of ethics). While the power of the membership has been used to curb those who would break the economic rules by accepting memorial or funeral society business, it is seldom used to control the unethical. A sensitive occupation—such as funeral directing—that fails to control its own members might experience an increasing amount of governmental intervention to protect its citizens.

A recent move by the NFDA, in its growing awareness of consumer issues, is its sponsorship of ThanaCAP, an independent organization that serves as an ombudsman for those who claim that they have been unfairly treated by a funeral home. This organization has been applauded by several consumer advocates for its response to the concerns of the consumer.

The polar positions held by the funeral industry and its critics are each representative of philosophical issues which typify classical liberal and conservative perspectives. While the funeral directors tend to emphasize a more conservative image of the world, their opponents reflect a more liberal viewpoint, stressing more secular and egalitarian values. The question of which attitudes toward death might be associated with each of these ideological positions has not yet been thoroughly studied. However, from the historical material we have discussed, it would be possible to hypothesize that the more conservative image of the world is linked to a more realistic acceptance of death, and that the more liberal image tends to be associated with a greater death denial.

By and large, Americans are getting the kinds of funerals that they wish. Both sides have argued that theirs is the most "mentally healthy" position. Today we have a great deal of belief in mental health, scrutinizing our every activity to make sure it's "OK." In this case, neither side has presented conclusive evidence that the funeral with the body present is or is not mentally healthy. Perhaps that is because the issue is a sentimental and not a scientific one. It is my position that people should have the kind of funeral that meets their sentimental needs; whether it is elaborate and costly or simple and frugal is not our concern.

From our examination of the functions of ceremony, it would seem important that some public recognition of the death should occur. The choice as to the disposition of the body and the appropriate ceremony should be made by those affected by the death, free from the pressures of funeral directors and social critics alike.

Notes

1. Robert Hertz, *Death and the Right Hand* (Glencoe, Ill: The Free Press, 1960), pp. 81–82.
2. Arnold A. van Genepp, *The Rites of Passage* (Chicago: University of Chicago Press, 1960).
3. David Sudnow, *Passing On: The Social Organization of Dying* (Englewood Cliffs, N.J.: Prentice-Hall, 1967).
4. Hertz, p. 79.
5. Paul N. Rosenblatt et al., *Grief and Mourning* (Human Relations Area Files Press, 1976), p. 8.
6. Emile Durkheim, *The Elementary Forms of the Religious Life* (New York: Collier Books, 1961), p. 439.
7. Geoffrey Gorer, *Death, Grief, and Mourning* (Garden City, N.Y.: Doubleday, 1965), pp. 126–135. See also John J. Schwab et al., "Funeral Behavior and Unresolved Grief" in Vanderlyn Pine, ed., *Acute Grief and the Funeral* (Springfield, Ill: Charles C Thomas, 1976), pp. 241–248.
8. Rosenblatt, p. 45.
9. Harriet Sarnoff Schiff, *The Bereaved Parent* (New York: Penguin, 1978), pp. 101–107.

10. Philip Slater, *Footholds* (New York: E.P. Dutton, 1977), p. 117.

11. Philippe Aries, *Western Attitudes toward Death* (Baltimore: Johns Hopkins University Press, 1974), pp. 1–25.

12. Robert W. Habenstein and William M. Lamers, *The History of American Funeral Directing* (Milwaukee: Bullfin, 1962), p. 116.

13. Robert Stannard, ed., *Death in America* (Philadelphia: University of Pennsylvania Press, 1976), p. 116.

14. Martha Fales, "The Early American Way of Death," *Essex Institution Historical Collection* 100, no. 2 (1964): 75–84.

15. Walter M. Whitehall, *Boston: A Topographical History* (Cambridge: Harvard University Press, 1968), p. 37.

16. Habenstein and Lamers, pp. 223–249.

17. LeRoy Bowman, *The American Funeral* (Washington, D.C.: Public Affairs Press, 1959), p. 114.

18. Alice M. Earle, *Customs and Fashions in Old New England* (New York: C. Scribner's Sons, 1904), p. 369.

19. Habenstein and Lamers, p. 436.

20. Ibid., p. 414.

21. Ibid., p. 415.

22. William M. Kephart, "Status after Death," *American Sociological Review* 15 (October 1950): 641.

23. James J. Farrell, *Inventing the American Way of Death: 1830–1920* (Philadelphia: Temple University Press, 1980), pp. 94–95.

24. Habenstein and Lamers, pp. 389–444.

25. Jessica Mitford, *The American Way of Death* (New York: Simon & Schuster, 1959), pp. 156–159.

26. Ibid., p. 60.

27. W. Lloyd Warner, *The Living and the Dead* (New Haven: Yale University Press, 1959), Chapter 8.

28. S.J. Kleinberg, "Death and the Working Class," *Journal of Popular Culture* 11, no. 1 (Summer 1977): 205.

29. Robert Blauner, "Death and Social Structure," in Robert Fulton, ed., *Death and Identity* (Bowie, Md.: The Charles Press, 1976), pp. 35–39. Also Geoffrey Gorer.

30. Orrin E. Klapp, *Collective Search for Identity* (New York: Holt, Rinehart & Winston, 1969), Chapter 1.

31. Robert Jay Lifton, *The Broken Connection* (New York: Simon and Schuster, 1979), passim.

32. Georg Simmel, "The Metropolis and Mental Life," in Richard Sennett,

ed., *Classic Essays on the Culture of Cities* (New York: Appleton-Century-Crofts, 1969), pp. 47–60.

33. Warner, p. 280.

34. Stanley French, "The Cemetery as Cultural Institution: The Establishment of Mount Auburn and the 'Rural Cemetery' Movement," in David E. Stannard, ed., *Death in America* (Philadelphia: University of Pennsylvania Press, 1975), pp. 69–91.

35. Ibid., pp. 71–74.

36. Ibid., p. 80.

37. Ibid., p. 82.

38. Ibid., p. 89. Also, Charles O. Jackson, "Death Shall Have No Dominion," *Omega*, 8 no. 3 (1977): 196.

39. Edmund Gillon, *Victorian Cemetery Sculpture* (New York: Dover Publications, 1972), p. 104.

40. Gillon. See also James S. Curl, *The Victorian Celebration of Death* (Detroit: Partridge Press, 1972); and John Morley, *Death, Heaven and the Victorians* (Pittsburgh: University of Pittsburgh Press, 1971).

41. Warner, p. 287.

42. Ibid., p. 293.

43. Ibid., p. 297.

44. Kephart, p. 642.

45. William J. Dean, "Potter's Field: Aisle of the Dead." *The New York Times*, 25 May 1981.

46. Habenstein, pp. 225–249; also Farrell, p. 147.

47. Habenstein, pp. 237–238.

48. Farrell, p. 170.

49. Ibid., p. 172.

50. Ibid., pp. 173–177.

51. Ibid., p. 176.

52. Ibid., p. 160.

53. Warner, p. 315.

54. Ibid.

55. *International Encyclopedia of the Social Sciences* (New York: Macmillan, 1968), Vol. 12, pp. 336–342.

56. Sudnow, pp. 51–64.

57. Vanderlyn Pine, *Caretaker of the Dead: The American Funeral Director* (New York: Halsted Press, 1975), p. 80.

58. Ibid., p. 141.

59. Ibid.

60. Ben M. Crouch, "Professionalism in Funeral Service: A Study of Work

Orientation (Ph.D. dissertation, Southern Illinois University, Carbondale, 1971).

61. Pine, p. 7.
62. Ibid., p. 39.
63. Ibid.
64. Lifton, p. 315.
65. Rosenblatt, pp. 34–37, 112.
66. Pine, p. 37.
67. William F. May, "The Sacral Power of Death in Contemporary Experience," *Social Research* 39, no. 3 (1972): 465–474.
68. William H. Porter, Jr., "Some Sociological Notes on a Century of Change in the Funeral Business," *Sociological Symposium* 1 (Fall 1968):36–46.
69. Crouch.
70. Mitford, passim.
71. Mitford, Chapter 15.
72. Federal Trade Commission Staff, Bureau of Consumer Protection, "Funeral Industry Practices," Washington, D.C., June 1978, pp. 107–109.
73. Mitford, p. 41.
74. Mitford; Bowman; Ruth M. Harmer, *The High Cost of Dying* (New York: Collier, 1963).
75. Mitford, p. 49.
76. Ibid., p. 169.
77. Ibid., Chapter 2.
78. Ibid., pp. 64–70.
79. Ibid., Chapters 7 and 8.
80. Crouch; Minnesota Office of Consumer Services, *Funerals in Minnesota: Customer Experiences* (Minneapolis: State of Minnesota, 1977); Baheej Khleif, "The Sociology of the Mortuary: Attitudes to the Funeral, Funeral Director, and Funeral Arrangements," in Otto S. Margolis, et al., eds., *Grief and the Meaning of the Funeral* (New York: MSS Information Corporation, 1975). (Khleif's work is drawn from a more extensive study, which served as his Ph.D. dissertation, University of Colorado, Boulder, 1971.)
81. Khleif.
82. Minnesota Office of Consumer Services.
83. Khleif, p. 226.
84. Federal Trade Commission, p. 169.
85. Ibid., pp. 275–277.
86. Gorer.

87. Lifton, p. 97.

88. Elizabeth Kubler-Ross, *Questions and Answers on Death and Dying* (New York: Macmillan, 1974), p. 101.

89. May.

90. May, p. 469.

91. Jeremy Main, "Curbing Funeral Costs," *Money* Magazine, March 1977, pp. 87–89. Also, Ernest Morgan, *A Manual of Death Education and Simple Burial* (Burnsville, N.C.: Celo Press, 1977).

CHAPTER EIGHT

Suicide: Deciding to Die

T HE SUICIDE RATE in the United States, according to government census data of 1980, is 11.9 per 100,000. This figure indicates a slight decrease since 1975, when the reported figure was 12.6 per 100,000. Most of the suicides are male, roughly three times the number of female suicides. The suicide rate for men increases with age, with those sixty-five or over having a rate of 35 per 100,000. The suicide rate for females has tended to be highest for women between the ages of forty-five and sixty-four. Blacks and other minorities tend to have a suicide rate much lower than whites, and there has been a dramatic increase in the number of suicides among teenagers, rising 250 percent for females and 300 percent for males.[1]

American society's anxiety-laden attitude toward death is most evident in the ways in which we relate to the subject of suicide. This anxiety stems from our overall death-avoiding attitudes, and the nature of the suicidal act itself. Suicide represents both a shameful act and rejection; rejection of those who survive the suicide, rejection of society, and rejection of life itself. The suicide, by the nature of his or her absolute act, calls into question our understanding of the meaningfulness of life. To those who hold a religious image of the world, suicide may be seen as a rejection of God by the individual, or at least an interference with God's plan.[2]

The term suicide, as popularly used, connotes a deliberate act to end one's life. The descriptor "deliberate" is important, because any serious student of suicide quickly realizes that suicidal behavior is not so easily defined. If, for example, an individual is reported as having died from a self-inflicted gunshot wound to the head, we would usually consider such an act a suicide. If, however, we learn that the act took place during a game of Russian roulette, on a dare, and was committed by a teenager who had been drinking heavily with a group of his peers, the label of suicide does not fit as easily. Certainly not as easily as it would to a seventy-two-year-old widower, in failing health, who deliberately takes his own life, leaving a note to explain his actions. What these examples point out is the importance of the *intention* of the suicidal person.

Still, there are types of suicides that imply a more subtle decision-making process than simply a "deliberate act" of self-destruction. Smoking, excessive consumption of alcohol, risk-taking behavior—all may imply a certain level of self-destructiveness. Shneidman classifies this kind of death as subintentioned, in which the person acts unconsciously or in hidden ways to bring about his or her own death.[3] This is not to imply that all who engage in risk-taking behavior are suicidal. Again, one must examine the intention behind the behavior. For example, a person may genuinely believe that the number of cigarettes he or she consumes will not cause any ill effects. On the other hand, I knew a person so badly afflicted by emphysema he had to carry an oxygen tank with him, who would remove the oxygen tube from his nose in order to smoke a cigarette. Although he died as a result of his emphysema, his death was not considered a suicide, at least by common standards. One could argue, however, that he chose to end his life as deliberately as did the seventy-two-year-old widower spoken of earlier.

Unless we are aware of what the actor intends by his or her behavior, we must be cautious in our labeling of that behavior. Farber argues that along with the intention of the actor, the outcome of the act also affects our definition of suicide.[4] To complicate the situation even more, the outcome, while easily known (one either dies or one doesn't), may disguise the actual intention of the act. Farber offers us a paradigm to describe the interface between outcome and intention:[5]

Cell A. The individual intends to kill him- or herself, and succeeds in carrying out his or her intentions. This is what Farber

OUTCOME

		Dies	Lives
	To Die	A	B
INTENTION			
	To Live	C	D

describes as the true suicide.[6] A suicide note left behind may often serve as evidence of the actor's intention.

Cell B. The individual intended to commit suicide, but for one reason or another was unsuccessful. This may involve being accidently discovered while attempting suicide. For example, a woman takes an overdose of sleeping pills and goes to bed, leaving a note explaining the reasons for her act. However, a fire in a nearby apartment leads the police to discover her body while evacuating the building. She is rushed to the emergency room of a nearby hospital, and survives. In this case, the intention was clearly to commit suicide, but the act was unsuccessful.

Cell C. The intention here is one of making a suicidal gesture, but not of killing oneself. The result, however, is contrary to the intention, and death follows. According to one account, Sylvia Plath, the poet, intended not to die, but was unsuccessful.[7] She had made an appointment with a new maid for the morning that she died. Shortly before the woman was due to arrive, she turned on the gas in her apartment and left a note telling how to reach her doctor. The maid, unable to get a response upon knocking and finding no name on the door, set out to locate a telephone to reaffirm the address with the employment agency. By the time her body was found, Sylvia Plath was dead. While this was labeled a suicidal act, there is much evidence that this was not Sylvia Plath's intention.

Cell D. The individual who does not intend to die, and who survives the suicidal gesture, is what Farber describes as the true attempter.[8] For example, the person who takes twenty-five aspirins and then walks into the next room and announces his act to his friends fits into this category. Clearly the intention was not to end his life, nor did the result conflict with the person's intention.

A word of caution is necessary concerning the survivors of a suicide attempt: Often it is difficult for the layman (and sometimes the professional as well) to discern the intentions of the suicidal person. (That is, to decide whether the individual belongs in Cell

B or Cell D above.) No suicidal act should be dismissed as a mere gesture. At best, it is a desperate cry for help; at least, it is an unsuccessful effort to end one's life. In either case, professional help is indicated. Many lay people feel a sense of helplessness when confronted with an attempted suicide, which may be fueled by their own sense of guilt and fear. As a result, others may be willing to enter into a conspiracy of sorts with the suicidal person by either rationalizing away the act (perhaps by labeling it a transient aberration) or developing a kind of pretense awareness whereby the reality of what has occurred is never acknowledged. Neither strategy aids the suicidal person in confronting his or her behavior, and either may in fact give a kind of subtle support to it. What is necessary is for the suicidal person's friends and family to recognize that a suicidal act is a severe form of acting out, and that without help the individual has a good chance of repeating the suicidal act. It may not be survived the next time.

Those surrounding the suicidal person can provide support, aiding the individual in getting the help he or she needs. Crisis centers, mental health associations, and suicide prevention agencies can provide information on resources available in the community, and may give helpful advice to those who find that they are witnessing suicidal indications or acts by a friend or relative.

Theories of Suicidal Behavior

Classical theories seeking to explain suicide can be placed in two general categories: those that use psychological factors as explanatory variables, and those which rely on sociological explanations. Sigmund Freud is typical of the first category; he argued that suicide is attributable to the psychological make-up of the individual. Emile Durkheim, on the other hand, maintained that the individual was a product of the social environment, and this was the key to understanding suicide. After discussing both Freud and Durkheim, we will examine further Farber's theoretical position, which is an attempt to resolve the divergent sociological and psychological arguments put forth by Freud and Durkheim.

Sigmund Freud, as we discussed earlier, developed the concept of an innate human drive toward destruction, commonly called the death instinct.[9] Early in his work, before he developed the concept of a drive toward death, Freud argued that suicide was a result of anger being turned inward.[10] According to Freud, the individual incorporates within his or her psyche an internalized image of a particular loved object. When the loved object itself ceases to exist or terminates the relationship, the anger over the desertion is turned inward, upon the internally held image of the object. Because the image is held in the mind of the person, the anger is turned inward, upon the self. As a result, suicide became, to Freud, the product of retroflexed anger. When he later developed his idea of a death drive, Freud modified his explanation of suicide: It became a product of the triumph of the death instinct over the life instinct. The death drive breaks through the defenses of the drive toward self-preservation, rendering the individual helpless before its powers. Understanding Freud's argument, we can appreciate how easily suicide could become categorized as a mental illness, and certainly not the act of a rational person.

Freud's death drive theory, as we saw when discussing theoretical work in thanatology, has not proved a fruitful concept and has few proponents today (Freud himself labeled it as "often far fetched speculation").[11] The concept has proved to be so abstract as to be untestable, and has been of little practical value in the treatment of mental illness. Also, beginning with Durkheim, sociological investigations began to raise questions concerning suicidal behavior that were not easily answered by the strictly psychological perspective of Sigmund Freud.

Emile Durkheim, seeking to refute the psychological interpretations of human behavior so popular in his day, choose to study suicide from a social perspective.[12] By demonstrating that social facts could account for the rate of suicide in a given population, Durkheim gave a legitimacy to sociology that is recognized as a milestone in the development of social science.

Durkheim claimed that suicide, as defined in official statistics, had a social basis. By examining suicide rates in comparison with other social indicators, Durkheim was able to derive four types of suicidal behavior: egoistic, altruistic, anomic, and fatalistic. Egoistic suicides occur when the bonds between the individual and his society are weak.[13] In this category Durkheim placed those such as the suicides of unmarried persons, who, theoretically at least, would not hold strong ties to the larger society. At the polar extreme from egoistic suicides are those Durkheim called altruistic suicides.[14] In this case, the social bonds are so strong that the individual ego is submerged beneath the values of the group. Committing suicide because of offenses against society or the heroic life-sacrificing deeds of a soldier both serve as examples of altruistic

suicide. These two forms of suicide—eogistic and altruistic—are
the polar extremes of what Durkheim called social integration, a
term that has been variously described as connoting the social bond,
the value context of society, or as a sense of moral community.[15]
When social integration is low, egoistic suicides prevail. When integration is high, then altruistic suicides predominate.

Anomic suicide, according to Durkheim, is a category of behavior which includes those suicides that take place in the context
of a sense of rootlessness; of a lack of a place in society.[16] The
individual is unrestrained by society, and as a result this disequilibrium leads to suicide. An example of anomic suicide is the businessman who takes his own life at a time of financial crisis. Weakened social regulation no longer meets the expanding needs of
the individual, and so he or she commits suicide.

At the polar extreme from anomic suicide is the category Durkheim called fatalistic suicide.[17] This is the suicide of the individual
who is over-regulated, such as the slave. The overbearing nature
of the social world makes life no longer worth living. Both these
categories of anomic and fatalistic suicide are extremes on a continuum which Durkhiem described as social regulation; the extent
of social control over the individual.

Douglas criticizes Durkheim's schema by pointing out that
the act of suicide has meanings that vary not only from one individual to the next (as Farber also argued), but also may vary between
segments of a society as well as between entire cultures.[18] For example, differing suicide rates in two cultures may not be measuring
the same thing; a suicidal act in one society may be concealed or
defined as an accident in another. While this may be easy for us
to comprehend on a cross-cultural basis, it becomes more difficult
when looking within one's own society. Most people hold a common-sense idea of what suicide is, and we tend to assume that
this image of suicide holds throughout society. This is not necessarily true; studies have shown a great variance within United States
society as to how suicides are defined. Douglas points out that
coroners often differ widely in what deaths they classify as suicidal
or accidental.[19]

If we agree that what is called "suicide" varies so greatly because a precise definition is lacking, then Durkheim's work, as
well as work by others who take a statistical approach, becomes
suspect. In addition, we are still confronted with the problem of
intention: to what degree does it matter how society labels a partic-

ular act, or is what the actor intended of prime importance? It appears that a strictly sociological approach which leaves little room for such psychological concepts as intention is doomed in its efforts to fully explain suicide.

Regardless of his critics, Durkheim still must be acknowledged as having demonstrated the importance of social factors in suicide. Suicides do not occur in a social vacuum; like all human deeds, they are a product, to a lesser or greater extent, of the social world in which they take place. Although Durkheim's study itself may be flawed in its overemphasis on social factors in explaining suicide, it did help establish a counterbalance to the view that human behavior is to be explained solely in terms of psychological theory.

A more balanced perspective is found in the work of Farber, who argues that suicide is a function of two factors: vulnerability and deprivation. Put in his own words, "The frequency of suicide is a function of the frequency of individuals possessing a certain vulnerability in that population, and of the extent of certain deprivations in that population."[20] While Farber rejects the Freudian notion of a death drive, he does acknowledge the importance of the individual's mental state. Psychological vulnerability accounts for the individual's sense of competence, a self-knowledge that one can (or can not) cope with the stresses and strains of life. "Basically," Farber writes, "such a person doubts that his powers are sufficient to handle the demands of life."[21]

Vulnerability

The more vulnerable the individual, the greater the chance of suicide. The individual's vulnerability affects and is in turn affected by deprivation, which is the diminishing or disruption of the person's living conditions. When the threat to acceptable life conditions is high, and one's sense of self-competence (the perceived ability to contend with the threat) is low, then there is a greater chance of suicide occuring. On the contrary, when one's self competence is high (low vulnerability) and the threat of deprivation is low, the chances of suicide diminish. "Suicide, then," Farber asserts, "is in the main an act of hopelessness, of despair and desperation."[22]

Farber uses the term "vulnerability" in describing the suicidal person because he or she is often psychologically damaged, either through mental disease or as a result of mental impairments developed while in a pathological environment. This does not necessarily indicate that a deprived childhood or mental illness causes suicide; rather, the psychologically impaired person is more vulnerable to threats or deprivations from the environment.[23] In other words, the individual believes he or she lacks the ability to cope with a hostile world. When the conditions of life become unbearable—when there is no hope of surmounting the threat—the individual perceives no way to improve his situation. Suicide may be seen as the only solution to the individual's dilemma. For example, Farber describes Ernest Hemingway as a man who was haunted by a deep sense of incompetence, which would surface as depression when he failed at some task.[24] This perceived incompetence made Hemingway vulnerable to feelings of hopelessness when he felt that he was a failure. Sudden, massive deprivation, on the other hand, may overwhelm an individual's normally adequate sense of competence. The person withdraws his or her emotional investment from a hostile world. Further deprivation results in an increase in psychic or physical pain, while reinforcing the individual's perception of his or her helplessness. With no positive image of the future, death may be perceived as the only alternative.

Further reinforcement for Farber's argument can be found in a study conducted by Robert and Beatrice Kastenbaum. They offer three hypotheses which are models concerning the relationship between the individual and his or her environment.[25] The *developmental hypothesis* states that "dependence upon the proximal environment is greatest at both extremes of the life cycle, infancy and advanced age."[26] At these points in the life cycle the individual is less able to take care of him- or herself, and is thus more dependent upon the environment. The *docility hypothesis* maintains that the lower the person's degree of competence, the more that person's behavior will be affected by changes in the environment. The *social echelon hypothesis* states that the lower the individual's socioeconomic status, the more susceptible he or she is to the environment. For example, the poor are more likely to suffer due to adverse weather conditions than are the more wealthy, who can buy whatever is needed to make the condition more livable.

What the Kastenbaums are indicating is that those who fall into their three categories are more vulnerable to threats from the environment, because they are unable to cope competently with those threats to their well-being. The Kastenbaums sum up their argument as follows:

The person who is low man in all three vulnerability models (developmental, docility, and social echelon) comes up against an establishment that acts upon him without truly acknowledging his existence. The very first point of contact may instantly convey the message: "You have no power." . . . Objectively, there could be many opportunities for the individual to achieve his own goals or to obtain a relevant response from the environmental system. But one quick encounter may be enough to freeze him into the learned hoplessness position. . . . This process is probably less certain and rapid in those who occupy a less vulnerable position at the beginning. But sooner or later some environmental cue may be interpreted as confirmation of one's self-suspected inability to impose his will on the world.[27]

An example of a person who is low on all three vulnerability scales is a poor black child in America. The child is dependent upon others in the environment for nurturance, and to teach him or her what the world is like. The limitations that are placed upon the child by the education he or she receives, and the poor self-image he or she is socialized to accept mean that the child has a low sense of competence. As a result, the child is likely to meet the world with apathy and resignation. Finally, being of a low socioeconomic status, the poor black child is unable to insulate himself or herself from threats from the environment, and more subject to being victimized by that environment.

A positive, humane social environment is one which connects with and validates the individual, and which responds to him or her as a significant, effective individual. A lack of such reinforcement of one's competence can indicate to the individual that that he or she has no emotional harbor of refuge, no place in the world where he or she is seen as having some importance.[28] To illustrate this point, Durkheim speaks of the egoistic suicide as one who is without family, and thus devoid of social support.[29] For example, the individual whose social relationships are based upon his or her personal wealth or fame may find him- or herself considering suicide when he or she is deprived of those supports. Social support facilitates our abilities to cope with life, and the lack of such a support system may leave us with a weakened sense of self-competence in the face of a world turned suddenly hostile. Studies of the grief process have emphasized the importance of a support system in resolving the loss.[30]

This discussion of vulnerability to environmental forces does not imply that one's behavior is determined by the environment. What it does demonstrate is the very powerful influence which the environment can have upon the individual—especially the individual who is unable to withstand such strong influences. There is still a decision process which goes on prior to the act of suicide. But as with most if not all decisions that we make, the social reality within which we exist has a powerful influence upon those decisions.

Hopelessness

When a person views him- or herself as hopeless, we can say that a desired outcome is not possible. There is nothing that he or she can do to affect the outcome of a given event or threat. The hopeless person is characterized as one who "expects or believes that nothing will turn out right for him, nothing he does will succeed, his important goals are unattainable, and his worst problems will never be solved."[31] What is implied in this definition is that hopelessness is learned; it is not that the person is born knowing that he or she is incompetent to deal with the vicissitudes of life. This is a lesson that has been taught, perhaps brutally, perhaps subtly. Nonetheless, the person has come to "know" that he or she is unable to cope with life.[32] Several empirical studies have shown that indications of a sense of hopelessness are more closely related to suicidal intent than is depression.[33]

What Durkheim called egoistic and anomic suicides also demonstrate the importance of hopelessness as a precursor to suicide. The individual, faced with certain death preceded by a period of pain and suffering, chooses not to experience that pain and suffering. While the individual in such a situation may not be severely depressed, he or she is certainly defining him- or herself as helpless to do anything about the present situation.

Durkheim's altruistic and fatalistic suicides can also be reinterpreted as a deprivation of other alternatives, at the same time that the individual's self-esteem is made dependent upon the one remaining alternative, which is to give his or her life for others. For example, a military officer leads a suicidal mission, knowing that this action will most certainly result in his death. I would contend that the officer has no real choice; no other alternatives are perceived to be open to him. As one dedicated to the military life, honor and courage are most highly prized. In *The Divine Wind*, Inoguchi and Nakajima's account of Japan's suicidal efforts near the end of World War II, we find that there existed a pervasive sense of doom over the war effort, and also a realization by the pilots that no other honorable course was open to them. Just before committing all of his outnumbered forces into a final offensive which he knew to be hopeless, one general wrote,

> With a burning desire to destroy the arrogant enemy, the men of my command have fought the invaders for almost three months. We have failed to crush the enemy, despite our death-defying resistance, and now we are doomed.[34]

The only way to atone for their failure, and at the same time give meaning to their lives, was to die in one last attack. To survive the war was to live in shame and ignominy. There was no alternative; the situation was hopeless.

Throughout our discussion, I have referred to the individual's *perceived* hopelessness. This is an important distinction, for it implies that the individual's sense of hopelessness may not be a totally valid assessment of the situation. Hendin points out that more suicides are committed by people who wrongfully *believe* that they have cancer than by those who actually do suffer from the disease.[35] A teenager, despondent at the break-up of a romance, may temporarily view his or her situation as hopeless; the pain is too great and can never be assuaged. Given time, however, he or she may modify this decision. Another example of the importance of perception in hopelessness was told to me by a former lifeguard, who remarked that he could understand those close to drowning who would cling to him with almost superhuman strength, but he failed to understand those who almost immediately upon perceiving their own danger seemed to give up and drown.

Seligman speaks of this kind of learned helplessness, where the individual decides that the outcome of a particular situation will occur regardless of anything he or she does to try to affect it.[36] Helpless (as Seligman defines it), the individual quickly succumbs to the hostile environment. In the example above, this meant allowing oneself to drown (at least making no effort to prevent that from happening). By contrast, another individual in the same situation may perceive him- or herself as competent enough to survive, and thus make more of an effort to do so. This individual will tend to be more effective in coping with life's deprivations.

Two important factors in the individual's deciding his or her degree of helplessness are how the person perceives the environment and him- or herself. The individual may decide that the environment is overpowering or controllable, or that he or she is helpless in being able to master the situation. Both of these factors are learned. We learn what situations are dangerous and overpowering. We also define ourselves as to whether or not we are helpless in a given situation. This means, in effect, that the decision to suicide may be predicated upon learned definitions, and that one may be able to redefine oneself as competent, or a given situation as manageable. The helplessness of the suicidal person may be redefined in the light of new, perhaps more accurate information. Melges and Bowlby describe different treatment modes for combating hopelessness, including insight-oriented therapy which aids the person in understanding the orgins of his or her feelings of helplessness. Also, behavioral techniques are being developed to aid the individual in redefining his or her sense of self-competence.[37]

Suicide as Deciding to Die

One of the benefits of our approach to understanding suicidal behavior is that it allows us to account for a great many behaviors which are decisions to end one's life, but where the action predicated upon such a decision is passive, rather than active. This includes "giving up on life"; deciding that the situation is hopeless, and that one is hopelessly doomed to die. Recall the emphysema victim described earlier who continued to smoke, ultimately causing his own death, and the case of the swimmer who decides not to try to survive. Seeing suicide as the result of a decision that the situation is hopeless allows us to include this kind of self-destructive behavior in our definition.

This theoretical schema allows us to consider as suicide a wide range of behaviors that result in the deliberate ending of one's life. For example, there are studies which describe the phenomenon known as "voodoo death."[38] These investigations tell of individuals who violate the rules of their society, and consider themselves to be doomed as a result. When this occurs, the individual usually dies within forty-eight hours, regardless of the medical aid received. Here we see an example of the individual's hopelessness becoming so totalistic as to be able to inhibit biological functioning.

Hope is the individual's belief in achieving a certain goal. Farber maintains that hope is a function of both competence and threat; and that both must be considered in order to understand it.[39] Where a person's perceived degree of competence is high, he or she will be able to withstand a higher level of threat; where self-competence is low, it will not take as great a degree of threat to render the individual hopeless. A knowledge of our own competence is, for most of us, our belief that we can cope with the challenges of daily existence; that we can bring about our desired ends. Where hope is low, however, we do not feel that we can control life; we are victims and not controllers.

The Deprivation of Competence

We might ask, in what ways does United States society teach us that we are helpless? One way that we have examined earlier is through the institutionalization of the old and sick. By this process, we have seen that the individual is robbed of his or her ability to have any control over his or her own body, and the greater social environment in which he or she has been placed. This learned helplessness may contribute to the increase in death rates among people soon after they enter a nursing home or are moved from one home to another.[40]

One defense against the invasiveness of the institution may lie in the mutual pretense context described earlier, wherein the patient and staff pretend that the patient is not dying. For the patient, to enter into such a pretense may allow him or her a measure of control over the situation, in that he or she can maintain some semblance of his or her old self, as well as a certain amount of personal privacy.[41] Rather than succumb to the helpless/hopeless condition of a dying patient, the pretense allows the individual to maintain some sense of competence over his or her existence.

Another example of a patient striving to maintain control over what is left of life was told to me by a hospital staff member: In the face of many intrusions into her life on the part of an overzealous social worker, and in order to preserve her own privacy and some control over what went on in her life, a dying patient set the social worker to work on what she knew to be an impossible task; reuniting her with her children prior to her death. The patient confided to a nurse that it kept the social worker busy, and allowed the woman to maintain the sense of privacy she desired until her death.

Both of the examples above point to the need that the individual has to maintain some control over his or her life; to have some sense of self-competence. To remove this, whether systematically by the institution or individually by overzealous professionals, is to heighten the individual's vulnerability in the face of a threat to his or her very life. The rapid pace and constant change of American life no doubt contribute to the hostile environment within which we try to survive. At the same time, the individualistic ethic values self-mastery, and tends to denigrate reaching out to others—the very behavior that can provide a more nurturing and responsive environment.

Another factor in our society that teaches us of our helplessness is society's emphasis upon competition. The competitive ethos states that only one wins, and everyone else loses. The increases in suicides among young adults may be attributed, in part, to a failure to be effective in a competitive world, where there is no surcease from the treadmill of competition.[42] By developing a world of artificial scarcity, a world where we can easily be deprived of society's rewards, we have created an environment wherein the individual must strive against his or her fellows in order to achieve those rewards. Failure—a sign of personal incompetence—is always present as a grim specter in the competitive society.[43] Here we see a facet of American society working against the need for Lifton's life-affirming human connection, and instead pitting us each against the other in competition for socially controlled scarce resources.[44]

For the elderly, the group with the highest completed suicide rate and the fewest attempted suicides, loneliness, grief, declining health, and increasing financial problems are a few of the reasons cited.[45]

But why suicide? If the individual perceives that he or she is helpless in a hostile world, why is suicide chosen over other alternatives, such as flying into a rage or passively accepting the situation? Suicide is the chosen alternative because it is the only alternative perceived to be left. To continue in the world means to continue to exist in a situation full of despairing helplessness, where things can only get worse and no one can be trusted to help. To live on is to live a life doomed to more misery. Deciding to die, the only act the person feels that he or she can control, may take an active form (hanging, shooting, overdosing) or a more pasive form (driving recklessly, excessive drinking, smoking, etc.). In American society, it appears that the more passive and extended over time the act of suicide, the more acceptable it is. The person with a liver ailment who continues to drink heavily despite his or her physician's advice is, by our definition, commiting as suicidal an act as the individual who slits his or her wrists. Socially, however, the former act is morally acceptable though regrettable; the latter is not acceptable, for society labels this as suicide—an immoral and abhorred act.

This chapter has provided an overview of suicidal behavior, and a general paradigm for understanding the suicidal act. This is by no means a definitive statement; a great deal more empirical work is necessary before we begin to comprehend suicide fully, which is by its very nature an intensely personal act. Shneidman, a leading figure in the field of suicidology, sums it up this way:

> No one really knows why human beings commit suicide. Indeed, the very person who takes his own life may be least aware at the moment of decision of the essence (much less the totality) of his reasons and emotions for doing so. At the outset, it can be said that a dozen individuals can kill themselves and "do" (or commit) twelve psychologically different deeds. Understanding suicide—like understanding any other complicated human act such as drug or alcohol misuse or antisocial behavior—involves insights drawn from many fields that touch on man's entire psychological and social life.[46]

Notes

1. *Statistical Abstracts of the U.S.,* 104th ed., United States Bureau of the Census, Washington, D.C., 1983, pp. 78,79,83. Also, Herbert Hendin, *Suicide in America* (New York: W. W. Norton), 1982, p. 19.

2. Jacques Choron, *Suicide* (New York: Charles Scribner's Sons, 1972), p. 3.

3. Edwin S. Shneidman, "The Enemy," in Sandra Wilcox and Marilyn Sutton, eds., *Understanding Death and Dying,* 2nd ed. (Sherman Oaks, CA: Alfred, 1981), pp. 329–340.

4. Maurice Farber, *Theory of Suicide* (New York: Funk & Wagnalls, 1968), p. 7.

5. Ibid.

6. Ibid., p. 9.

7. A. Alvarez, *The Savage God* (New York: Bantam, 1973), pp. 35–38.

8. Farber, p. 9.

9. Sigmund Freud, *Beyond the Pleasure Principle,* Vol. 18 of *The Standard Edition*

of the Complete Psychological Works of Sigmund Freud (London: Hogarth, 1955), pp. 7–84.

10. Sigmund Freud, Mourning and Melancholia, Vol. 14 of The Standard Edition, pp. 243–258.

11. Freud, Beyond the Pleasure Principle, p. 24.

12. Emile Durkheim, Suicide (New York: The Free Press, 1951).

13. Ibid., pp. 208–216.

14. Ibid., pp. 217–228.

15. Whitney Pope, Durkheim's Suicide: A Classic Analyzed (Chicago: University of Chicago Press, 1976), pg. 30.

16. Durkheim, pp. 246–276.

17. Durkheim, p. 276 (footnote).

18. Jack D. Douglas, The Social Meanings of Suicide (Princeton: Princeton University Press, 1967), p. 155.

19. Ibid., pp. 191–231. Also, "The Reliability of Suicide Statistics: A Bomb-burst" (Editorial Comment), Suicide and Life-Threatening Behavior 10, no. 2 (1980): 67–69.

20. Farber, p. 10.

21. Ibid., p. 29.

22. Ibid., p. 26.

23. Ibid., pp. 10–11.

24. Ibid., pp. 30–32.

25. Robert and Beatrice Kastenbaum, "Hope, Survival, and the Caring Environment," in Erdman Palmore and Frances C. Jeffers, eds., Prediction of Life Span (Lexington, Mass.: D. C. Heath, 1971), p. 262.

26. Ibid.

27. Ibid., p. 267.

28. Ibid., p. 251.

29. Durkheim, pp. 180–189.

30. P. J. Clayton et al., "The Depression of Widowhood," British Journal of Psychiatry 120 (1972): 71–78.

31. Kenneth Minkoff, et al., "Hopelessness, Depression, and Attempted Suicide," American Journal of Psychiatry 130, no. 4 (1973):455.

32. Warren Breed, "Suicide and Loss in Social Interaction," in Edwin Shneidman, ed., Essays in Self-Destruction (New York: Science House, 1967), pp. 198–199.

33. Minkoff, et al., pp. 455–59. Also, R. Wetzel, "Hopelessness, Depression, and Suicide Intent," Archives of General Psychiatry 33 (1976):1069–1073. Cf. A. Pokorny et al., "Hopelessness and Attempted Suicide:

A Reconsideration," *American Journal of Psychiatry* 132, no. 9 (1975):954–956.

34. Rikihei Inoguchi and Takashi Nakajima, *The Divine Wind* (Annapolis, Md.:United States Naval Institute, 1963), p. 148.

35. Hendin, p. 214.

36. Martin P. Seligman, *Helplessness* (San Francisco: W. H. Freeman, 1975), pp. 166–169.

37. Frederick Melges and John Bowlby, "Types of Hopelessness in Psychopathological Process," *Archives of General Psychiatry* 20 (1969):697.

38. M. J. Walters, "Psychic Death," *Archives of Neurology and Psychiatry* 52 (1944):84–85; T. X. Barber, "Death by Suggestion," *Psychosomatic Medicine* 23 (1961):153–155; also, N. Younger, "Emotions as the Cause of Rapid and Sudden Death," *Archives of Neurology and Psychiatry* 36 (1936):875–879.

39. Farber, pp. 15–16.

40. Richard Schulz and David Aderman, "Effect of Residential Change on the Temporal Distance to Death of Terminal Cancer Patient," in Robert Fulton, ed., *Death and Identity* (Bowie, Md.: The Charles Press, 1976), pp. 317–322.

41. Barney Glaser and Anselm Strauss, *Awareness of Dying* (Chicago: Aldine, 1978), p. 77.

42. Richard Seiden and Raymond Freitas, "Shifting Patterns of Deadly Violence," *Suicide and Life-Threatening Behavior* 10, no. 4 (1980):207.

43. Philip Slater, *The Pursuit of Loneliness* (Boston: Beacon Press, 1970), pp. 81–95.

44. Robert Jay Lifton, *The Broken Connection* (New York: Simon & Schuster, 1979), p. 249.

45. William McMordie, "The Highest Suicidal Risk—The Elderly." Paper presented at the Central Iowa Directors of Nursing for Long Term Care, Knoxville, Iowa, 13 September, 1978.

46. Edwin S. Shneidman, "Current Overview of Suicide," in Edwin Shneidman, ed., *Suicidology: Contemporary Developments* (New York: Grune & Stratton, 1976), p. 5.

CHAPTER NINE

Euthanasia

The patient, a 21-year-old, left the hospital in November after treatment for leukemia and came back on New Year's Eve of the same year. At that time she was not expected to live through the night. When the psychiatrist went to visit her parents in the waiting room outside of the intensive treatment unit, she found the father to be in so much agony and pain that he could not relate. . . .

When the psychiatrist visited the patient, she realized what the parents had been trying to say. The woman lay half-naked on the bed, hooked up on tubes, a tracheostomy [breathing through a tube inserted through an opening made in the throat], and a respirator, staring desparately around the room. The psychiatrist's first impulse was to cover her with a bed-sheet, but a nurse appeared and said, "Don't bother—she will push it off again in a minute." The psychiatrist approached the patient, who took her hand and pointed to the ceiling. The psychiatrist looked up and asked if the light was bothering her. The patient grabbed her hands and kissed them, communicating that her impression was correct. When the psychiatrist asked for the light to be switched off, however, the nurse reminded her of the rules and regulations of the intensive treatment unit, which required that the light stay on. Then the psychiatrist asked for a chair for the mother to sit with her daughter. She was told that they could not give her a chair anymore because during the previous visit the mother had stayed more than five minutes.

The woman died eight hours after the physicians had informed the parents of her imminent death—she died with the room lights in her eyes, the tubes in her mouth and her veins, and the parents sitting outside in the waiting room.[1]

This true story, used as a case study in a discussion of euthanasia, dramatically points to some of the issues involved in the treatment of persons who are in the process of dying. One alternative is euthanasia—the intentional ending of a person's life. Kluge offers the following definition: "Euthanasia is the act of deliberately killing a person in as painless a manner as possible where the act of killing is the result of full deliberation and is for the sake of that person, rather than that of anyone else."[2] Most usually, the individual under consideration is suffering from a terminal illness and the quality of his or her life has disintegrated to the point that the individual is experiencing great pain and/or mental torment. For many reasons some of which we will investigate below, the question of euthanasia has become entangled in a web of ethical, religious, social, political, technological, and medical considerations. These factors have contributed to the difficulty of developing a public policy toward euthanasia which can be accepted by the general public as well as by medical, legal, and religious leaders.

Euthanasia is often broken down into four general categories:

1. *Voluntary active euthanasia.* The patient is able to request that his or her life be terminated. To fulfill that wish may or may not require an action on the part of another. For example, a terminally ill individual in great pain asks a relative to shoot him. The relative complies.

2. *Voluntary passive euthanasia.* In this category, the individual asks that nothing be done to extend his or her life. An example of this would be a woman who asks of her doctor that he not attempt to resuscitate her if she should stop breathing. The doctor agrees, and orders a "no code" instruction be attached to her hospital file. As a result of this order, when the patient stops breathing, no efforts are made to revive her.

3. *Involuntary active euthanasia.* The individual cannot indicate that he or she does not want to continue to live. Someone else makes that decision, and then acts on it. For example, a baby is born suffering from severe retardation. The father kills the child.

4. *Involuntary passive euthanasia.* As in involuntary active euthana-

sia above, the individual cannot indicate whether or not he or she desires to go on living. The decision is made by others, who then withhold treatment which might continue life. An example of this might be an aged woman, suffering from multiple serious ailments and a major terminal disease, who enters the hospital in a coma. Medical personnel decide not to treat the diseases present, but to provide only support systems (nourishment, water) and pain relievers until the illnesses cause the patient's death.

Even this comparatively simple categorization leads to a good deal of controversy, and there is much disagreement as to just what is involved in active versus passive euthanasia. We will use the categories in an referential manner, allowing us to have a common terminology when discussing euthanasia.

Active versus Passive Euthanasia

It is argued by some that the difference between active and passive euthanasia is nonexistent. What difference does it make if a person dies as a result of an act of omission or one of commission? In one well-known example, a philosopher describes the following situation: Mr. Smith stands to inherit a great deal of money upon the death of his young nephew. He decides to murder him, and so he enters the bathroom while the boy is taking a bath, holds the boy's head under water, and drowns him. Mr. Jones is in the same situation, and he also decides to murder his nephew. As he enters the bathroom, however, he sees the boy slip and fall into the tub, hitting his head and becoming unconscious. He stands there and does nothing to save the boy. Smith is guilty of murder. Is Jones? Smith actively sought to end the boy's life. Jones, by an act of omission, brought about the same end.[7] Morally, at least, they are both guilty of the same thing. According to United States law, however, Jones has not committed a crime. Based upon this example, the argument is made that there is no difference between active and passive euthanasia.

There are two further arguments that are made in favor of doing away with the distinction between active and passive euthanasia: One is that to force the individual to go on living is to do greater harm than to end the person's suffering as quickly and as painlessly as possible. One situation that has arisen on more than one occasion in the United States involves a baby who is born defective. Either because the parents refuse permission for lifesaving treatment, or because the medical staff decides that the child would be better off not to have to suffer, nothing is done to save the child's life. Instead, the child is wheeled off to a corner of the nursery, with an order placed on its records that it is to receive no food or water. In other words, the baby is left to die. This is an act which would be considered passive euthanasia. Proponents of doing away with the distinction between active and passive euthanasia argue that such an act is wrong. Better to bring about the end of the child's life, than to force the child to go through a process of slow, painful dehydration. Yes, killing the child is a harmful act, but not nearly so harmful as forcing the child to suffer a painful end because no one is willing to help the child to die. In fact, in this kind of a situation, we treat animals better than we do people.

Joseph Fletcher, a leading proponent of eliminating the difference between active and passive euthanasia, points out the inconsistency which exists when we approve of therapeutic abortions to terminate the existence of a deformed fetus, and yet we refuse to terminate the existence of a delivered neonate who is obviously doomed to a subhuman existence.[8] Fletcher sums up his argument in this manner:

> The plain hard logic of it is that the end or purpose of both negative and positive euthanasia is exactly the same: to contrive or bring about the patient's death. Acts of deliberate omission are morally not different from acts of commission. But in the Anglo-American *law*, it is a crime to push a blind man over a cliff. It is not, however, a crime to deliberately not lift a finger to prevent his walking over the edge. This is an unpleasant feature of legal reasoning which is alien to ethics and to a sensitive conscience. Ashamed of it, even the courts fall back on such legal fictions as "insanity" in euthanasia cases, and this has the predictable effect of undermining our respect for the law.[9]

Robert Veatch replies to the above arguments by raising several important points.[10] First, acts of commission and omission are *psychologically* different. Simply put, we feel differently about letting someone die than we do about killing him or her. These feelings of guilt should not be dismissed, according to Veatch. They are an indication of our perceptions of right and wrong. Veatch does concede that this perception may be a product of our socialization, a point with which I would tend to agree. (Descriptions of Eskimos putting their elderly out to die in the snow do not indicate a great deal of guilt is present. Were this done by people in a different culture, however, it might be met with a good deal of guilt.)

Veatch also points out that active killing on the part of the physician violates the Hippocratic Oath, by which a doctor vows not to kill. Also, we have to ask if it is proper to ask physicians to take life. Doctors are dedicated to saving lives. As a result of their dedication to this principle, they are somewhat removed from the position of making judgments concerning who should live and who should die, at least in an ethical sense. It would seem to me to be a dangerous act to redefine the doctor's role in such a way as to make them arbiters over life and death. I recognize that doctors do have a good deal of power over life and death. However, that power does not legitimately extend to actively killing people.

Trammel argues the differences between active and passive euthanasia further, raising an important distinction between the two:

> He who acts to end life presumes to know what is best for the person he is trying to kill. He who fails to act to provide treatment which might reasonably be thought to extend the life of the patient does not necessarily presume to know what is best for the patient. The person who acts to end life has a definite outcome in mind for the patient, and his action is not successful until that outcome is achieved. The person who refrains from acting is not necessarily aiming at a definite outcome. His inaction is not rendered "unsuccessful" by an unexpected survival or improvement of the patient.[11]

Trammel is pointing out the finality of killing a person, and contrasting it with the possibility that exists in any human situation: A miracle, a new cure, or a spontaneous remission are all impossible if the person is dead.

Another point of concern in active euthanasia is when such an act involves another person. There have been cases of people who have begged their doctors to end their lives, only to be thankful at a later time that the doctor refused. When an individual asks another to aid in ending his or her life—to assist in voluntary active euthanasia—the legal issues become more involved. Since the person will end up dead, he or she cannot complain that the death was a murder. By legalizing assisting someone to die, we run the risk of people asserting that the killing of another was committed at that person's request. Yet it is impossible for us to know the state of mind of the dead person at the time of the killing. People in pain, facing death, or having experienced some traumatic events may vacillate in their feelings for a while. Also, if active voluntary euthanasia were to be sanctioned, it could lead to situations where the law is abused for personal gain of the other person.

A Modern Dilemma: "High Tech Dying"

In the past, the questions with which we concern ourselves today were irrelevant for two reasons: First, one usually did not live long in a suffering condition. Pneumonia, which used to be known as "the old man's friend," often would quickly set in and end the person's life. Second, it was not considered "bad" to suffer. In fact, as we saw when we discussed the dying behaviors of the Puritans, suffering was sometimes seen as something bestowed upon the individual by God. To interfere with the dying process by bringing it to an early end would have been considered a direct act against God, who had chosen to purge the individual of his or her sinfulness through earthly suffering. As a result, euthanasia was simply not an issue.

As our technology has allowed us to keep people alive longer, we have come to realize that longer is not necessarily better; the quality as well as the length of life must be taken into consideration. The technology that has been in the medical world sees death as something to be defeated. Charmaz points out that in the medical world, prolonging life is considered to be the best use of technology.[3] No decisions are made about about the quality of life that is extended as a result of implementing new technologies. Respirators do not make value judgements. We are also aware that people live a social existence as well as a physical one. To be socially dead and yet biologically alive is a terrible way to exist. Yet technology offers us no solution to the dilemma, except when technology can no longer "help" the person, and he or she dies anyway.

The Machine in the Garden

Our new-found technology has produced situations in which individuals are being kept alive who no longer can be considered persons. Some estimate that as many as 5000 people are being kept alive today although they are permanently unconscious.[4] The dilemmas of euthanasia do not allow for a resolution of their conditions, and so they continue to exist as what are known in the medical world as "vegetables." They exist solely because they are hooked up to machines that force them to breathe, and they are invaded by tubes that provide nourishment and carry off wastes. Because the brains of these individuals continue to show some indication of activity, they do not fall into the category of being brain dead. The following case history portrays some of the hardships that can result when an individual is caught in a technological limbo somewhere between life and death:

> On October 28, 1966, a 27-year-old Illinois woman riding in an arena was thrown from her horse and sustained severe head injuries. A doctor, also riding in the arena, administered artificial respiration and she was taken by ambulance to a nearby community hospital where she remained paralyzed and unconscious.
> . . . She was examined by a number of neurologists and neurosurgeons and was evaluated at the University of Illinois Research Hospital where she was diagnosed as having received a probable contusion of the cerebral cortex, the thinking part of the brain, and other brain damage. A year later she was taken to another medical center with no change in diagnosis, and was again returned to the community hospital. In the years that followed, this patient received medical and nursing care which made it possible for her to survive numerous episodes of aspiration pneumonia, urinary tract infection, convulsions, dermatitis and other disorders associated with immobility and brain trauma. In 1974, 18 years after the accident, at age 45, she developed a genitourinary infection and acute respiratory symptoms. She was maintained on oxygen, respirator therapy and antibiotics for 10 days, and died.[5]

One ethicist, commenting on this case, stated that the expenses involved were probably well over $6 million. A physician considered it the doctor's duty to do all that was possible to help the family cope with the feelings that might arise in a situation like this, but also to help the family realize that after a year at most, "the chances for recovery of cognitive functioning were essentially non-existent."[6] One can only imagine the toll that such a lingering dying must have had upon the family.

In response to this problem, some would opt for euthanasia,

believing that to keep a person in such a state of non-being is inhumane treatment. Others, regarding life as a sacred trust, would protest such a decision, calling it murder.

Extraordinary Medical Treatment

One of the many issues confounding the problem of euthanasia is that of the use of exotic, untried procedures in order to sustain life. While it is argued by some that we do not have to use such procedures, it is difficult to define strictly just what is meant by extraordinary treatment. Many rather ordinary procedures, such as heart by-pass surgery, have been in common use for only a relatively short period of time. Fifty years ago, incubator babies were exhibited at sideshows and amusement parks.[12] Today's experiment may be tomorrow's common practice. And so arguing that untried or extraordinary techniques are not always required in order to save lives does not clearly resolve the issue.

The Use of Euthanasia

To what extent is euthanasia practiced today? While few doctors approve of or have carried out active euthanasia, one study shows that 87 percent of the doctors asked approved of passive euthanasia, and 80 percent admitted to having done so. Passive euthanasia appears to be a rather widespread activity in contemporary medicine.[13]

In order to produce the effects of euthanasia without actually making a decision which would be considered active euthanasia, a doctor can issue what is called a "TKO" order. This means that the nurses should endeavor "to keep open" the patient's intravenous tubes, but at a minimal level. This technically does not shut off the food supply, but the amount given is not enough to keep the patient alive.[14]

Another way in which doctors are able to avoid the label of euthanasia is the practice of what is called "snowing." When a patient is suffering from pain, the doctor may order an increase in painkillers, even exceeding the lethal dosage level. The intent is not to end the patient's life, but to alleviate pain. Eventually, however, the patient may die from the medication. The moral reasoning behind the practice of snowing is called the double-effect argument. The position taken is that when there is both a good and a bad effect from a particular act, it is morally acceptable to undertake the action for the good that it will do, and allow the bad effect to result as well. The crux of the argument is the intention of the actor. The doctor must truly intend to ease the patient's pain, and not to kill the person. Kluge argues that such an argument is morally indefensible; that it is a kind of utilitarian argument, weighing the values of good versus bad outcomes against each other. Further, he argues that an act such as snowing is done in bad faith, wherein the bad effects are ignored in a kind of self-deception.[15]

The double-effect argument is the basis for the position taken by the Roman Catholic Church, which approves of the use of pain relievers that might shorten the person's life in the process.[16] Opposing arguments stress the importance of patient self-determination in deciding these issues, with the doctor taking a more advisory role.[17]

The Living Will

An increasingly popular way to deal with the problem of prolonged suffering induced by the application of life-sustaining technology is the living will. The living will serves as a statement of the person's wishes, should he or she be in such a situation and unable to speak for him- or herself. Since the courts recognize the individual's right to control his or her own life, the living will is recognized in many states as a boda fide expression of the individual's feelings concerning being kept alive on life-support systems.[18]

DECLARATION

Declaration made this _____ day of _____ (month, year).

I, _____ , being of sound mind, willfully and voluntarily make known my desire that my dying shall not be artificially prolonged under the circumstances set forth below, do hereby declare:

If at any time I should have an incurable injury, disease, or illness certified to be a terminal condition by two physicians who have personally examined me, one of whom shall be my attending physician, and the physicians have determined that my death will occur whether or not life-sustaining procedures are utilized and where the application of life-sustaining procedures would serve only to artificially prolong the dying process, I direct that such procedures be withheld or withdrawn, and that I be permitted to die naturally with only the administration of medication or the performance of any medical procedure deemed necessary to provide me with comfort care.

In the absence of my ability to give directions regarding the use of such life-sustaining procedures, it is my intention that this declaration shall be honored by my family and physician(s) as the final expression of my legal right to refuse medical or surgical treatment and accept the consequences from such refusal.

I understand the full import of this declaration and I am emotionally and mentally competent to make this declaration.

Signed _____

City, County, and State of Residence

_____

The declarant has been personally known to me and I believe him or her to be of sound mind.

Witness _____

Witness _____

The model legislative bill, developed by the Society for the Right to Die, of which the above declaration is a part, requires that two physicans confirm the person's terminal condition, the document be witnessed, and states that physicians who act in accordance with the patient's desires are free from civil and/or criminal liability.

Euthanasia Pro and Con

Kluge's analysis of the arguments in favor of and opposed to euthanasia describes the following key issues:[19]

Arguments in Opposition to Euthanasia

1. *The Religious Argument.* The religious opposition to euthanasia relies upon a definition of God. Some argue that the simple commandment, "Thou shalt not kill," precludes any acceptance of euthanasia. Others argue from a moral code based upon religious principles; it is wrong to kill anyone except when unjustly attacked. Another religiously based position is that suffering may serve to develop one's better qualities. It may also be argued that life itself

is a gift from God; we have no right to reject such a sacred gift. Finally, there are those religious arguments which hinge upon accepting death as God's sole prerogative. We have no right to interfere with what is a sacred decision.

2. *Moral Arguments.* Personhood—that unique state of rational human beings—is a sacred state, which means that it has absolute value. Nothing should be done to interfere with the condition of personhood (i.e., to bring about the end of such a state). Also, it must be realized that the absolute value of life supersedes the question of the quality of that life. Put another way, any life of a person is better than no life at all.

Another moral argument is based on the fact that we are fallible. As such, it is possible that we could make an error in our decision to employ euthanasia. We must not run this risk, the argument continues, because the possible consequence (needless killing) is too great. The difficulty, according to Kluge, with the former argument lies in the assumptions that it makes about what it means to be a person. The latter argument implies that we should never take risks because, to a greater or lesser degree, risks may threaten our existence.

3. *Ignorance of Other Minds.* Under this title, Kluge places those arguments against what is called substituted judgment. The case of Joseph Saikewicz is a good example of this.[20] The sixty-seven-year-old Saikewicz had been institutionalized all his life. His mental age was judged to be under three years, his IQ 10, and his communication skills were limited to simple noises and gestures. He did not usually react to people, and he easily became disoriented. When he developed a terminal form of leukemia, his guardian petitioned the courts of Massachusetts to withhold treatment. The guardian claimed that the extremely doubtful beneficial effects of the suggested chemotherapy were outweighed by the serious side effects of the treatments, which he would not understand. Saikewicz would most likely have to be tied down during the daily treatments. The court held that the wishes of Saikewicz himself were not and could not be known. As a result, there was a basis for substituting his guardian's decision, and withholding treatment. Saikewicz died without pain four months later.

The opposing argument is made that the court had no right to impose what it thought to be correct upon an innocent person, any more than the individual has a right to guess what another is thinking, and to act upon that guess.

In many cases, such a difficult decision is avoided through the testimony of witnesses that the individual in question had previously stated that he or she would not want to be kept alive by artificial means. Here one can see the power of the living will, which is evidence of the person's wishes on this issue. However, this evidence or testimony reflects the person's wishes at an earlier time. Kluge points out that those opposed to euthanasia argue that we do not know the wishes of the person at the moment of crisis; only what he or she has felt at an earlier time.[21]

4. *The Argument from Social Utility.* This argument claims that euthanasia is a threat to society. First, the individual may make a decision that is wrong, and as a result society may lose a valuable member. Second, and more important, there is the danger of the abuse of such legislation, as we saw earlier. A powerful historical example is the Nazis' use of euthanasia laws as legitimization for their efforts at genocide. The permissibility of euthanasia was a part of German law prior to Hitler's rise to power. It was a simple matter to redefine antisocial diagnosis to include anyone who did not embrace Nazism. As a result, the Nazi-promulgated holocaust was a legal action, under the laws in force at the time.[22]

5. *Appropriateness.* In his final category of arguments opposing euthanasia, Kluge describes the argument that death should occur in its own appropriate time, and that we must not interfere with this natural process. The fallacy of this argument lies in the fact that we do, in fact, interfere with natural processes every day in many ways, from digging tunnels through mountains to medical surgery.

Arguments Favoring Euthansia

1. *Personal Dignity.* One of the most popular arguments favoring euthanasia centers on the value of a dignified existence. The description of the undignified death of a young woman at the beginning of our discussion of euthanasia is the kind which assaults our sensibilities. While most people would opt for a dignified existence (to include the dying process), defining (or operationalizing) such a concept is another matter. Also, assuming we have arrived at a mutually agreeable definition of dignity, we have to ask whether this implies that all who lead undignified lives should be killed, in the reasoning that an undignified life is not worth living.

I believe that many of the problems of being denied a dignified existence do not result from the dilemmas of euthanasia as much as from a lack of humanistically oriented care of the terminally ill. Many of the examples one finds in the arguments favoring euthansia involve assaults on the person's dignity not only from efforts to prolong life, but also on the part of those who place other values, such as organizational efficiency and policies, above the needs of the terminally ill.

2. *The Moral Argument.* This argument holds that we each have the right to control our own lives. One who chooses to engage in risky or unhealthy behavior has the right to do so. By the same token, one has the right to choose not to undergo a particular medical treatment, even if doing so means that one will live a shorter length of time. A derivative argument holds that because a person has a right to control his or her own life, he or she also has a right to make out a living will to be implemented at a later time.

Another moral argument is that the larger society has a right to control and, if necessary, limit the amount of its resources that it uses on those who are hopelessly ill. Both these arguments are based upon assumptions about the rights of the individual and the state.

3. *The Biological Argument.* Ths position holds that artificially supported life—life sustained by machines—is not genuine life. Therefore, it is ethically permissible to terminate such an existence, because it is not really life. The problem with this argument is that many active people, such as those who undergo periodic blood cleansing by means of hemodialyis machines, rely upon those machines to keep living. A second biological argument is based upon a concern with eugenics, which favors euthanasia in order to prevent the spreading of genetically transmitted diseases or unhealthy conditions. This argument, popular in the past, is flawed, in that it fails to consider other ways of preventing transmission besides murder; it assumes that we should interfere in the gene pool. In the first case there are many alternatives for preventing further transmission, such as contraception. In the second, we do not have enough information concerning the make-up of human genes to make the kinds of decisions necessary for the genetic argument to prevail.

4. *Social Utility Argument.* Society relies upon people to perform in ways that are useful to it. The social utility argument contends

that no social system can carry everyone; indeed, society should be able to rid itself of those who are totally useless. Difficulties in this position lie in the fact that someone who is useless and a burden upon society at one point in time may not be so at a later point. Another issue, one brought up earlier, is the problem of defining what is considered as "socially useless," and of determining who should make such a decision?

Another argument that Kluge puts in this category is that society's resources are finite. To spend resources upon the hopelessly ill means that someone else is deprived in some way. This argument is becoming increasingly popular as more exotic (and expensive) medical technologies *which will actually service only a small number of people* are being developed. A popular magazine recently noted that some hospitals are deciding not to offer such treatments, because of the high costs involved in benefiting comparatively few people. It cited the decision of some hospitals not to set up burn units, which can provide highly effective treatment, but for comparatively patients.[23] Burn units and other specialized technologies can be centrally located so that a person who needs such treatment can be transported to the providing institution, but there is a larger issue which involves providing large numbers of people with life-saving, expensive treatments.

A physician, writing in a medical journal, took an unpopular stand by arguing that society is reaching a point where it can no longer afford to support the hopelessly ill.[24] He describes terminally ill, aged, often mentally incapacitated patients who are shuttled back and forth between extended care facilities such as nursing homes, and acute care hospitals. Often subject to decubiti (bedsores), these people will be placed in a hospital for treatment. The doctor states that a cost of $20,000 is not unusual in such cases. The people are cured of their presenting symptoms and are returned to the nursing home to continue their dying. He estimates the total cost of this kind of treatment to be $730 million per year in the United States.

Kluge attempts to answer these objections by pointing out that while the premise is certainly valid—that is, that we have only finite resources—the conclusion that euthanasia is the solution does not necessarily follow.[25] A reallocation of resources from other areas, or such actions as birth control can also solve the problem without taking any human lives.

This overview of the arguments central to the issue of euthanasia demonstrates the complexity and the many ramifications which the various positions entail. There is a larger social issue involved in our efforts to resolve the controversy over euthanasia. This issue is our image of death, which as we have seen is one that avoids the reality of death and is permeated with fear and anxiety. As a result, we avoid taking a realistic view of death, and coming to grips with the issues that need to be faced. We prefer, instead, to opt for a technological solution to the problem. But ultimately technology can no longer support a meaningful existence, and we are confronted with the value judgments involved in the question of whether life would be prolonged, allowed to run its natural course, or terminated.

Euthanasia and the Defective Newborn

An issue that appears to exist between the questions of abortion and euthanasia is that of allowing malformed or diseased newborns to continue living. Approximately 15 in every 1000 births are either malformed or stillborn.[26] A problem that also crops up in abortion controversies is the degree to which parents are autonomous in making decisions concerning their children's welfare. (Note that the mother, it is often argued, has an absolute right to determine what is done with her body while pregnant, and this would include the right to kill the fetus. However, when the baby is born, the father also becomes involved in decisions about how the baby will be treated.) However, obviously the parents do not have total freedom of choice because there are legal consequences if the baby is treated in ways which are against the child's best interests (i.e., abuse or neglect).

The legal system is not the only institution that may intervene in parental decision making. Medicine has become involved in this process as well. Silverman describes a case of what he calls "thoughtless benevolence" on the part of a hospital staff, who fought the parents' desire not to place their fifteen-and-a-half week, 800-gram baby on a respirator. The court battle, which involved attacks on the character of the parents, was moot: the baby died of continuing medical problems after living six months.[27]

We will not detail the ethical arguments surrounding infant euthanasia; for the most part they are similar to those outlined above. There are pressing social issues, however, which are unique to the problem of defective neonates. One such issue is the degree to which medicine should intrude upon the moral issue faced by the parents. Silverman argues that overzealous hospitals and medical professionals are advocating a kind of "Reverse Social Darwinism," by promulgating a goal of preserving all neonates, regardless of their condition.[28] (This is often the view of religious institutions as well.) If Silverman is correct, then we have to ask by what right does a hospital or medical staff become involved? Silverman points out that there is no formal recognition by American society that the institution of medicine has a right to so involve itself. For example, if a physician is opposed to an individual's decision to have some elective surgery performed, he or she can withdraw from the case. The physician is not ethically or legally obligated to pursue the case in a court of law. But Silverman describes cases involving the parents' decision to withhold treatment from a neonate where medicine has taken an advocacy position.[29]

I would argue that the parents in such a case have a far greater right to make the decision to withhold treatment than the physician or medical institution. First, the parents are the ones who must live with the results of their decision. Their financial, social, and emotional resources must be taken into account. Second, the expertise of the physician is medical, not ethical. While medical information and expertise should be a part of any decision of this nature, the moral beliefs of the participating medical staff should not be imposed upon others.

Robertson points out several aspects of infant euthanasia that need to be considered:[30] First, this kind of passive euthanasia is common practice in medicine. Letting severely malformed or diseased infants die is favored and practiced by many physicians. Second, the issue is morally ambiguous for many, with others holding very strong views as to its rightness or wrongness. This increases the difficulty of reaching a decision concerning the treatment of a defective newborn.

Another factor contributing to the complexity of the issue is that birth defects exist along a continuum. While few would argue for the rightness of allowing a child to die for the want of a simple operation to eliminate a life-threatening condition, and few others would argue for extraordinary treatments for a newborn so badly deformed as to be barely recognizable as a human being, there are many more ambiguous cases between the two extremes. Also, Robertson notes that these decisions to treat or not to treat the defective newborn are made under stressful conditions. There may be a sense of urgency that puts great pressure on the parents, who are also dealing with the emotional trauma of having a joyfully anticipated event turn into a sad and perhaps horrifying experience.[31] Relevant information may not be available at the time when people are feeling a need to reach closure on the problem. This may be further complicated by the knowledge that withholding treatment at the outset is probably much easier than considering active euthanasia later on.

The decision-making process, typically involving the parents and the physician, does not usually involve an advocate for the child; the one who perhaps has the most at stake. This is an important point, not only for the obvious reason of protecting the child's rights, but also because having an advocate present may allow the parents to make a more considered judgment at the time. (The presence of an advocate may also produce a great deal of anguish in the parents.) Finally, the threat of possible legal prosecution further beclouds the issue, as nontreatment of defective newborns can be a criminal offense. All of these factors make the decision whether or not to withhold treatment difficult at best. While some more zealous advocates of life-prolonging treatment for all defective newborns may try to portray the parents in these cases as hard and selfish people, more often than not they are caring people who find themselves faced with an agonizing dilemma, and who try to make a decision that will be in the best interests of all those, including the baby, who are involved.

Conclusion

The issue of euthanasia has become "an ethical thicket, a tangled swamp overgrown with extraneous moral distinctions which entrap those who try to reflect on the moral dilemmas in the care of the dying."[32] Our ability to prolong life has outstripped our ethical framework, and we struggle for answers to complex questions which challenge our understandings of such concepts as the quality of life, the meaning of suffering, and the rights of the individual. The answers to the questions raised by those in favor of euthanasia as well as those opposed will require society to rethink some of its most fundamental understandings of the meaning of life and death.

Notes

1. Robert M. Veatch, *Case Studies in Medical Ethics* (Cambridge, Mass.: Harvard University Press, 1977), pp. 326–327.

2. Eike-Henner W. Kluge: *The Practice of Death* (New Haven: Yale University Press, 1975), p. 173.

3. Kathy Charmaz, *The Social Reality of Death* (Reading, Mass.: Addison-Wesley, 1980), pp. 102–103.

4. "Doctor's Dilemma" *U.S. News and World Report*, 6 December 1982, p. 54.

5. *Newsletter*, NY: *Concern for Dying*, 8, no. 3 (Summer, 1982): 3.

6. Ibid.

7. James Rachels, "Active and Passive Euthanasia," reprinted in Tom L. Beauchamp and Seymour Perlin, eds., *Ethical Issues in Death and Dying* (Englewood Cliffs, N.J.: Prentice-Hall, 1978), p. 243.

8. Joseph Fletcher, "Ethics and Euthanasia," in James P. Carse and Arlene B. Dallery, eds., *Death and Society* (New York: Harcourt Brace Jovanovich, 1977), p. 165.

9. Ibid., p. 173.

10. Robert M. Veatch, *Death, Dying, and the Biological Revolution* (New Haven: Yale University Press, 1976), pp. 80–106.

11. Richard L. Trammell, "The Presumption against Taking Life," *The Journal of Medicine and Philosophy*, 3, no. 1 (1978): 64–65.

12. William A. Silverman, "Mismatched Attitudes about Neonatal Death," *The Hastings Center Report*, December 1981, p. 14.

13. William W. Weddington, Jr., "Euthanasia," *Journal of the American Medical Association* 246, no. 17 (1981):1949–1950.

14. *Los Angeles Times*, "Life-Support Court Edict Leaves Physicians Cautious", 31 October, 1983.

15. Eike-Henner W. Kluge, *The Practice of Death* (New Haven: Yale Univ. Press, 1975), pp. 63–65.

16. Frank Harron, John Burnside, and Tom Beauchamp, *Health and Human Values* (New Haven: Yale University Press, 1983), pp. 52–59.

17. Ibid.

18. Society for the Right to Die, 250 W. 57th St., New York, NY, 10019.

19. Kluge, pp. 133–169.

20. George J. Annas, "The Incompetent's Right to Die: The Case of Joseph Saikewicz," *Hastings Center Report*, February 1978, pp. 21–22.

21. Kluge, p. 148.

22. Leo Alexander, "Medical Science under Dictatorship," *New England Journal of Medicine* 241 (1949):39–47.

23. *U.S. News and World Report,* "Doctor's Dilemma," 6 December 1982, p. 56.

24. Howard Caplan, "We Can't Afford to Prolong so Many Helpless Lives, *Medical Economics,* 2 December 1982, pp. 62–66.

25. Kluge, p. 168.

26. Robert C. Coburn, "Morality and the Defective Newborn," *The Journal of Medicine and Philosophy* 5, no. 4 (1980):340–357.

27. Silverman, pp. 12–16.

28. Ibid., p. 14.

29. Ibid., p. 16.

30. John A. Robertson, "Dilemma in Danville," *The Hastings Center Report,* October 1981, p. 508.

31. Ibid.

32. Veatch, *Case Studies in Medical Ethics,* p. 325.

Bibliography

ALVAREZ, A. *The Savage God*. New York: Bantam, 1973.

ARIES, PHILIPPE. *Western Attitudes toward Death*. Baltimore: Johns Hopkins University Press, 1974.

BECKER, ERNEST. *The Denial of Death*. New York: The Free Press, 1973.

BLUBOND-LANGNER, MYRA. *The Private Worlds of Dying Children*. Princeton, New Jersey: Princeton University Press, 1978.

BLUMER, HERBERT. *Symbolic Interaction*. New York: Prentice-Hall, 1969.

BOULDING, KENNETH E. *The Image*. Ann Arbor: University of Michigan Press, 1961.

BOWLBY, JOHN. *Attachment and Loss* Volume I (1969), Volume II (1973), Volume III (1980). New York: Basic Books.

BEAUCHAMP, TOM L. AND SEYMOUR PERLIN, eds. *Ethical Issues in Death and Dying*. Englewood Cliffs, Prentice-Hall, 1978.

BRIM, ORVILLE G., JR. et al. *The Dying Patient*, New York: The Russell Sage Foundation, 1970.

CAIN, ALBERT C., ed. *Survivors of Suicide*. Springfield, Ill: Charles C Thomas, 1972.

CAMUS, ALBERT. *The Plague*. New York: Random House, 1948.

CARSE, JAMES P. AND ARLENE B. DALLERY, eds. *Death and Society*. New York: Harcourt, Brace, Jovanovich, 1979.

CASSIRER, ERNST. *Mythical Thought* (Volume 2 of *The Philosophy of Symbolic Forms*). New Haven: Yale University Press, 1953–57.

CASTLES, MARY AND RUTH MURRAY. *Dying in an Institution*. New York: Appleton-Century-Crofts, 1979.

CHARMAZ, KATHY. *The Social Reality of Death.* Reading, Mass: Addison-Wesley, 1980.

CHORON, JACQUES. *Suicide.* New York: Charles Scribner's Sons, 1972.

COHEN, KENNETH. *Hospice: Prescription for Terminal Care.* Germantown, Maryland: Aspen Systems Corp., 1979.

CURL, JAMES S. *The Victorian Celebration of Death.* Detroit: Partridge Press, 1972.

DATAN, NANCY AND NANCY LOHMANN, eds. *Transitions in Aging.* New York: Academic Press, 1980.

DAVIDSON, GLEN, ed. *The Hospice.* Washington, D.C.: Hemisphere, 1978.

DOUGLAS, ANN. *The Feminization of America.* New York: Alfred A. Knopf, 1977.

DOUGLAS, JACK D. *The Social Meanings of Suicide.* Princeton: Princeton University Press, 1967.

DUBOIS, PAUL. *The Hospice Way of Death.* New York: Human Sciences, 1980.

DUMONT, RICHARD AND DENNIS FOSS. *The American View of Death.* Cambridge, MA: Schenkman, 1972.

DURKHEIM, EMILE. *Suicide.* New York: The Free Press, 1951.

———. *The Elementary Forms of the Religious Life.* New York: Collier, 1961.

EASSON, WILLIAM M. *The Management of the Child or Adolescent Who is Dying.* Springfield, Ill.: Charles C Thomas, 1970.

EPSTEIN, SAMUEL S. *The Politics of Cancer.* San Francisco: The Sierra Club, 1978.

FARBER, MAURICE. *Theory of Suicide.* New York: Funk and Wagnalls, 1968.

FARRELL, JAMES J. *Inventing the American Way of Death: 1830–1920.* Philadelphia: Temple University Press, 1980.

FEIFEL, HERMAN. ed. *The Meaning of Death.* New York: McGraw-Hill, 1959.

FEIGENBERG, LOMA. *Terminal Care.* New York: Bruner-Mazel, 1980.

FRANKL, VIKTOR F. *The Doctor and the Soul.* New York: A.A. Knopf, 1972.

FREIDSON, ELIOT. *Professional Dominance: The Social Structure of Medical Care.* New York: Atherton, 1970.

FREUD, SIGMUND. *An Outline of Psychoanalysis.* New York: W.W. Norton, 1949.

———. "Beyond the Pleasure Principle," in *The Standard Edition of the Complete Psychological Works of Sigmund Freud,* vol. 18. London: Hogarth, 1955.

———. "Mourning and Melancholia," in *The Standard Edition,* op. cit., vol 14.

———. "Thoughts for the Times of War and Death," in *The Standard Edition,* op. cit., vol. 14.

FULTON, ROBERT. ed. *Death and Identity.* Bowie, MD: Charles Press, 1976.

FURMAN, ERNA. *A Child's Parent Dies.* New Haven: Yale University Press, 1974.

GERMAIN, CAROL. *The Cancer Unit: An Ethnography.* Wakefield, MA: Nursing Resources, 1979.

GILLON, EDMUND. *Victorian Cemetary Sculpture.* New York: Dover Publications, 1972.

GLASER, BARNEY G. AND ANSELM L. STRAUSS. *Time for Dying.* Chicago, Aldine, 1968.

———. *Awareness of Dying.* Chicago: Aldine, 1978.

GLICK, IRA O., ROBERT S. WEISS, AND C. MURRAY PARKES. *The First Year of Bereavement.* New York: Wiley, 1974.

GORER, GEOFFREY. *Death, Grief and Mourning.* Garden City, New York: Doubleday, 1965.

GUBRIUM, JABER F. *Living and Dying at Murray Manor.* New York: St. Martin, 1975.

GUNTHER, JOHN. *Death Be Not Proud.* New York: Harper and Row, 1949.

HABENSTEIN, ROBERT W. AND WILLIAM M. LAMERS. *The History of American Funeral Directing.* Milwaukee: Bullfin, 1962.

HARMER, RUTH M. *The High Cost of Dying.* New York: Collier, 1963.

HARRIS, DIANA K. AND WILLIAM E. COLE. *Sociology of Aging.* Boston: Houghton Mifflin, 1980.

HARRON, FRANK, JOHN BURNSIDE, AND TOM BEAUCHAMP. *Health and Human Values.* New Haven: Yale University Press, 1983.

HENDIN, HERBERT. *Suicide in America.* New York: W.W. Norton, 1982.

HENRY, JULES. *Culture Against Man.* New York: Random House, 1963.

HERTZ, ROBERT. *Death and the Right Hand.* Glencoe, Ill.: The Free Press, 1960.

HOFSTADTER, RICHARD AND MICHAEL WALLACE, eds. *American Violence.* New York: A. A. Knopf, 1970.

ILLICH, IVAN. *Medical Nemesis.* New York: Random House, 1976.

JACKSON, CHARLES O. *Passing.* Westport, Conn.: Greenwood Press, 1977.

JACO, E. GARTLY, ed. *Patients, Physicians, and Illness.* New York: The Free Press, 1979.

JOHNSON, ELIZABETH S. AND JOHN R. WILLIAMSON. *Growing Old.* New York: Holt Rinehart Winston, 1980.

KASTENBAUM, ROBERT AND RUTH AISENBERG. *The Psychology of Death* (Concise Edition). New York: Springer, 1976.

KLAPP, ORRIN E. *Collective Search for Identity.* New York: Holt, Rinehart and Winston, 1969.

KLUGE, EIKE-HENNER W. *The Practice of Death.* New Haven: Yale University Press, 1975.

KOLLAR, NATHAN. *Songs of Suffering.* Minneapolis: Winston Press, 1982.

KRAUSE, ELLIOTT A. *Power and Illness.* New York: Elsevier, 1977.

KUBLER-ROSS, ELIZABETH. *On Death and Dying.* New York: Macmillan, 1969.

——. *Questions and Answers on Death and Dying.* New York: Macmillan, 1974.

KUSHNER, HAROLD S. *When Bad Things Happen to Good People.* New York: Schocken, 1981.

LAMM, MAURICE. *The Jewish Way in Death and Mourning.* New York: Jonathan David, 1969.

LEWIS, C. S. *A Grief Observed.* New York: Bantam, 1976.

LIFTON, ROBERT JAY. *Death in Life.* New York: Touchstone, 1976.

——. *The Broken Connection.* New York: Simon and Schuster, 1979.

LYNCH, JAMES J. *The Broken Heart.* New York: Basic Books, 1977.

MACK, ARIEN, ed. *Death in American Experience.* New York: Schocken Books, 1973.

MARGOLIS, OTTO S. et al., eds. *Grief and the Meaning of the Funeral.* New York: MSS Information Corporation, 1975.

MARTOCCHIO, BENITA C. *Living while Dying.* Bowie, MD: Robert J. Brady, 1982.

MAY, WILLIAM F. *The Physician's Covenant: Images of the Healer in Medical Ethics.* Philadelphia: Westminster Press, 1983.

McNULTY, ELIZABETH G. AND ROBERT A. HOLDERBY. *Hospice: A Caring Challenge.* Springfield, Ill: Charles C Thomas, 1983.

MITFORD, JESSICA. *The American Way of Death.* New York: Simon and Schuster, 1959.

MORGAN, ERNEST. *A Manual of Death Education and Simple Burial.* Burnsville, North Carolina: Celo Press, 1977.

MORLEY, JOHN. *Death, Heaven and the Victorians.* Pittsburgh: University of Pittsburgh Press, 1971.

PATTISON, E. MANSELL. *The Experience of Dying.* Englewood Cliffs, New Jersey: Prentice-Hall, 1977.

PEPPERS, LARRY G. AND RONALD J. KNAPP. *Motherhood and Mourning.* New York: Praeger, 1980.

PHIPPS, JOYCE. *Death's Single Privacy.* New York: Seabury, 1974.

PINE, VANDERLYN. *Caretaker of the Dead: The American Funeral Director.* New York: Halstad Press, 1975.

POPE, WHITNEY. *Durkheim's Suicide: A Classic Analyzed.* Chicago: University of Chicago Press, 1976.

PRESTON, RONALD PHILIP. *The Dilemmas of Care.* New York: Elsivier, 1979.

QUINT, JEANNE C. *The Nurse and the Dying Patient.* New York: Macmillan, 1967.

RAPHAEL, BEVERLY. *The Anatomy of Bereavement.* New York: Basic Books, 1983.

ROBERTSON, LEON S. AND MARGARET C. HEAGARTY. *Medical Sociology: A General Systems Approach.* Chicago: Nelson-Hall, 1975.

ROSENBLATT, PAUL C. *Bitter, Bitter Tears.* Minneapolis: University of Minnesota Press, 1983.

ROSENBLATT, PAUL N. et al. *Grief and Mourning in Cross-Cultural Perspective.* New Haven: Human Relations Area Files Press, 1976.

ROSSMAN, PARKER. *Hospice.* New York: Association Press, 1977.

RUTTER, MICHAEL. *Maternal Deprivation Reassessed* (2nd ed). New York: Penguin, 1981.

SAHLER, OLLIE, ed. *The Child and Death.* St. Louis: C.V. Mosby, 1978.

SCHIFF, HARRIET SARNOFF. *The Bereaved Parent.* New York: Penguin, 1978.

SCHOENBERG, BERNARD et al., eds. *Bereavement: Its Psychosocial Aspects.* New York: Columbia University Press, 1975.

SELIGMAN, MARTIN P. *Helplessness.* San Francisco: W.H. Freeman, 1975.

SHEEHAN, P.W., ed. *The Function and Nature of Imagery.* New York, Academic Press, 1972.

SHNEIDMAN, EDWIN, ed. *Essays in Self-Destruction.* New York: Science House, 1967.

———. *Deaths of Man.* New York: Quadrangle, 1973.

———, ed. *Suicidology: Contemporary Developments.* New York: Grune and Stratton, 1976.

———, ed. *Death: Current Perspectives.* Palo Alto: Mayfield, 1984.

SIMOS, BERTHA. *A Time to Grieve.* New York: Family Services, 1979.

SLATER, PHILIP. *The Pursuit of Loneliness.* Boston: Beacon, 1970.

STANNARD, DAVID E., ed. *Death in America.* Philadelphia: University of Pennsylvania Press, 1975.

———. *The Puritan Way of Death.* New York: Oxford University Press, 1977.

SUDNOW, DAVID. *Passing On: The Social Organization of Dying.* Englewood Cliffs: Prentice-Hall, 1967.

TOLSTOY, LEO. *The Death of Ivan Ilych.* New York: Health Sciences, 1973.

TOYNBEE, ARNOLD. *Man's Concern with Death.* New York: McGraw-Hill, 1969.

VAN GENEPP, A. *The Rites of Passage.* Chicago: University of Chicago Press, 1960.

VEATCH, ROBERT M. *Death, Dying, and the Biological Revolution.* New Haven: Yale University Press, 1976.

———. *Case Studies in Medical Ethics.* Cambridge, MA: Harvard University Press, 1977.

WALLACE, SAMUEL E. *After Suicide.* New York: John Wiley, 1973.

WARNER, W. LLOYD. *The Living and the Dead.* New Haven: Yale University Press, 1959.

WASS, HANNELORE, ed. *Dying: Facing the Facts,* Washington, D.C.: Hemisphere, 1979.

WEISMAN, AVERY D. *On Dying and Denying.* New York: Behavioral Publications, 1972.

WERNER, EMMY S. AND RUTH S. SMITH. *Vulnerable but Invincible.* New York: McGraw Hill, 1982.

WILCOX, SANDRA AND MARILYN SUTTON. *Understanding Death and Dying* (2nd ed.). Sherman Oaks, CA: Alfred, 1981.

WOLFF, SULA. *Children Under Stress.* London: Penguin, 1969.

ZINNER, ELLEN AND STEPHEN STEELE, eds. *Selected Proceedings of the First National Conference of the Forum for Death Education and Counseling.* Lexington, MA: Ginn, 1979.

Index

281

Printed in the United States
By Bookmasters